Marek J. Murawski

Messerschmitt
Bf 109 F
The Ace Maker

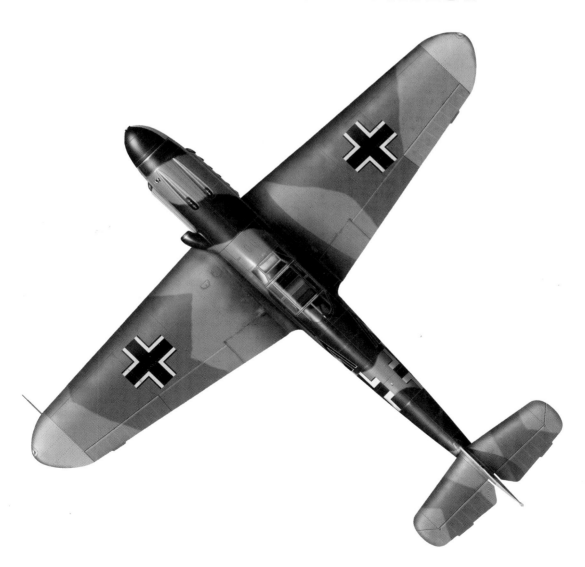

KAGERO

MORE FROM KAGERO

www.kagero.pl • phone ++48 81 50 1 21 05

Messerschmitt Bf 109 F. The Ace Maker • Marek J. Murawski • First edition • LUBLIN 2012

© All rights reserved. With the exception of quoting brief passages for the purposes of review, no part of this publication may be reproduced without prior written permission from the Publisher. Nazwa serii zastrzeżona w UP RP • **ISBN 978-83-62878-49-9**

Editing: **Marek J. Murawski, Maciej Góralczyk** • Translation: **Tomasz Szlagor, Maciej Góralczyk** • Cover artwork: **Janusz Światłoń**
• Color profiles: **Arkadiusz Wróbel** • Photos: **Marek J. Murawski's archive, Kagero's archive**
• Design: **KAGERO STUDIO, Łukasz Maj, Marcin Wachowicz**

Oficyna Wydawnicza KAGERO
Akacjowa 100, Turka, os. Borek, 20-258 Lublin 62, Poland, phone/fax (+48) 81 501 21 05
www.kagero.pl • e-mail: kagero@kagero.pl, marketing@kagero.pl
w w w . k a g e r o . p l
Distribution: **KAGERO Publishing Sp. z o.o.**

Introduction

Twelve Spitfires reported over Berck-sur-Mer! We could still have a go at these lads... Gathering speed while descending from an altitude of 8000 meters down to 5000, we intend to cut off the English. We are already over the middle of the Channel when a squadron of Spitfires looms ahead. Their tight, rigid formation gives them away for miles. We're moving up-sun to stay hidden in its blinding rays and position ourselves for a bounce. We're trailing the enemy formation like a shadow. Over Dungeness, when the English make a wide turn to starboard, the machine on the right flank falls slightly behind the others. Our *Geschwaderkommodore*[1] closes in to point-blank range and from a distance of no more than 50 meters, opens up. The stricken Spitfire falls over on its port wing and plummets towards the ground streaming a long white trail.

Our commander immediately breaks away and pulls up in a steep, right turn, so that the others can also engage. I go straight for the next Spitfire but when I line him up in my sights, the English pilot gets wise and breaks away to starboard. I lay off a lot of deflection and press the trigger. I can see my rounds rake across his fuselage and cockpit. The Spitfire hurtles down and I follow him in his dive. Then I cast a quick glance over my shoulder – just in time! A swarm of Spitfires trails after me in hot pursuit. With all my strength I push the stick into the right corner of the cockpit and ram the throttle lever forward. After several anguished moments I outdistance my pursuers and head for home.

The commander arrives over our airfield shortly afterwards and waggles the wings of his Messerschmitt. Everybody is excited - the ground crews rush to shake his hand. Pity I didn't see what happened to the Spitfire I had fired at. Perhaps he didn't make it back, just like the one knocked down by our CO. Either way, I pumped a lot of lead into mine[2].

Designing the 'Friedrich'

In the autumn of 1938 the design team of the Bayerische Flugzeugwerke in Augsburg began work on a development version of the Messerschmitt Bf 109 E, which at that time was entering service as the primary fighter of the German Luftwaffe. Prof. Willy Messerschmitt, the company's founder, and Robert Lusser, chief of project planning, sought to develop an improved version of the aircraft which could outperform earlier variants by means of an aerodynamically refined airframe and a more powerful engine.

The new fighter, designated Bf 109 F, was to be powered by the Daimler-Benz DB 601 E engine, a development version of its successful predecessor, the DB 601 A, used on the Bf 109 E. The new DB 601 E was an inline engine with direct fuel injection to the cylinders. Displacement was 3390 cm³ and maximum output at 17,750 ft (4,800 m) was 1,350 horsepower. This was a remarkable 23% increase in power[3]. The new engine was longer by 17.2 inches (452 mm), which necessitated a major redesign of the engine bearers and cowling. The 'Friedrich' (German phonetic name for the letter 'F') also incorporated a propeller spinner similar to that designed for the Me 209. The final result was an aerodynamically clean, superbly streamlined machine, which offered ground crews easy access to its powerplant. Furthermore, the chin oil cooler scoop was redesigned and the distinctive tailplane bracing struts of the Bf 109 E, re-

Messerschmitt Bf 109 F-0, coded PH+BE, in flight. The distinctive feature of the F variant was partially retractable tailwheel.

moved. Introduction of the un-braced horizontal stabilizers required further modifications to the rear section of the fuselage.

An important factor in Messerschmitt's quest for aerodynamic perfection were the revised wing-mounted coolant radiators, wider but flatter for less drag. The two-piece flaps, located at the rear of the radiators to regulate airflow, could be raised by 17° and dropped by 23°. The lower piece also acted as a regular wing flap. Concurrently, new wings with semi-elliptical wingtips, reshaped ailerons, leading edge slats and flaps, were designed. In order to save weight and increase the new fighter's manoeuvrability, wing armament was discarded.

When it became clear that series production of the DB 601 E engine was far behind schedule, the Messerschmitt team had to resort temporarily to the readily available DB 601 A engine of 1100 hp instead. On 26th January 1939, the new airframe went through a series of flight tests. On that day Messerschmitt Bf 109 V22 (W.Nr. 1800, registered as D-IRPQ) took to the air for the first time, with test pilot *Dipl. Ing.* Heinrich Beauvais at the controls. The machine featured a new supercharger air intake scoop intended for the F-series and was powered by the older DB 601 A engine. The second prototype to be flown was the Bf 109 V23 (W.Nr. 1801, D-ISHN), fitted with one of the still-experimental DB 601 E units. Finally, the Bf 109 V24 (W.Nr. 1929) and V25 (W.Nr. 1930, D-IVKC) incorporated all the distinctive external features of the Bf 109 F, which included the modified fuselage and new wings with rounded wingtips[4].

Flight test results were promising and the RLM placed an order for a pre-production batch of 15 Bf 109 F-0s. They were to be delivered to the Luftwaffe in the period between November 1939 and April 1940. However, due to Hitler's decision to curtail development work

on all combat aircraft designs, completion of the first batch of 'Friedrichs' was delayed until June 1940 – February 1941[5]. Four more Bf 109 F-0s were assembled between March and June 1941[6]. Most of them subsequently served as test-beds. At least five of these aircraft were converted standard Bf 109 E-3 airframes (W.Nr. 5601 through 5605). Messerschmitt Bf 109 F-0, W.Nr. 5601, was earmarked for "further constructional development" (*Weiterentwicklung des Baumusters*); it was powered by a DB 601 A engine and featured wings identical to that of the Bf 109 E variant. Bf 109 F-0, W.Nr. 5602, was used to test the new radiator systems intended for the F-series. It was lost during trials at Rechlin (the Luftwaffe's main testing ground for new aircraft designs).

The first prototype of the definitive series-production Bf 109 F-1 was the Bf 109 F-0, W.Nr. 5603 (coded CE+BP) powered by a DB 601 N engine. This powerplant was an upgraded DB 601 A, rated at 1,175 hp. It ran on 96-octane C3 fuel (the octane number of the Luftwaffe's standard B4 fuel was 87). Upon completing the tests the aircraft was returned to the Messerschmitt plant, where it was later used to develop the Me 309, being subsequently fitted with a new landing gear and nose wheel. Another Bf 109 F-0, W.Nr. 5604 (coded VK+AB), was used for testing the wing slats and radiator flaps. Messerschmitt Bf 109 F-0, W.Nr. 5605 (VK+AC), fitted with the standard wings of an E variant, served as a test-bed for the engine cooling system; it was also experimentally fitted with several different types of supercharger air intake.

The major difference between the 'Friedrich' and its predecessor was the onboard armament. The twin wing-mounted 20 mm MG FF/M cannons of the E variant were replaced by a single 15 mm Mauser MG 151 cannon installed between the engine cylinder banks and firing through the

Messerschmitt Bf 109 F-0, W.Nr. 5604, coded VK+AB, used for testing slats and radiator flaps. The aircraft was fitted with clipped wingtips. The first flight took place on 10th July 1940, with test pilot *Dipl. Ing.* Heinrich Beauvais at the controls.

hollow propeller shaft. The new cannon, despite its smaller calibre, gave more firepower. This was due to the considerable increase in the rate of fire – from 530 rds/min to as many as 700! Furthermore, the increased muzzle velocity (1020 m/sec, compared to the previous 718 m/sec) gave the new weapon greater accuracy. Nevertheless, the process of preparing the MG 151 cannon for mass production was handicapped by numerous delays, as was the case with the DB 601 E engine. This left the Messerschmitt team with no option but to initiate production with the DB 601 N engine and the MG FF/M cannon.

Messerschmitt Bf 109 F-1

The Bf 109 F-1 was the first series-production 'Friedrich'. In accordance with the aircraft production program issued on 1st April 1939,

production was to begin as early as June 1940 with machines being manufactured by the Messerschmitt plant at Regensburg, the Arado plant at Warnemünde and the WNF plant at Wiener-Neustadt. It was estimated that 1072 aircraft of the type would have been constructed by March 1942.

The Messerschmitt Bf 109 F-1 was powered by a Daimler-Benz DB 601 N engine. It was a 12-cylinder, inverted-vee, inline engine with a displacement of 3390 cm³. It developed a maximum output of 1,175 hp. Maximum rpm at take-off/emergency power was 2600 at a boost pressure of 1.35 ata. "Climb and Combat Power"[7] at 5400 meters was 1060 hp at 2400 rpm and 1.3 ata. Continuous power rating was 950 hp at 2300 rpm and 1.2 ata. The DB 601 N was similar to the earlier DB 601 A; its higher power was attained through the use of higher-octane C3 fuel and higher compression

Another shot of the Messerschmitt Bf 109 F-0, W.Nr. 5604. Note the main tank fuel filler point below cockpit. Of further interest are characteristic clipped wingtips.

Messerschmitt Bf 109 F-0, coded PH+BE, during factory tests. Note squared-off supercharger air intake.

ratios. Its production continued until October 1939. The engine drove a VDM 9-11207A three-bladed metal propeller of constant speed type, with a diameter of 9 ft 10 in (3000 mm). The aircraft was equipped with a lever for manual adjustment of the propeller pitch in case the constant speed governor failed.

The oil tank of 56.5 litre capacity (it was normally filled with 50 litres of 'Intava 100', 'Rotring' or 'Aero Shell mittel' oils) was moved on top of the engine reduction gear's housing. The oil had to be changed every 8-10 hours of engine running time. The oil cooler was built into the lower cowling. Airflow through it was automatically regulated by means of a thermostat and a hydraulically operated cooling flap. The engine was cooled by a mixture of water and ethylene glycol (in 1:1 proportion), together with 1.5% of Schutzöl 39 anti-corrosion additive. The coolant mixture was stored in two header tanks with a total capacity of 35 litres, located on either side of the engine. The underwing radiators were installed behind the main spar and fitted with flaps to regulate the airflow. The split flaps located behind the radiators were operated via hydraulic actuators and thermostatically controlled.

The airframe was made of duralumin with fabric-covered control surfaces. The semi-monocoque construction of the fuselage copied that of the Bf 109 E. The fuselage shell comprised two halves, seamed at the axis of symmetry. Each half shell consisted of eight sections with integral formers. The construction was stiffened by longerons, five in each

fuselage half. There were two additional longerons at the upper and lower seam of the two fuselage halves. The end part of the fuselage housed an oval-shaped former, which supported the tailfin. The rear section of the fuselage also housed the tail wheel bay and the wheel retraction mechanism. The 290 x 110 mm tail wheel was mounted on a strut fitted with an oleo shock absorber and semi-retracted into the fuselage by means of a hydraulic mechanism.

The cockpit set of navigational, flight control and engine control instruments was very similar to that of the Bf 109 E-4. The gauges had a slightly differently layout and some new instruments were added - such as an electric bank indicator and a Patin master compass. Electronic equipment consisted of a FuG VIIa radio set (mounted at the fourth fuselage seam), which comprised an S 5b transmitter and an E 5a receiver powered by a U 4b/24 converter.

The cockpit was partially protected by three armoured plates screwed to the floor and a 10 mm armoured bulkhead located between the cockpit and fuel tank. The canopy consisted of three pieces. In the lower corners of the windshield two small triangular windows were installed to let more light in on the instrument panel. Although the Bf 109 F-1 manual stated that on the starboard side the triangular glass panel was removed and replaced by a solid metal panel supporting the Walther flare pistol port, in practice this solution was not in use before the arrival of the F-3 variant. In order to enhance the pilot's protection, from mid-1941, a supplemental slab of armoured glass was often screwed to the front of the windshield.

The centre section of the canopy – the hood – was hinged to open sideways to starboard and fitted with a 6 mm armour plate, which protected the pilot's head from the rear. The front side panels of the canopy could be slid open. The centre and rear sections of the canopy could be jettisoned in an emergency with one pull of a lever located inside the cockpit.

The main, self-sealing 400 litre fuel tank was located beneath and behind the pilot's seat. The fuel was fed to the engine by an FBH membrane pump. The fuel filler point was located aft of the cockpit, on the port side of the fuselage.

The fuselage section behind the cockpit housed three cylindrical oxygen bottles each of 2 litres capacity. Their filling valve was located on the starboard side of the fuselage. The oxygen was delivered to the oxygen apparatus mounted on the cockpit floor by the starboard sidewall. The sixth, rear section of the fuselage, housed a 7.5 Ah battery, which together with 2000 W Bosch generator (powered by the aircraft's engine) delivered 24 Volts to the electrical installation. Automatic safety fuses protected all electrical circuits.

The two-piece, single-spar tapered wing was fitted with rounded wingtips and automatic leading edge slats. The wings were covered with a skin of duralumin sheets, flush-riveted to the ribs and longerons. The ailerons were metal framed and covered with fabric, mass-balanced and operated by means of actuators. The slotted flaps were synchronized with the two-piece flaps regulating the airflow through the underwing radiators. The wingtips were fitted with position lights. The wing area was 16.05 m² (as compared to 16.35 m² of the Bf 109 E). The main landing gear wheel wells, of

circular section where they housed the wheel, began at the wing root between the leading edge and the main spar. The undercarriage was fitted with oleo shock absorbers and mounted on the lower sides of the fuselage frame. The 650 x 150 mm wheels were equipped with hydraulic drum brakes. The undercarriage legs were 1975 mm apart. Wheel covers, originally mounted on the legs, were often removed to prevent clogging by mud and snow. The hydraulic retraction mechanism was equipped with an emergency system for lowering the landing gear.

The cantilevered, tapered vertical stabilizers had rounded tips and were of similar construction to that of the wing. The tailplanes' angle of incidence could be adjusted in flight (from + 1°10' to - 6°) by means of a manually operated handwheel located in the cockpit. The tailfin was of asymmetric cross section in order to provide an aerodynamic counter to engine torque. The rudder was operated via control cables, while the elevators were moved up and down by means of actuator rods. The Bf 109 F-1's armament consisted of a single, 20 mm MG FF/M cannon with 60 rounds and two 7.92 mm MG 17 machine guns with 500 rounds per gun.

As soon as the first series-production Messerschmitt Bf 109 F-1s were delivered to front-line units, it transpired that there were many early development snags to be sorted out. The aircraft could not exceed 250 kph with its landing flaps lowered, though it could reach 350 kph with just its landing gear down. The maximum authorized dive speed was 750 kph; however, due to the control surfaces' tendency to 'freeze' in one position, reaching such a speed was highly inadvisable and as events were to show, deadly dangerous.

The first prototype of the definitive series-production Bf 109 F-1 was the Bf 109 F-0, W.Nr. 5603 (coded CE+BP) powered by a DB 601 N engine. It basically differed from the series-production machines in a relatively small supercharger air intake.

The Bf 109 F-0, W.Nr. 5603 (CE+BP) was subsequently to be used in the Me 309 program for testing the installation of a tricycle undercarriage with front wheel.

In February 1941 three Bf 109 F-1s were lost in fatal accidents. In all three cases pilots had reported over the radio that violent engine vibrations were rocking the airframe. Subsequent investigations revealed that the fuselage longerons had deformed so badly that the tail assembly had broken off. These structural failures were so sudden the pilots had no chance to bail out. Finally, the crash of the fourth machine revealed that the rivets fastening the aft fuselage skinning were torn loose or missing and that the metal sheets in this spot were cracked or badly deformed. The reason behind this was the insufficiently stiffened joint between the fuselage and empennage. Hence, at certain engine rpm levels, the resonant vibration of the non-braced horizontal stabilizer tended to literally tear off the tail at the junction of seam number nine. Two external stiffen-

ers were added to each side of the troublesome area, i.e. the joint between the last former and the tail bracket.

Another common problem was frequent jamming of the MG FF/M cannon, caused by insufficient cooling of the weapon, as well as failures in the hydraulic braking system fitted to the main landing gear.

Series production of the Bf 109 F-1 variant commenced in August 1940 at the Messerschmitt Werk Regensburg plant. The following month, in September 1940, the Wiener-Neustädter Flugzeugwerke GmbH (WNF for short) also began assembling the machine. Of the 207 aircraft ordered, 157 were manufactured by the Messerschmitt plant and a further 50[8] by WNF. They received serial numbers from the following blocks: 5601-5790 (Messerschmitt Regensburg) and 6601-6650 (WNF). The price of one Bf 109

F-1 was 63,000 RM. A distinctive feature of the WNF produced machines was the squared-off supercharger air intake.

In May 1941, the Bf 109 F-1/U1 variant was tested, armed with twin, cowl-mounted 13 mm MG 131 machine guns in place of the standard 7.92 mm MG 17s. Initially, two aircraft were selected for this purpose: W.Nr. 5711 (tested at Rechlin) and W.Nr. 5712 (tested at the Luftwaffe's proving ground at Tarnewitz). Shortly afterwards, another F-1, W.Nr. 5720, was rebuilt to F-1/U1 standard. It was used for testing new ammunition feed systems and cartridge ejection chutes.

Messerschmitt Bf 109 F-2

Series production of the Bf 109 F-2 variant started in November 1940 at the WNF plant and AGO plant at Oschersleben concurrently with the first deliveries of the MG 151/15 cannons. Initially, only 120 machines of this variant were planned but, eventually, as many as 1350 were ordered.

The F-1 and F-2 were externally very similar. Both variants were powered by the DB 601 N engine, which gave the two practically the same performance. The only noteworthy difference was the armament, for the Bf 109 F-2 sported the engine-mounted 15 mm MG 151/15 cannon with 200 rounds. The ammunition was stowed within the port wingroot and belt fed into the fuselage. The storage bin for the spent cartridges and belt links was located beneath the cockpit's floor. Some factory-fresh aircraft, as well as machines modified in the field, featured a system of valves that allowed coolant to be cut off from a damaged radiator. If one of the two radiators was shot through, the pilot could eliminate it from the cooling system and let the

The first series-production Messerschmitt Bf 109 F-1 manufactured by Wiener-Neustadt plant.

Messerschmitt Bf 109 F-2s at a factory airfield of the Wiener-Neustadt plant.

Messerschmitt Bf 109 V31, W.Nr. 5642 (SG+EK), used for testing undercarriage in the Me 309 program

Messerschmitt Bf 109 F-2, W.Nr. 8195 (VD+AJ), produced in Erla plant, was tested with ski landing gear fitted.

coolant circulate through the other, undamaged radiator.

The fighter-bomber variant, designated Bf 109 F-2/B or Bf 109 F-2/Bo, was fitted with the ETC 500/IXb centreline-mounted bomb rack, which could carry a single 250 kg (551 lb) SC 250 bomb, or the ETC 50/VIIId rack for carrying four 50 kg SC 50 bombs. It is not clear if a tropicalized Bf 109 F-2/trop variant was officially produced, or whether tropical filters for the supercharger air intakes were retrofitted to some machines in field workshops. Certainly such filters were present on several aircraft operated by 2.(H)/Aufklärungsgruppe 14 (including

WNr. 5445). It has to be noted that the tropical filter could not be attached to the standard supercharger air intake of the Bf 109 F-2 and the early Bf 109 F-4.

In order to extend the Bf 109 F-2's range, 300 litre under-belly drop tanks were introduced in the late summer of 1941. Fuel from the auxiliary tank was "pumped" by compressed air from the main fuselage fuel tank, so there was no need to install an extra fuel pump.

An equally common addition was the FuG 25 IFF radio set. Some aircraft from the last production runs were not fitted with the external tail stiffeners, which had been made redundant

Messerschmitt Bf 109 F-2, W.Nr. 9246 fitted with experimental armament – underwing RZ 65 rocket launchers.

Messerschmitt Bf 109 F-2 of I./JG 51 shortly before the start of the Operation 'Barbarossa'.

Aircraft of Stab I./JG 51 at Krefeld aerodrome in May 1941. In the foreground the machine flown by *Gruppenkommandeur* Hptm. Hermann Joppien. Engine cowling and rudder are yellow.

by revised internal construction of the fuselage. Many Bf 109 F-2s had circular wheel wells, while others received the squared-off wheel wells.

Some publications claim that several aircraft were fitted with a GM 1 installation, which enabled nitrous oxide to be directly injected into the engine's cylinders in order to boost its high-altitude performance. Such aircraft – supposedly – bore the Bf 109 F-2/Z designation and were produced at the WNF plant[9]. However, there is no information in the source data to confirm that these machines existed.

Three Bf 109 F-2s were converted to the Bf 109 F-2/U1 variant armed with two cowl-mounted 13 mm MG 131 machine guns in place of the standard 7.92 mm MG 17s. After the trials at the

Resupplying ammunition to MG 151 cannon in a Messerschmitt Bf 109 F-2. Note construction details of radiator flaps.

Tarnewitz test facility the three aircraft were returned to the Messerschmitt factory with a note that the armament mounting was "too weak". After the arrival of the Bf 109 G variant further tests with the Bf 109 F-2/U1 were discontinued. One of the upgunned 'Friedrichs', W.Nr. 6711, was combat flown over France by none other than Obstlt. Adolf Galland, *Geschwaderkommodore* of JG 26.

The F-2s from the first production runs were troubled by numerous teething problems, as described in the report written in early April 1941 by the commander of *Luftflotte 2* Generalfeldmarschall Kesselring:

"In connection with the model Bf 109 F the following main complaints have been reported to me:

1.   On one aircraft the tail-plane complete with tail section was torn off at the fuselage disconnecting point (panel 9). The fuselage disconnecting point was found to be too weak.

2.   The external elevator bearing is breaking away and must be reinforced.

3.   The bearing flange for the elevator bearing must also be reinforced.

4.   The parking brake is completely inadequate. A mere reinforcement of the spring would hardly be sufficient.

5.   The pilot's seat is too far to the front. It must also be pointed out that, due to the present position of the seat, a pilot in full flying kit will be unable to move the control column fully backwards and one result of this is that only wheel landings are possible.

6.   The breathing tube is too short for pilots of average and above average height.

7.   The breathing equipment for high-altitude flying is also inadequate. An additional pressure-oxygen unit is urgently required.

8. The front and rear bolts holding the wingtip edges deflect and rattle.

9. The ammunition boxes fitted in the wings are loose and have jammed. This was temporarily remedied in the unit by means of wooden blocks fitted underneath, but this does not present a permanent solution.

10. The oil radiator is inadequately secured.

11. A solution of the wing surface deformation problem, which since the unit reported adverse flying qualities with a deformed aircraft, has also been observed on the right-hand wing.

12. Securing of plating on landing gear, oil radiator and water cooler.

13. Thermostat must be secured more firmly.

14. The welding of aileron horns on aircraft supplied is to be subjected to a test by the unit based on instructions to be issued by the Generalluftzeugmeister.

15. The distance between the ribs of the aileron is larger on the model F than on the model E. Due to poor quality stitching the fabric tends to pull out of shape.

16. Tyre wear is extremely high due to the pronounced toe-in, this is particularly noticeable among aircraft using concrete runways where a tyre change is necessary after 20 sorties.

17. The fuel consumption varies considerably for different aircraft, e.g. the aircraft produced by Arado require 70 litres per hour more than others. It is assumed that the aircraft companies will carry out, belatedly, a more thorough tuning of engines.

18. The red fuel warning lamp shows inaccurate readings. It was found that in one case the lamp did not light up until the fuel had dropped to 10 litres, whereas in another case the lamp was observed to light up with 60 litres in the tank.

19. Complaints regarding the automatic propeller system.

20. Cable securing screws on the valve body are too long, so that the cylinder wall is pierced when the screws are tightened. Result: oil running through.

21. Since the 15 mm bush and the deep-groove-type radial ball-bearing of the supercharger are frequently being deflected, an order must be given to have the end clearance checked, if possible, after five hours operating time. Within one quarter, 30 superchargers out of 400 have shown such faults and had to be replaced.

22. One unit proposes a higher basic setting of the supercharger to improve high altitude performance.

23. Due to leaking valves there is relatively high wear of N-engines (which have a life of about 40 hours). This leads to an increased demand for spare engines.

24. Reduced altitude performance was observed with repaired engines. It is assumed that the performance is not re-tested on altitude test stands but merely by recalculation. Random checks seem essential."[10]

The deficiencies listed in Kesselring's report were, by and large, fixed in the later series and in the F-4 variant.

A belly-landed Messerschmitt Bf 109 F-2, coded 'Black 9' of 11./JG 51, summer 1941. This shot offers a good view of the camouflage scheme on the wing upper surface.

DB 601 N engine check in a Messerschmitt Bf 109 F-2 of 7./JG 2, St. Pol-Brias.

Messerschmitt Bf 109 F-2/B of 2./JG 51, which from mid-August 1941 began to specialize in fighter-bomber missions. Note under-belly ETC 50/VIIId bomb rack for four SC 50 bombs.

MONOGRAFIE MONOGRAPHS SPECIAL EDITION

In the period between November 1940 and August 1941 1334 machines of the F-2 variant[11] were manufactured by the Messerschmitt plant at Regensburg, Arado plant at Warnemünde, WNF plant at Wiener-Neustadt, AGO plant at Oschersleben, and Erla Maschinenwerk plant at Leipzig. The aircraft received serial numbers from the following blocks: 5601-5790, 8901-9001, 9151-9250 (aircraft from all three preceding blocks were produced by Messerschmitt Regensburg), 6651-6822 (WNF), 8075-8266 (Erla), 5401-5558, 9535-9734 (aircraft from both pre-

2./JG 51 getting ready for an operational sortie; Schalatovka airfield, August 1941. Seen on the cowling of this Bf 109 F-2/B is the *Geschwader* badge, with the *Gruppe* emblem below the cockpit. Also note lowered underwing radiator flaps.

Shackling up 50 kg bombs onto ETC 50/VIIId bomb rack under the fuselage of a Messerschmitt Bf 109 F-2/B of 2./JG 51. Of special interest are the whistles mounted along the bomb stabilizing fins, which magnified the shriek of a falling bomb.

Front view of the lower part of a Messerschmitt Bf 109 F-2/B with visible ETC 50/VIIId bomb rack and SC 50 bombs. This photo also offers excellent view of landing gear wheel struts and oil cooler scoop. Note the starter crank on the port side. further aft open canopy with in-built armor plate protecting pilot's head.

ceding blocks were produced by Arado), and 12601-12978 (AGO).

Messerschmitt Bf 109 F-3

The F-3 variant was a direct development of the Bf 109 F-1. It was fitted with a Daimler-Benz DB 601 E rated at 1350 hp, which drove a three-bladed VDM 9-12010A propeller. The armament consisted of one 20 mm MG FF/M and twin machine guns. Since that type of cannon had proved very troublesome, production of the F-3 ceased as soon as the superb MG 151/15 became available. Only 15 F-3 machines were assembled between October 1940 and January 1941. It remains unclear if they were actually built at the WNF plant or by Messerschmitt Werk Regensburg[12].

Messerschmitt Bf 109 F-4

The most numerous variant of the 'Friedrich' was the Bf 109 F-4. It was almost identical in appearance to its predecessor, the F-2. Later Bf 109 F-4s dispensed with the tailplane reinforcement strips, the internal structure of the tailplane being redesigned to eliminate the vibration problem. During the series production of the aircraft the supercharger air intake was also revised. It was enlarged and strenghtened, allowing to fit it with the tropical filter. The F-4 was often fitted with extra armour for the pilot. Many aircraft flew with a bolt-on armoured glass plate added to the windscreen

and retrofitted in the field. A factory-installed innovation was a 5 mm thick armour plate "hood" installed inside the cockpit to protect the pilot's head. The majority of Bf 109 F-4s had circular wheel wells.

The F-4 was powered by the long-awaited Daimler-Benz DB 601 E rated at 1350 hp, which drove a three-bladed VDM 9-12010A propeller. The standard armament consisted of twin, cowl-mounted 7.92 mm MG 17 machine guns with 500 rounds per gun and an engine mounted 20 mm MG 151/20 cannon with 200 rounds, firing through the propeller's hub. The aiming device was a Revi C/12D reflective gunsight. Radio equipment included a FuG VIIa radio and a FuG 25 IFF transponder (in spring 1942 changed to a FuG 25a).

Approximately 600 aircraft were completed in the Bf 109 F-4/Z configuration. These machines were fitted with the GM 1 installation, which boosted the engine's performance for short periods and gave additional 20 kph at altitudes above 6000 metres. The nitrous oxide reservoir was mounted in the wings, aft of the wheel wells. The aircraft equipped with GM 1 boost are easily recognizable by their deeper Fö 870 oil cooler, mounted under the forward cowling. Many of them were also equipped with the VDM 9-12087A propeller with wider blades.

A Messerschmitt Bf 109 F-2/B coded 'Black 1' of 2./JG 51 flown by Lt. Heinz Schumann. The aircraft is armed with four SC 50 bombs mounted under its belly.

Cranking the engine of a Bf 109 F-2/B coded 'Black 1' of 2./JG 51.

Messerschmitt Bf 109 F-4, W.Nr. 13388, coded 'White 5', was the regular mount of Lt. Gerhard Barkhorn, *Staffelkapitän* of 4./JG 52 in June 1942. The aircraft was named 'Christl' for his girlfriend. The most interesting feature of this machine is the unusual triple wire antenna installation, which is also known to be mounted on a few other machines of JG 52 and JG 54.

There were also other modifications of the basic F-4 variant, which featured the so-called *Rüstsätze* (add-on kits) in order to meet local demands. These included:

Bf 109 F-4/R1 – could be upgunned with two 15 mm MG 151/15 cannons mounted in FGB (Flügelgondelbewaffnung) underwing gondolas streamlined with wooden fairings, offering 135 rounds per gun. However, since the system was prone to jamming, usually only 100 rounds per gun were carried. A total of 240 aircraft of the F-4/R1 variant were built by the WNF plant in 1942, but the gondolas with cannons were actually rarely used. The Tarnewitz facility also tested underwing gondolas armed with 20 mm MG 151/20 cannons. These gondolas, delivered by rail to Tarnewitz in March 1942, were experimentally mounted on Bf 109 F-4 W.Nr. 7449. In the period between 24th March and the end of April 1942 the aircraft carried out some 60

flight tests. In early May 1942 a further four machines armed with underwing MG 151/20s arrived at Tarnewitz, where they performed at least 27 flight tests. Also at Rechlin, in the period between 11th and 16th May 1942, four machines rigged with add-on MG 151/20 cannons were test flown (including Bf 109 F-4/R1 W.Nr. 9246). Later on these machines were issued to I./JG 52, which at that time was operating over the eastern front, for combat trials. In late May 1941 the Tarnewitz facility tested another WNF produced Bf 109 F-4/R1 (W.Nr. 13149), this time fitted with additional anti-dust protection in the form of leather covers over the spent cartridge chutes. Between 28th May and 2nd June 1942 this modification was tested during 15 firing exercises and deemed satisfactory for frontline service. The Tarnewitz tests of Bf 109 F-4s armed with MG 151/20s in underwing gondolas were not officially terminated before 1st Octo-

Messerschmitt Bf 109 F-4 trop at one of German airfields prior to its delivery to Africa to serve with JG 27. Note the 300 liter under-fuselage drop tank.

ber 1942, and in fact, this modification only saw widespread use when the Bf 109 G-2 variant entered service.

Bf 109 F-4/R2 – a photo-reconnaissance variant equipped with an Rb 20x30 camera. Due to the weight of the photo equipment, the R2 variant was stripped of its radio apparatus. Five Bf 109 F-4/R2s were assembled by the Erla plant.

Bf 109 F-4/R3 – a photo-reconnaissance variant equipped with an Rb 50x30 camera. This variant, too, lacked a radio. The production run

Messerschmitt Bf 109 F-4/B of II./JG 51 armed with four SC 50 bombs. Apparently the aircraft was fitted with a replacement wing as it features two different types of wheel wells.

Knight Cross holder Lt. Josef 'Pepi' Jennewein of I./JG 51 in cockpit of a Messerschmitt Bf 109 F-4.

This Messerschmitt Bf 109 F-4 coded 'Black 2' of 2./JG 51 made an emergency landing on a Russian steppe. Clearly visible are details of DB 601 E engine and 7.92 mm MG 17 cowl machine guns.

of the Bf 109 F-4/R3 totalled 36 machines (all by the Erla plant).

Bf 109 F-4/R4 – a photo-reconnaissance variant equipped with an Rb 75x30 camera, devoid of FuG VIIa radio. The Erla plant built only one specimen of this variant.

Bf 109 F-4/R8 – a photo-reconnaissance variant equipped with an Rb 75x50 camera and with the FuG VIIa radio set.

Bf 109 F-4s that were not fitted with GM 1 nitrous oxide boost or underwing gondolas with cannons could perform the role of a fighter-bomber (designated F-4/B). As in the case of the F-2/B variant, the F-4/B could deliver a single 250 kg SC 250 bomb when fitted with a centreline ETC 500/IXb rack, or alternatively, could carry four 50 kg SC 50 bombs under its belly when fitted with an ETC 50/VIIId rack.

Beginning in August 1941, the Erla plant started production of the tropicalized Bf 109 F-4 trop. This variant was fitted with an anti-dust filter and a pilot survival kit in case of emergency landing. Stored in the rear fuselage, the kit included food, water and a Mauser rifle.

In the period between May 1941 and May 1942 1841 machines of the F-4 variant were manufactured by the WNF plant at Wiener-Neustadt and Erla Maschinenwerk plant at Leipzig. The aircraft received serial numbers from the following blocks: 6999-7250, 7251-7660, 13001-13391 (aircraft from all three preceding blocks were produced by WNF), 8267-8399,

Messerschmitt Bf 109 F-2/B of I./JG 54 fitted with underfuselage ETC 500/IXb bomb rack for carrying a 250 kg SC 250 bomb. Wheel covers were removed to prevent clogging the wheels by mud and snow

MONOGRAFIE MONOGRAPHS SPECIAL EDITION

8400-8806, and 10001-10290 (aircraft from all three preceding blocks were produced by Erla).

Messerschmitt Bf 109 F-5

During a Messerschmitt company board meeting in summer 1941, Willi Messerschmitt came up with the idea of designing a dedicated, high-altitude interceptor and reconnaissance aircraft based on the Bf 109 F-2. The aircraft was to be powered by a DB 601 N engine running on 100-octane fuel, and fitted with a VDM 9-11207A propeller. It was to be armed with a 20 mm MG 151/20 cannon and take advantage of GM 1 boost. The suggested designation was Bf 109 F-5. However, the aircraft met with little interest from the Reich's Air Ministry. According to RLM documents, only one aircraft of this version was built[13].

Messerschmitt Bf 109 F-6

In accordance with the Luftwaffe's fighter aircraft production programme, issued in October 1940, the Messerschmitt plant was to produce 1281 machines of the Bf 109 F-6 variant. This variant was to be based on the Bf 109 F-2 airframe and make use of the DB 601 N engine running on 100-octane fuel. The basic difference between the two was the more powerful armament of the former, which comprised an engine-mounted 20 mm MG 151/20 cannon, twin cowl-mounted 7.92 mm MG 17 machine guns and two additional machine guns mounted in the wings and firing outside the propeller's disc.

The designation Bf 109 F-6/U was used at the unit level for a Bf 109 F-2 which had been equipped with two wing-mounted 20 mm MG FF/M cannons. The aircraft was serial-numbered W.Nr. 6750 and in the autumn of 1941 it was delivered to Stab/JG 26 in France, to be tested in combat by the Kommodore himself, Obstlt. Adolf Galland. On 18th November 1941, at 12:32 hrs, Galland shot down a Spitfire whilst flying this very aircraft. It took a burst of 14 rounds from the MG 151/20 cannon, 22 rounds from the MG FF/M cannons and 62 rounds from the MG 17 machine guns to down the British fighter.

Experimental aircraft and test-beds

Many Bf 109 Fs served as experimental aircraft. Among them was the Bf 109 V23, W.Nr. 1801 (coded CE+BP), one of the prototypes of the F-series. It was subsequently to

Another shot of Messerschmitt Bf 109 F-4s during engine check at Briansk airfield, February 1942.

Hot air generators enabled ground crews to start engines of their Bf 109 F-4s even during the severe winter of 1941/42.

Armorers of II./JG 51 loading 20 mm MG 151/20 cannon of a Messerschmitt Bf 109 F-4, Briansk, February 1942.

be used in the Me 309 program for testing the installation of a tricycle undercarriage with front wheel. So modified, the machine flew no fewer than 23 times, with, alternatively, test pilots Wurster and Baur at the controls. In January 1941 the front wheel leg was shortened and the tests continued. The aircraft was eventually lost in the summer of 1944 at Mühlacker aerodrome during a strafing attack by Allied fighters.

Two machines (Bf 109 F-1, W.Nr. 5716 and Bf 109 F-1, W.Nr. 5717) designated respectively the V30 and V31, were adapted in 1942 to test pressurized cockpit installations for the future Me 309. The V31 (Bf 109 F-1, W.Nr. 5642. coded SG+EK) was in turn equipped with new landing gear, a pressurized cockpit and a completely revised engine cooling system, in which the radiators and oil coolers were built into the fuselage and only extended in flight. A wide track undercarriage was tested (from 13th June 1941) at Regensburg on Bf 109 F-2 W.Nr. 9161, while the V24 prototype (W.Nr. 5604), was fitted with a single radiator mounted under the fuselage and tested in the wind tunnels at Göttingen and Chalasis-Meudon.

In July 1941, Bf 109 F-4 W.Nr. 7003 fitted with a DB 601 E engine, was used to test the Me P6 propeller. Yet another early 'Friedrich', Bf 109 F-2 W.Nr. 8195 (coded VD+AJ) was tested with ski landing gear fitted.

In 1942, Bf 109 F-2, W.Nr. 9246, was used to test the effectiveness of a new air-to-air weapon: the 73 mm Rheinmetall-Borsig RZ (*Rauchzylinder*) 65 unguided rocket missile. The rockets were fired in fours by tubular launchers under the wings.

Another noteworthy conversion was the Bf 109 F-0 (W.Nr. 5608, D-ITXP) airframe, which was modified by the Messerschmitt factory to accept a BMW 801 A-0 engine, in an attempt to meet the RLM's requirement for a radial-engined fighter. The rebuilt aircraft was designated 'Bf 109 X'. It was first flown on 2nd September 1940, with the Messerschmitt test pilot, Dr. Hermann Wurster, at the controls. In his opinion, the aircraft's performance was similar to that of the Bf 109 E, though it handled better during landings. Nevertheless, the aircraft was plagued by persistent engine problems. Overall, it was flown on 25 test flights and spent a total of 7 hours and 48 minutes in the air.

Another intriguing (though never completed) project was the Bf 109 W, a fighter floatplane design. A note mentioning such a project, dated 18th June 1941, was written after a meeting of Messerschmitt factory representatives with Gen. Christensen, and it is documented in the RLM's archives. The aircraft was to be a Bf 109 F airframe rigged with floats taken from an Arado Ar 196, the standard German shipboard reconnaissance aircraft throughout the Second World War.

By the end of the war the Germans found yet one more curious use for the Bf 109 F-4 – that of the piloted, top element of a twin-aircraft Mistel system, also known as the *Huckepack*

Lt. Horst Wunderlich in cockpit of a white-camouflaged Bf 109 F-2, coded 'White 4', of 4./JG 51. Note the main tank fuel filler point visible under cockpit.

or *Vater und Sohn*. The idea was to load a war-weary Junkers Ju 88 A-4 bomber with explosives and guide it to its target by means of a fighter aircraft, in this case a Bf 109 F-4, mounted above it on a set of struts. Take-off and flight to the target area was achieved using the engines of the lower element, the pilotless bomber. Upon reaching the target the pilot had to start the engine of the fighter, release the bomber, aim it via radio-controlled servos - and return to base.

Messerschmitt Bf 109 F-2 of JG 51, coded 'Black 10', at Briansk, February 1941. Of interest are the unit's emblem and a dent in propeller's spinner.

A propaganda photograph of a Bf 109 F-2, reproduced in Luftwaffe's magazine *Adler*, was to make an impression that also this type is used in the night fighter role.

By June 1942, when production of the 'Friedrich' was phased out, approximatelly 3400 Bf 109 Fs of all sub-variants had been manufactured, this number including uncertain amount of F-0s, 207 F-1s, 1334 F-2s, and 1841 F-4s.

Combat debut over the Channel

The *Oberkommando der Luftwaffe*[14] issued the first series-production Messerschmitt Bf 109 F-1s to JG 51, which in the autumn of 1940 was stationed in France near the English Channel. During that period it was the most active *Jagdwaffe* unit engaged in operations against Great Britain. The new mounts were delivered to Stab/JG 51 in early October 1940. At that time the *Geschwader* was led by Maj. Werner Mölders, the Luftwaffe's highest-ranking ace. His operational career had begun on 14th April 1938 during the Spanish Civ-

il War. During that campaign he served with 3./JG 88, which formed part of the Condor Legion. By the 5th of December 1938 he had claimed 14 Republican aircraft shot down, which made him the Legion's most successful fighter pilot. He scored his first victory in the Second World War at 14:50 hrs on 20th September 1939 over Apach-Bündingen, when he knocked down a French Curtiss H-75A fighter of GC II./5 flown by Sgt. Queguiner. By the end of September 1940 Mölders had racked up an impressive tally of 42 victories scored during the Second World War, plus another 14 during the Spanish Civil War.

Maj. Mölders flew his first two combat sorties in Bf 109 F-1, W.Nr. 5628, coded SG+GW, on 9th October 1940. Only two days later, on 11th October 1940 at 12:30 hrs, Mölders bagged a Spitfire over Folkestone for his 43rd victory. His victim was Spitfire Mk I, s/n X4562, of No 66 Sqn RAF, flown by P/O J.H.T. Pickering, who suffered injuries during this encounter. The

A pair of Messerschmitt Bf 109 F-4s at an airfield somewhere in Western Europe. Lowered wing flaps and radiator flaps are clearly visible.

MONOGRAFIE MONOGRAPHS SPECIAL EDITION

A reconnaissance Messerschmitt Bf 109 F-4/R3, coded 4U+TL of 3.(F)/123 equipped with auxiliary 300 l. drop fuel tank.

following day Mölders claimed three Hurricanes during two sorties. The first of them belonged to No 249 Sqn and was flow by Adj. Perrin, a Frenchman in the RAF; the second one was lost to the strength of No 605 Sqn RAF (its pilot Sgt. McIntosh was killed in action) while the third, of No 253 Sqn RAF, was badly damaged but managed to limp back to base. Its pilot, P/O Gaudry, was injured in his legs by shrapnel from cannon rounds. More victories promptly followed. On 15th October 1940 a Spitfire of No 601 Sqn fell to his guns (its pilot Sgt. Fenemore perished) and on 17th another Spitfire, this time of No 66 Sqn (the pilot, P/O Reilley, was KIA). On 22nd October 1940 it took Maj. Mölders three minutes to claim three Hurricanes (at 15:40, 15:41 and 15:42 hrs). Those were his 49th, 50th and 51st aerial victories. This time only one of the three claims could be positively verified – a Hurricane of No 605 Sqn RAF, which crash-landed due to combat damage (the pilot, P/O Milne, was injured in the crash).

Extracting the Rb 50x30 camera from the fuselage of a Messerschmitt Bf 109 F-4/R3 upon its return from a sortie. Of note id the lack of FuG VIIa radio antenna and mast.

MONOGRAFIE MONOGRAPHS
SPECIAL EDITION

A pair of reconnaissance Messerschmitt Bf 109 F-4/Z/R3s of 1.(F)/Aufkl.Gr. 122, which in the summer of 1942 was stationed in Sardinia.

With his victory tally surpassing the 50 mark, on 25th October 1940 Mölders was promoted to the rank of Oberstleutnant (Lieutenant Colonel). On the same day he added two more victories to his score. During the first mission, at 10:45 hrs, he flamed a Hurricane of Polish No 302 Sqn flown by F/Lt Franciszek Jastrzębski. W/Cdr Mümler noted in the squadron's diary: "Task for today – fighting German Me-109s. Clouds at 3000 ft, 50/50 overcast, visibility very good. A patrol over Biggin Hill at 20,000 ft. Upon reaching the prescribed altitude the 'Ballerina'[15] warned us of enemy aircraft approach-

ing from the east at a higher altitude. Off to one side flew No 229 Sqn, which engaged in a dogfight with a bunch of Me-109s, while I kept an eye on the Messerschmitts above us. The Germans, however, turned back towards France and disappeared in the distance. Then we turned for England. We were passed by a flight of Me-109s, flying some 500 meters above, but it scurried towards France. We landed at Northolt at 10:30 hrs., where we learned that over the Channel F/Lt Jastrzębski and P/O Bernaś had separated from the squadron. Jastrzębski was seen to dive steeply towards the French coast, while Bernaś

An umbrella shading the cockpit of a Messerschmitt Bf 109 F-4/R3 coded F6+UH of 1.(F)/122 from the scorching Mediterranean sun.

turned for England. Jastrzębski didn't report over the R/T. The squadron did not register any contact with the enemy. Jastrzębski failed to return to Northolt, perhaps due to engine problems"[16].

Mölders' second quarry was P/O Yule of 145 Sqn RAF, shot down at 13:20 hrs. The injured English pilot wrecked his fighter during an emergency landing. Obstlt. Mölders last victory in October was scored four days later, on 29th, at 13:55 hrs.

It was at this time that the first Bf 109F-1s were received by I./JG 51. The first machine of this type was lost in action on 11th November 1940. It was Bf 109 F-1, W.Nr. 5635, flown by the *Staffelkapitän* 1./JG 51, Oblt. Georg Clausen (a 17-victory ace). He successfully ditched his fighter in the Channel but eventually drowned. This incident was described by Maj. Fritz von

Forell in his book dedicated to Mölders and his *Geschwader*:

"The 11th of November proved one of the blackest days in Oberstleutnant Mölders' career. For weeks, owing to a bad case of flu, he had to stay out of the cockpit of his Messerschmitt. Finally, he felt fit enough to direct his fighters from the ground control room. In the meantime the best of his boys, Oberleutnant Claus, took command of the first *Staffel*. Despite adverse weather conditions in November, the *Geschwader* flew many tough escort missions for the benefit of bomber units. Claus excelled in his new post, proving that, even without his tutor around, he was a capable *Kapitän* and an excellent fighter pilot.

On that fateful day the *Geschwader* again took to the air to shepherd dive-bombers to their target at the mouth of the Thames river.

Beginning with early October 1941, this Messerschmitt Bf 109 F-1, W.Nr. 5628, coded SG+GW, became a regular mount of *Geschwaderkommodore* JG 51 Maj. Werner Mölders.

The same aircraft with partially overpainted fuselage code letters. Engine cowl, wingtips and rudder are yellow. Note 54 victory bars on the rudder.

Maj. Werner Mölders among JG 51 pilots describing his latest victory.

Messerschmitt Bf 109 F-2, coded 'Black 2' of 2./JG 51, Coquelles airfield, France, April 1941. Engine cowling and rudder are yellow. The aircraft in early RLM 71/02/65 camouflage.

Banks of thick cloud hung low over the Channel and intermittent rain squalls limited the already poor visibility even more. Finally the bomber formation located its target, a coastal convoy. A burst of excited voices over the R/T betrayed a fight breaking out in the air. Someone declared a victory; then someone else feverishly shouted a warning. The intense radio traffic suggested that the skirmish was particularly heavy. Then... what happened? One of the pilots reported that he was hit. Moments later another report followed – a ditching in the Channel!

Mölders anxiously left the ground control room and walked out towards the landing ground. The first of the returning machines, rocking its wings, came into sight. This was Oberleutnant Eberle, who was announcing his victory over a Spitfire in the usual Luftwaffe manner. As soon as he clambered out of the cockpit, he reported with a shaken voice that Oberleutnant Claus had ditched in the Thames estuary because of a coolant leak from his shot-up radiator. Mölders listened no longer. He rushed to a telephone; for the first time Mölders men saw their *Kommodore*, known for his steel nerves, look apprehensive. With his hand trembling he gripped the receiver, instructing the air sea rescue service. He would go to any lengths to save his best pilot. He immediately ordered the ground crew to ready an aircraft for him - and, accompanied by Oblt. Eberle, took to the air for the first time in two weeks to search for the man who was closer to him than any other pilot in his *Geschwader*. The two Messerschmitts skimmed the land beneath them, going flat out towards the murky waters of the English Channel. They flashed past the Cape of Margate and approached the Thames estuary. Mölders seemed unconcerned about six Spitfires still circling above the convoy. He kept on looking around, scanning ever-larger areas of empty sea. He stayed over the spot until his Bf 109 had no more fuel to remain, straining his excellent eyesight in the hope of picking

The 'Black 2' of 2./JG 51. Wheels hubs of the main landing gear are covered with RLM 66 varnish. Spinner and propeller blades are painted with RLM 70.

Messerschmitt Bf 109 F-2s of 2./JG 51 at Coquelles, April 1941. In the background aircraft coded '10' and '5'.

up a trace of the missing man against the dark surface of the water. Finally, with a heavy heart, he returned to base. This loss was a personally disheartening blow to him. They were friends and comrades in combat, for good and for bad. So many times they had fought side by side, protecting each other."[17]

From February 1941, Messerschmitt Bf 109 Fs gradually re-equipped the Luftwaffe fighter units stationed along the English Channel. Stab and I./JG 51 received their machines in February, to be followed by III. and IV./JG 51. In March 1941 the new fighters were delivered to Stab and I./JG 3, III./JG 26 as well as Stab, I., II. and III./JG 53. By the end of June 1941 practically all the *Jagdwaffe*'s frontline units in the West had exchanged their 'Emils' – Bf 109 Es – for 'Friedrichs'.

Pilots received the new aircraft with mixed emotions. The Bf 109 F offered better performance than the reliable, but ageing, Bf 109 E. However, the weaker armament of the new version was commonly considered insufficient. Initially, there were also problems with the new fighter's cooling system and fragility of construction, which led to several fatal crashes. The latter deficiency was partially solved by installing external stiffeners on the fuselage of the F-2 variant, but the problem wasn't entirely solved until the introduction of the F-4. Peter Bremer of JG 54 witnessed one such accident:

Engines lasted 20 hrs.

"On 4 June 1941, shortly after we had received our new Bf 109 F-2 aircraft, the *Staffelkapitän*, Oberleutnant Hein, took the entire *Staffel* in tight formation up to maximum altitude. We were flying over the North Sea at 12,500 metres and dived down steeply in formation, our airspeed indicators registering the maximum, about 1000 km/h. We had dived to about 5000 metres, when the *Kapitän* ordered us to pull out slowly. We gradually eased back on our control columns in order to bring the aircraft to a normal attitude, but one excited voice on the radio stated that his aircraft would not pull out. It was Harry Krause. The *Kapitän* told him to keep calm and to slowly and firmly pull back on his stick, but we heard Harry Krause crying: *It's not responding, it's not responding!*

At this point the *Staffelkapitän* told him to bale out. We saw Krause's canopy come away but, to our horror, saw two separate dots falling down followed more slowly by one loosely fluttering parachute. He had pulled his ripcord immediately after he'd left his aircraft (Messerschmitt Bf 109 F-2, W.Nr. 12690) but due to the high speed of his fall, the straps of his parachute had been torn apart and he plummeted to his death. His body was later discovered in a sand dune. Only his flight suit kept him in one piece; there was not a single bone unbroken.

Later, an enquiry determined that, on a specific factory series of the Bf 109 F-2, the fabric

Messerschmitt Bf 109 F-2 of Stab JG 51. In the cockpit *Geschwaderkommodore* Obstlt. Werner Mölders, Mardyck, 4th May 1941. On that day Mölders scored his 65th aerial victory – a Hawker Hurricane of No 602 Sqn RAF.

on the lower area of the rudder ballooned at high diving speeds and jammed the elevators. However, there was no court-martial to determine the question of guilt."[18]

Nevertheless, slowly but steadily, the 'Friedrich' was winning its pilots' trust. The new machine easily outperformed the British Supermarine Spitfire Mk. II. This fact proved particularly welcome in the face of the RAF's increasingly evident numerical superiority. A spell of fair weather in February 1941 allowed for increased activity over the Channel. On 10th February 1941, near Calais, Maj. Werner Mölders and his wingman of Stab/JG 51 shot down a Hurricane apiece. Oblt. Hans-Karl Keitel of 10./JG 51 also claimed a Hurricane, whilst Fw. Heinz Wiest of 12./JG 51 claimed a Spitfire. On that day it was noted in the unit's combat diary, with a tone of triumph: *"Es geht wieder los!"*[19]

Ten days later, on 20th February 1941, during a sweep over the English coast, Maj. Mölders bagged two out of five patrolling Spitfires. These were his 57th and 58th victories. Both machines belonged to No 51 Sqn RAF. The pilots, Sergeants Angus and McAdams were killed in action.

In the early morning of 25th February 1941 six Blenheims escorted by three RAF fighter squadrons struck off for Dunkirk. Another five squadrons indirectly supported their formation. The invading British were challenged by Bf 109 Fs of JG 51; Maj. Mölders chalked up one Spitfire, serial-numbered X4592 of No 611 Sqn RAF (its pilot, P/O Stanley, was killed).

Messerschmitt Bf 109 F-4/Z of JG 2 with 300 l. fuel drop tank.

Messerschmitt Bf 109 F-2, W.Nr. 12 764, flown by *Kommandeur* of I./JG 26, Hptm. Rolf Pingel, after an emergency landing in Kent on 10th July 1940.

The following day, 26th February 1941, six Hurricanes of No 615 Sqn were bounced by Bf 109 Fs of I./JG 51 near Maidstone. One of the British pilots who participated in the ensuing skirmish was F/O Christopher Foxley-Norris:

"Six Hurricane Mk. IIs of 615 Squadron took off from Kenley, flying in two 'vics' of three aircraft. I was flying in the rear 'vic' with Wing Commander Holmwood, our Australian CO, leading and Pilot Officer 'Alfie' Hone weaving as rear cover. We never saw or heard anything of the latter after take-off, which accounted for our later vulnerability.

We were controlled to over 30.000 feet over Kent, heading west and were vectored onto a formation of German fighters alleged to be quite close dead ahead of us and encouraged to 'buster' (full throttle) to overhaul them. 'You must be able to see them now!' I have always suspected that the two plots were confused by control, because at that moment we were jumped by numerous Me 109s from behind. My attacker shot off my propeller at the hub, which was unusual, and did a lot of other damage. I baled out at great height, probably over 25,000 feet, with some initial trouble disentangling my oxygen and radio leads. I finally landed heavily in a field near Ashford, where I received a mistakenly hostile reception from some of the local worthies (I was wearing a black flying suit)."[20]

The German pilots shot down three Hurricanes of No 615 Sqn. during this engagement.

The victors were: Hptm. Hermann-Friedrich Joppien, *Gruppenkommandeur* of I./JG 51 (with a double score) and Oblt. Horst Geyer of Stab JG 51. Moments later some Spitfires of No 610 Sqn joined the fray. P/O Grey was immediately jumped and blasted out of the sky by Maj. Mölders hiding high up in the sun.

More scraps over eastern England followed on 3rd March 1941, when Hptm. Joppien again claimed a brace of Spitfires. One of them was flown by P/O Lockwood of 54 Sqn, who perished in the wreck of his Spitfire (P7300) in the vicinity of Maidstone.

Another resounding success was the mission flown by IV./JG 51 on 5th March 1941, in the area of Boulogne. On that occasion Messerschmitt Bf 109 F-1s engaged the escorts of six Blenheims (of No 139 Sqn) flying as Circus No 6. Slashing through the formation of No 610 Sqn's Spitfires, they took four out in one firing pass. Five days later, on 10th March 1941 (at 17:25 hrs), the commander of IV./JG 51, Maj. Friedrich Beckh, claimed his second Spitfire over France. It was s/n P7381 of No 54 Sqn; its pilot, Sgt. Cooper, was killed.

On the evening of 12th March 1941 two *Schwärme* of Bf 109 Fs on a "free hunting" foray swept over Kent. The first of them, from Stab JG 51, tangled with a pair of Spitfires of No 91 Sqn, which were promptly given aid by the entire strength of No 74 Sqn. Despite their overwhelming numerical advantage, the Brit-

The same aircraft being examined by British experts. Of interest is the painting scheme on the upper surfaces. The spinner is painted in RLM 70 with one third segment of white. The aircraft was restored to flying condition and test-flown. It eventually crashed on 20th October 1941 at Fowlmere, killing its pilot.

A group of 1./JG 26's pilots. Standing fifth from the left is Oblt. Josef Priller. In the background Messerschmitt Bf 109 F-2.

ish failed to down a single Messerschmitt. On the other hand, Maj. Mölders and Hptm. Geyer each claimed a victory. Sgt. Glendinning flying Spitfire P7506 of No 74 Sqn was killed, whereas Sgt. Mann of No 91 Sqn crashed his Spitfire P7693 during a forced landing and suffered injuries. At the same time the leader of the second *Schwarm*, Hptm. Joppien of I./JG 51, knocked down Spitfire P7689 of No 54 Sqn (its pilot, Sgt. Burtonshaw, was killed). The following day,

13th March 1941, the RAF undertook Circus No 7, which targeted the Calais/Marck aerodrome. While countering this raid, Maj. Mölders and Oblt. Hermann Steiger of 7./JG 51 shot down a Spitfire apiece.

At noon on 18th March 1941, six Hurricanes of No 17 Sqn took off from Croydon for a training flight. Twenty minutes later their pilots spotted five fighters closing in from the direction of Bexhill. At first they took the ap-

Maj. Walter Oesau, from 20th July 1941 the *Kommodore* of JG 2, in cockpit of a Bf 109 F-2 at St. Pol-Brias.

Pilots of *Stabsschwarm* JG 2: (from left) Oblt. Erich Leie, Maj. Walter Oesau, Oblt. Rudolf Pflanz and Fw. Günther Seeger.

Messerschmitt Bf 109 F-4 of Stab JG 2, flown by *Geschwader Adjutant* Oblt. Erich Leie, St. Pol, August 1941. Of interest is the partially visible, non-standard tactical marking of the aircraft.

proaching aircraft for Spitfires, which proved a fatal mistake. The five roving Bf 109 Fs of I./JG 51 moved in for the kill. In a lightning attack, Hptm. Joppien and Oblt. Rudolf Busch, both of Stab I./JG 51, shot down one British fighter each. The British pilots, Sgt. Hughes and Sgt. Bartlett, both bailed out with injuries.

Jagdgeschwader 53 claimed its first success with the Bf 109 F as early as 19th March 1941, when the *Gruppenkommandeur* of II./JG 53, Hptm. Heinz Bretnütz (flying Bf 109 F-2 W.Nr. 6674), downed a Spitfire over the Channel off Dunge-

ness (at 17:20 hrs). It was a machine from No 610 Sqn RAF, flown by Sgt. Hale. Despite injuries, the British pilot managed to nurse his crippled Spitfire back to Hailsham, where he bellied in. Five days later, on 24th March 1941, JG 53's pilots again 'mixed it up' with the British. For Lt. Franz Schieß it was his first taste of combat:

"Heavy, laden clouds roll low over the 'creek'[21]. There's probably nothing happening on the other side, but one never knows. Either way, we climb into our machines and take off. The overcast layer between 2000 and 6000 me-

Messerschmitt Bf 109 F-4s and their pilots: (from left) Oblt. Helmut-Felix Bolz, *Staffelkapitän* of 5./JG 2 and Ofw. Kurt Bühlingen, at readiness; Abbeville-Drucat, September 1941.

tres is so thick that it's hard to even see one's own wingman. It doesn't make any sense; we turn around and descend. Then we slip below the cloud cover towards the steep banks of the English Channel between Dungeness and Dover. Over the port we can see barrage balloons, swaying calmly but ominously in the air. Two Spitfires ahead! There they are. The *Kommodore* instantly engages one of them but his opponent banks away and runs for it. Tracers flash past the English pilot's cockpit, but the distance is still too great to do him any harm. One has to close in to 100, or even 50 metres. Now the

other Spitfire moves in, and it seems he has picked on me as his target. He opens up. The leading edges of his wings flicker like burners of a gas cooker. The Spitfire has eight machine guns and when they rip out a burst, smoke streams back from his wings for some 50 meters and fire flashes from the muzzles. I'm not taken aback and also thumb down my triggers. In that very instant I don't mind whether I hit him or not, my shooting itself gives me a boost of self-confidence. Overexcited, I didn't even flick on my gunsight. The Spitfire whizzes past me, no more the a dozen meters to one side. None of

Oblt. Helmut-Felix Bolz, *Staffelkapitän* of 5./JG 2, in cockpit of his Messerschmitt Bf 109 F-4.

us scored a single hit, which was very fortunate; it would be unpleasant to get clobbered on my very first sortie.

Instead of banking to port, the Tommy[22] peels to starboard. I guess he's as much of a greenhorn as myself and he's happy to get through this shoot-out in one piece. The whole situation takes barely a couple of seconds and suddenly the sky around us in empty. The fuel is getting low, it's high time to get out of here. As soon as we land, everybody has his own story to tell. Our 'black men'[23] gather around us, eager to hear the details of our fight. This is their war as much as ours, and we share with them stories about everything we experienced up there."[24]

On 31st March 1941 another Messerschmitt Bf 109 F-1 was lost due to structural failure. At around 09:20 hrs a lone Spitfire of No 91 Sqn RAF flown by Sgt. Jack Mann, patrolling over Cap Griz Nez, was bounced by a *Schwarm* of Bf 109 Fs of 7./JG 51. The English pilot spotted the incoming danger at the last moment and threw his machine in a vertical dive. His manoeuvre was so violent that his cockpit canopy broke loose, whereupon the rushing air tore the goggles and leather helmet off his head. Mann chanced a quick look in his rear view mirror and saw a single Bf 109 latched onto his tail. The Englishman levelled off just above the waves and when he looked over his shoulder, he saw a grey mottled German fighter slam into the water. Lt. Enzio von Saalfeld, at the controls of Bf 109 F-1, W.Nr. 6624, coded 'White 3' was killed instantly.

On the same day, at 11:35 hrs, northwest of Calais, the commander of JG 53, Maj. Günther von Maltzahn, shot down a reconnaissance Spitfire of 1 PRU, which was returning from its mission over Rotterdam. Its pilot, P/O Punshon, was killed. In early April 1941 the RAF intensified its offensive fighter sweeps over France, known

A pair of Messerschmitt Bf 109 F-4s of 6./JG 2 taxiing out. In the foreground 'Yellow 1', in the background 'Yellow 12'.

Hydraulic mechanism of landing gear retraction in a Bf 109 F-2, coded 'Black 8', of 8./JG 2 under surveillance by a ground crew member. lower cowling and rudder are yellow.

Messerschmitt Bf 109 F-4, W.Nr. 7334, marked with 'Black <-+-', flown by *Kommodore* of JG 2, Maj. Walter Oesau; St. Pol-Brias, autumn 1941.

as 'Rhubarbs'. One of these raids was recalled by Lt. Hans Strelow of 5./JG 51 in the following words:

"We saw an aircraft come quite smoothly out of the clouds. A Hurricane. He was already very close and sprayed the airfield with his eight guns. As he turned towards us, we hastily vanished behind the barracks and, as we emerged, we saw him go straight up into the clouds again. During the attack the airfield loudspeaker played merrily and a voice stressed our air superiority on the Channel Front!"[25]

On 4th April 1941, one of the Luftwaffe's future top aces in the West, Fw. Josef Wurmheller of II./JG 53, scored his sixth victory – his first

in a Bf 109 F. At 11:18 hrs he claimed a Spitfire over the Channel, 20 km north of Wissant. By 7th May 1941, he had added four more British aircraft to his tally, making him one of the first Bf 109 F aces.

In the early hours of 15th April 1940, Obstlt. Adolf Galland the *Kommodore* of JG 26, took to the air in an example of the new Messerschmitt for the first time. He flew Bf 109 F-2, W.Nr. 6714. In the afternoon, he climbed into the cockpit again, taking it for a ride to remember. Galland himself recalled:

"April 15th was Osterkamp's birthday (he was then *JaFü*[26] at Le Touquet) and he invited me to come over. As a present I packed a huge

Oblt. Werner Stöckelmann of Stab III./JG 2 posing in cockpit of a Messerschmitt Bf 109 F-2. Note the Gruppe badge, a cockerel head. Lower cowling and rudder are yellow.

Messerschmitt Bf 109 F-2 of *Adjutant* of III./JG 2; St. Pol-Brias, autumn 1941.

basket of lobsters with the necessary bottles of champagne into my Me 109 F and took off, with Oberfeldwebel Westphal on my wing. Again it was too tempting not to make a little detour on the way and to pay a visit to England. Soon I spotted a single Spitfire. After a wild chase, fate decided in my favour. My tough opponent crashed in flames in a little village west of Dover.

A few moments later we saw a flight of Spitfires climbing ahead of us. One of them lagged behind the formation. I approached him unnoticed and shot him to smithereens from a very short distance. We flew right on close to the formation, where I shot down a third Spitfire, which I nearly rammed. I was unable to observe the crash. Westphal was now in a good firing position but suddenly all his guns jammed. Now it was time to bolt as the Spitfires waded in on us. Throttle full open in a power dive down to the Channel! We were heavily attacked. Westphal was noticeably faster than me. Something was wrong with my crate.

As I came in to land at Le Touquet the ground staff waved frantically and let off red flares. At last I understood their gestures: I had

Messerschmitt Bf 109 F-4, 'Black < +-' of Stab II./JG 2; Abbeville-Drucat, October 1941.

Minor field work at Coquelles airbase, where III./JG 26 was stationed. In the background Bf 109 F-4s coded 'White 1' and 'White 4' of 7./JG 26.

nearly made an involuntary crash landing. When I worked the mechanism to let down the undercarriage it did not go down but retracted instead. It must have been down the whole time. I must have touched the landing gear button with my left knee during the action over England. I remembered that I had had to readjust my trimmer tabs because at one time the aircraft's handling suddenly changed. The lobster and champagne bottles were safe. Hunter's luck! Together with the report of the Spitfires I handed the birthday present to Osterkamp".[27]

On the morning of 4th May 1941, the pilots of Stab and I./JG 51 were ordered to carry out a strafing attack against the British airfield at Manston, located near the mouth of the River Thames. In order to avoid detection by British radars, the Messerschmitts skimmed the waves of the Channel while heading for Manston. The surprise was complete; the Germans raked the dispersed aircraft and hangars with gunfire. On the return leg, however, they had to fight their way through alarmed RAF fighters. Maj. Mölders took the opportunity to shoot down a Hurricane for his 66th victory.

Aft fuselage section of the Bf 109 F-4 coded 'White 4' of 7./JG 26

On 7th May 1941, during a "free hunting" sweep over eastern England, Oblt. Franz Götz, *Staffelkapitän* of 9./JG 53, notched up a Spitfire for his 66th kill. In the afternoon of 9th May 1941, during a fighter sweep along the English coast in the area of Dungeness, pilots of the *Geschwaderstab* of JG 53 ran into some Spitfires. Lt. Schieß reminisced:

"Dogfight with five Spitfires over Dungeness. I have no idea why the Tommies fly so foolishly at 8000 metres or higher, pulling thick contrails, which give them away for miles. We climbed above them and struck down with the advantage of altitude. A lone Spit loitered some distance away from his formation, so we swooped down on him from an altitude of 10,500 metres. When our *Kommodore* closed in to 200 metres, the Englishman did two quick rolls and hurtled vertically down. We followed him, gathering speed, until my controls 'froze'

Messerschmitt Bf 109 F-4 of Stab/JG 2 being re-fuelled at St. Pol-Brias; October 1941.

Empennage of Messerschmitt Bf 109 F-4, W.Nr. 7205, from by *Staffelkapitän* of 1./JG 26, Oblt. Josef Priller. On the rudder 54 victory bars. Priller scored his 54th and 55th victories – a brace of Spitfires – on 21st October 1941.

Messerschmitt Bf 109 F-4 z 3./
JG 26. Note the name 'Helga'
painted under cockpit.

Messerschmitt Bf 109 F-2,
W.Nr. 5749, was the personal
mount of Hptm. Hans 'Assi'
Hahn, *Gruppenkommandeur*
of III./JG 2. The photo was
taken at St. Pol-Brias in mid-
July 1941.

Mechanics moving
a Messerschmitt Bf 109 F-2
('Yellow 4') of 6./JG 2 to its
revetment.

Mechanic painting ninth victory bar on the yellow rudder of Bf 109 F-4 of 3./JG 26, flown by Lt. Paul Schauder.

solid. I don't know how I managed to break the dive and pull up. I levelled off at 4000 metres. Where's everybody? The sky was empty, far and wide. Fooling around over England alone was suicide. Our machines have a poor field of vision to the rear - the first one would know of an enemy being near would be when one's aircraft burst into flames.

Our bunch scattered during the scrap. Oblt. Pufhal returned alone, followed shortly after by the *Kommodore*. Now we only wait for 'Jul' (Lt. Julius Heger). Where on Earth did he go... is he trying to win the air war over England all by himself? We remain at the landing ground, smoking one cigarette after another. Time barely crawls, while we listen attentively for the buzz of an aircraft engine. Time after time it's not the machine we're waiting for. 'He's out of fuel by now', murmured the commander, checking his watch. We walk towards the ground control room - perhaps Jul put his crate down on some beach. It's evening already and he has made no call to report that he landed somewhere else. Every time the phone rings, I grab the receiver frantically. I refuse to believe that Jul went down, it's too depressing to accept. It was his 20th combat sortie. Our mood sagged; there was one empty chair by the table during supper."[28]

It was not until 19th May 1941 that Stab JG 53 received the information that Lt. Heger was alive and well, albeit in British captivity.

Hptm. Wolf-Dietrich Wilcke, *Kommandeur* of III./JG 53 at Jever on 9th November 1941, during a visit to I./JG 1. The aircraft is marked with double chevron, which denoted the machine of a *Gruppenkommandeur*.

Uffz. Karl Willius of 3./JG 26 by his Bf 109 F-4, W.Nr. 7194, 'Yellow 6'. Note the 'Annemarie' name painted under cockpit.

During the skirmish related above, the *Kommodore* of JG 53, Maj. von Maltzahn, shot down a Spitfire for his 17th victory. On 17th May 1941, Hptm. Wilhelm Balthasar, the new *Kommodore* of JG 2, shot down a Spitfire of No 54 Sqn over the Channel for his first Bf 109 F victory. It was also his 30th 'kill' scored during the Second World War. Balthasar had assumed command of JG 2 on 16th February 1941, and was a famed veteran of the Condor Legion – over Spain he had chalked up seven Republican aircraft. With 23 aerial victories and a further 13 enemy machines destroyed on the ground,

he was also the Luftwaffe's most successful fighter pilot of the French campaign.

On 8th May 1941, and for the two weeks thereafter, I./JG 3 was ordered to perform fighter-bomber missions against RAF airfields in eastern England. The *Kommandeur* of the *I. Gruppe*, Hptm. Hans von Hahn, vividly recalled the absurdity of such tactics:

"We were tasked with bombing and strafing enemy aerodromes until the English were forced to abandon them. It was a perfect assignment for a ground attack aircraft, which the Bf 109 was certainly not, We had to contend with

Messerschmitt Bf 109 F-4, W.Nr. 7194, 'Yellow 6' being pushed out of its revetment onto the field.

Rudder of Bf 109 F-4, W.Nr. 7194 sporting 11 victory bars tallied by Uffz. Willius (this number including 4 over British aircraft and seven from Russia).

heavy anti-aircraft fire - possibly followed by a 30 to 40-minute return flight over the open waters of the English Channel in a limping crate. The Tommies were a long way from abandoning their airfields. On the contrary, they studded them with more and more Flak guns. My boys, one after another, were being forced to ditch in the Channel. Few of them could be picked up by our air sea rescue service - most landed in the water right by the English coast. Worse still, only a few of them were actually saved by the English: most of them drowned. Unfortunately, among the latter was Oblt. Sprenger, the valiant *Kapitän* of my 1st *Staffel* - and Obfhr. Pöpel, the best young pilot of my *Gruppe*. Another of my pilots managed to fly his crippled machine back to France, only to crash and burn during a failed attempt at a belly-landing. To cap it all, Lt. Bucholz nosed over during take-off. We cursed St. Pol! There were only losses for us there, and very few victories."[29]

Mounting losses, suffered by I./JG 3 in that period, are evident in the unit's diary:

"May 16, 1941:

– 09:10 and 09:12 hrs – two *Rotten* scramble to intercept raiders reported in the vicinity of St. Pol, no contact with the enemy.

– 11:00 hrs – five aircraft sweep over enemy territory. During landing, Lt. Bucholz of 2. *Staffel* stalls his machine and crashes. The pilot is slightly injured, the aircraft 95% destroyed. One pair takes off on a patrol.

– 12:19 hrs – one pair strikes at Hawkinge airfield in a low-level attack. Two or three enemy aircraft strafed (see Lt. Bock's combat report dated 16th May 1941)

– 14:00 hrs – a flight from 1. *Staffel* (Oblt. Sprenger, Lt. van Kück, Fw. Lüth and Ofhr. Neumayer) takes off on an armed reconaissance mission, performing a low-level attack on Hawkinge. Lt. van Kück was hit by AA fire and baled out of his badly smoking machine. He was last

Schwarm of Messerschmitt Bf 109 F-2s of 7./JG 2 scrambling at Theville, late November 1941.

Messerschmitt Bf 109 F-2, coded 'White 1' flown by *Staffelkapitän* of 7./JG 2, Oblt. Egon Mayer. Note the CO pennant (adorned with *Staffel* badge) fitted to the antenna mast. Of note is the section of the fuselage aft of the exhaust stacks painted in black. Lower cowling is yellow. Mayer was killed on 2nd March 1944 in combat with American P-47s. At the time of his death he held the rank of Oberstleutnant and his victory tally stood at 102. He was also the holder of the Knight's Cross with Swords and Oak Leaves and a renowned expert in fighting the USAAF heavy four-engined bombers.

Messerschmitt Bf 109 F-4, coded 'Yellow 10' of 2./JG 26, under camouflage netting; St. Omer-Arques, November 1941.

seen drifting in the Channel, with his parachute still attached to his body, some 13 km south of Dover. Oblt. Sprenger failed to return. He was probably bounced by the enemy while supporting a rescue mission low over the sea (see Fw. Lüth's combat report dated 16th May 1941). Two remaining aircraft landed at 15:00 hrs, one with combat damage to its fuselage."[30]

By the end of May 1941 the *Jagdwaffe* units began to pull out of France in preparation for Operation 'Barbarossa'. On the afternoon of 4th June 1941, pilots of JG 53 flew their last mission over the Channel. Ofw. Litjens of *4. Staffel* claimed one Spitfire (not confirmed), whilst the Germans lost Bf 109 F-2, W.Nr. 6707, coded 'Black <3-+-'; its pilot, Fw. Heinrich Rühl, was posted missing.

Meanwhile, the RAF stepped up its activities. On 14th June 1941 the British mounted Circus No 12, a raid by ten Bristol Blenheim bombers against St. Omer. This foray marked the beginning of the RAF's great summer offensive across the Channel, aimed at debilitating the German fighter units stationed in northern France, of which only two *Jagdgeschwadern* – JG 2 and JG 26 – remained. The unprecedented intensity of the RAF's operations and the meagreness of their own forces compelled the German pilots to fly several sorties a day - against enemies who enjoyed overwhelming numerical superiority. While such a situation allowed the Luftwaffe's top scorers to amass more victories (for example, in a period of only five days, between 21st and 25th June 1941, JG 2 claimed 55 victories), the inevitable combat attrition took its toll and the roster of experienced pilots began to thin out. On 9th June 1941, whilst attacking a coastline convoy with a 250 kg bomb, Oblt. Werner Machold - *Staffelkapitän* of 7./JG 2 and a Knight's Cross holder - was hit off Portland by an anti-aircraft barrage from the destroyer HMS 'Blen-

Messerschmitt Bf 109 F-2s of 8./JG 2 at Theville airfield, November 1941.

Messerschmitt Bf 109 F-4s of 7./JG 26 at Coquelles, November 1941.

Messerschmitt Bf 109 F-2, W.Nr. 9553, coded 'Yellow 9', flown by *Staffelkapitän* of 9./JG 2, Lt. Siegfried Schnell, Theville, November 1941.

cathra'. Machold was forced to ditch and was promptly taken prisoner.

On 14th June 1941, Robert Menge of 3./JG 26, an 18-victory ace, was jumped by a Spitfire Mk V while taking off from Marquise-Audembert and shot down. Although the Spitfire Mk II was still predominant in RAF Fighter Command at that time - and barely a match for the Bf 109 F-2 - the increasingly numerous Spitfire Mk Vs posed quite a different challenge. The Messerschmitts still enjoyed the advantage of diving and climbing speed, which allowed their pilots to disengage at any given moment - but Spitfires of all variants, even outdated Hurricanes, had the edge over their German opponents in a turn fight. Therefore, the Germans practiced

the only effective tactic they could use to retain a combat advantage: 'Hit & Run'.

The Luftwaffe pilots learned to wait high up against the sun for an unaware victim to appear in a favourable position. The network of German 'Freya' early warning radars, located along the Channel coast, usually detected British formations approaching the Continent well in advance. This enabled German interceptors to scramble in time and reach a suitable altitude, which guaranteed them the initial, all-important advantage of height and initiative in attack. Even when the British struck off for a target of importance, the German fighters took their time, patiently waiting for some momentary confusion in the enemy formations. Such tac-

Middle section of the fuselage of the same aircraft. Interestingly, this machine was produced by Arado plant in Rostock as F-2 but was fitted with DB 601 E engine as indicated by the 87-octane fuel triangle.

tics were notably different from that of the RAF a year earlier, during the Battle of Britain, when the British had striven to shoot down bombers at almost any cost. Nevertheless, the new German tactics offered minimal own losses.

The tactic was perfected by the *Kommodore* of JG 26, Obstlt. Adolf Galland. His pilots always tried to position themselves higher and to the rear of their unsuspecting prey, with the blinding sun against their backs. As soon as this was achieved, they slashed through the fighter screen towards the bombers, firing as they dived down. Although, on Göring's orders, German fighters were to engage only bombers, Galland quickly managed to bypass this limitation to give his pilots more freedom of action. After the bounce the German fighters would continue down, outdistancing any pursuers due to their speed accumulated in the dive. Another attack technique devised by Galland was far more risky. It required that the majority of his fighters stayed up above the enemy, attracting the attention of the British escorts, while Galland led a pair (or flight) from his Stab to attack from below. This manoeuvre worked best with a cloudy sky, which enabled the stalking fighters to approach their prey stealthily.

On 16th June 1941, during Circus No 13, RAF Coastal Command despatched six Blenheims, covered by six fighter squadrons, over Boulogne. The British raid was challenged by JG 26, which claimed 11 victories (the RAF actually lost five), while losing a Bf 109 F-2 and a Bf 109 E-7.

The following day the RAF summoned up a force of 14 fighter squadrons and 23 Blenheims. Their target was a chemical factory at Chocques. While contesting this incursion, the Germans claimed 15 enemy fighters shot down: Obstlt. Galland and Oblt. Sprick each claimed a 'double'. On the same day pilots of III./JG 2 claimed a further three RAF fighters: Oblt. Carl-Hans Röders, *Staffelkapitän* of 9./JG 2, claimed two Hurricanes, whilst Lt. Egon Mayer of 7./JG 2 shot down a Spitfire. The actual losses registered on that day by the RAF amounted to nine machines lost and one damaged.

On 21st June 1941, the RAF carried out two Circus operations. During heavy engagements pilots of JG 26 and II./JG 2 claimed a total of 11 victories. Obstlt. Galland was credited with two, but during the afternoon mission was himself shot down and slightly injured. British losses of that day were six fighters and one bomber, plus four fighters and two bombers heavily damaged. On the other hand, RAF pilots claimed as many as 26 Messerschmitts destroyed, plus seven 'probables' and a further six damaged (the Luftwaffe's actual losses were confined to nine fighters destroyed and four damaged).

At 16:37 hrs, Galland shot down Spitfire Mk II, P7730, of No 616 Sqn RAF (flown by P/O E.P.S. Brown) for his 70th victory. Before the day was out, the *Kommodore* of JG 26 had received a telegram announcing that, as the first soldier of the Wehrmacht, he had earned the newly constituted decoration for valour in combat – the Oak Leaves to the Knight's Cross.

Meanwhile, the RAF ceaselessly pressed on with similar operations, day after day. They offered the *Jagdwaffe*'s pilots ample opportunity to raise their scores - but more and more frequently, at a cost. On 28th June 1941, during a scrap with some Spitfires, Oblt. Gustav Sprick, *Staffelkapitän* of 8./JG 26 and a Knight's Cross holder, perished. His Bf 109 F-2 (W.Nr. 5743, coded 'Black 4') tumbled from the sky as its starboard wing sheared off when he pulled into a violent manoeuvre. At the time of his death Sprick was credited with 31 victories.

Five days later, on 3rd July 1941, Hptm. Wilhelm Balthasar, *Geschwaderkommodore* of JG 2, lost his life in nearly identical circumstances – while dogfighting a couple of Spitfires, he whipped into a tight spiral and tore off a wing from his Bf 109 F-4. Only a day earlier, this 40-victory ace had celebrated receiving the Oak

Leaves to his Knight's Cross. He was buried at a German military cemetery in Flanders, next to his father, who was killed during the First World War. He was succeeded by Hptm. Walter Oesau, hastily recalled from the eastern front, where he had commanded III./JG 3.

A day earlier, on 2nd July 1941, JG 2 and JG 26 teamed up to battle the RAF's Circus No 29, which was a raid by 12 Blenheims on Lille. The pilots of Stab and I./JG 26 managed to position themselves against the sun and get through to the bombers. The *Kommodore* of JG 26 Ob-

Scoreboard with 57 victories proudly displayed on the rudder of a Bf 109 F-2. This is the tally of Lt. Siegfried Schnell by the end of 1941. In the background another 'Friedrich', marked with 'Yellow 2'.

stlt. Adolf Galland and Hptm. Rudolf Bieber of Stab I./JG 26 shot down a Blenheim apiece. Three other pilots of I./JG 26 (Oblt. Josef Priller, Gefr. Ernst Christof and Hptm. Johannes Seifert) claimed victories over fighters (one apiece). II. and III./JG 26 contributed with single victories by each *Gruppe* over Spitfires. JG 2's claims of six Spitfires had to be offset against the loss of three Bf 109s (though all three pilots safely baled out). The RAF's actual losses on that day amounted to eight fighters and two bombers. Apparently, among the victims of JG 2 were three machines of Polish No 303 Sqn, including that of S/Ldr Łapkowski. Obstlt. Adolf Galland was forced to jump out of his aircraft during the scrap, although his parachute brought him down to the ground unscathed. It transpired that his assailant was Larry Robillard of the RCAF:

"On 2nd July 1941, I slugged it out with Adolf Galland - with deplorable results for both of us. I saw his Messerschmitt 109 F attacking our Blenheims and latched onto his tail. He sliced down in a sharp descending turn, twisting and turning as he went to shake me off his tail. Still, I managed to close the gap, squeezed the trigger and saw flashes of impacting rounds tearing into the starboard side of his cockpit. I was about to finish him off when, suddenly, I saw tracers go whizzing by – there were more Jerries hurtling down out of the sun. I veered back just in time to meet four Me 109s coming at me head-on. They were closing in at a tremendous speed. Their leader opened up, I returned fire and hit him. Miracuously we didn't collide. I hauled around in a tight turn and headed for the deck. At that moment I felt a violent shudder to the rear of my crate – part of one wing tore off. My Spitfire went into a vicious, uncontrollable spin while I blacked out. When I came to, I saw the ground rushing at me. I pulled the ripcord. The parachute deployed, but my heavy boots got tangled in the cords and I was

descending head down. After a bit of a struggle I straightened up. I landed on a railway embankment, while Me 109s circled above my head".[31]

The following day, 3rd July 1941, the British went ahead with Circus No 30, this time targeting the Luftwaffe's airbase at St. Omer. The invading formation comprised six Blenheims escorted by no fewer than seventeen fighter squadrons! Over the target area they were intercepted by Bf 109 Fs of I. and III./JG 26 as well as JG 2. The Germans claimed three Spitfires, of which two were credited to JG 26's pilots: Lt. Hans-Joachim Harder and Lt. Johannes Naumann.

On 10th July 1941 a formation of three four-engined Short Stirling bombers of No 7 Sqn RAF, shepherded by a large group of Spitfires, headed for a powerplant at Chocques. Over the target one of the bombers was shot down by Flak, while two others dumped their load and beat a hasty retreat towards England, chased by Messerschmitts of JG 26. One of the pursuers was Knight's Cross holder and *Kommandeur* of I./JG 26, Hptm. Rolf Pingel. At that time Pingel's score stood at 22 Second World War victories, in addition to four chalked up in Spain. He recalled:

"I followed one of the *dicken Brummer* (fat buzzers) as it made its way back to England, and hoped to be able to carry out an attack. But then I was hit. Whether by one of its gunners or by an English fighter, I don't know. Perhaps both. My engine started to run unevenly, and oil and coolant temperatures began to climb.

I tried to escape close to the ground, as I had done many times before. There were many English machines in the air around Dover. While still at low-level my engine came to an almost complete stop. Unable to bail out, I had no other choice but to belly-land."[32]

Pingel landed wheels-up in a field by the Dover-Deal road. He immediately attempted to set his machine on fire but was seized by

A line-up of Messerschmitt Bf 109 F-4s of 1./JG 26 at St. Omer-Arques, November 1941.

Messerschmitt Bf 109 F-2, coded 'White 5' of 7./JG 2 at Theville, late November 1941. Note two victory bars on the rudder.

The same aircraft being refueled.

a group of British soldiers who quickly arrived at the scene of the crash. Pingel's Messerschmitt Bf 109 F-2, W.Nr. 12764, was restored to flying condition, duly repainted in RAF markings and registered under designation ES906, whereupon it was flight-tested until lost in an accident on 20th October 1941.

The period between 16th June and 11th July 1944 provided a string of successes for Oblt. Josef 'Pips' Priller, then Staffelkapitän of 1./JG 26, all of them scored at the controls of his Bf 109 F-2. Within less than four weeks he claimed 19 British aircraft, including 17 Spitfires, which increased his tally to 39. His 40th victory, scored at 09:47 hrs on 14th July 1941, earned him the highly coveted Oak Leaves to the Knight's Cross. What follows is an excerpt from his combat report:

"I wanted to attack two Spitfires that were high above us in the vapour trails. But my engine was acting up, and it was impossible to overtake them. The Spitfires turned about and came toward us. I pulled my aircraft's nose up and opened fire from about 100 meters, directly in front of them. I hit one in the cockpit and engine, and its pilot bailed out. I then had to dive away steeply, as I came under attack by the second Spitfire, which was firing at me from very close range.[33]

Priller's 40th victim was a Spitfire Mk V of No 72 Sqn RAF flown by F/Sgt W.M. Lamberton. The British machines were just returning from a sweep over St. Omer, with the sun behind their backs. Lamberton spotted a group of 11 Bf 109s climbing towards the Spitfires but in the same instant his own aircraft was hit and set on fire. He managed to take to his parachute and was made a PoW.

On 18th July 1941, Fw. Ernst Jäckel of 2./JG 26, flying a factory-fresh Bf 109 F-4, achieved the Luftwaffe's first success against the RAF's new four-engined bomber, the Short Stirling (a machine of No 15 Sqn). For this deed he was awarded a bonus of 500 RM and the Luftwaffe's Silver Honour Goblet (Ehrenpokal für besondere Leistungen im Luftkrieg). After returning to his home base, Fw. Jäckel described the combat in the following words:

Staffelkapitän of 1./JG 26, Hptm. Josef Priller bidding farewell to one of his subordinates prior to another combat mission. To the right Lt. Robert Unzeitig.

"I was with my *Schwarm* on a convoy protection mission. The ships were moving north west of Dunkirk. At 11:15 hrs we received information that numerous enemy aircraft were approaching the convoy at altitudes ranging from 0 to 2000 metres. Hence, we climbed up to 2500 metres and began to circle directly above the ships. At about 11:20 hrs I spotted four bombers in line astern, skimming barely 3-5 metres above the water from a north-westerly direction and heading straight for the convoy. Approximately 15 Spitfires flying at 2000 metres covered the bombers. I engaged the fighter escort, performing a surprise attack from the rear and above. Without much aiming I opened fire on the Spitfires, which flew in a tight formation of four-aircraft flights. When attacked, the British aircraft broke to either side. Together with my *Schwarm* I continued down and with a huge speed advantage closed in on the bombers. The aircraft - which I recognized as Bristol Blenheims - had just released their bombs over the convoy. I was about to engage one of them, when, to the north-west of the convoy, at a distance of some 2-3 kilometres, I noticed another machine of a type unknown to me, which also flew towards the convoy at a height of 3-5 metres, escorted by four Spitfires. I immediately turned towards this other aircraft and closed in from the rear starboard side. The Spitfires broke away. I was already close to the enemy bomber but held

Mechanic helping his commander to settle in the cockpit and strap seat belts. Messerschmitt Bf 109 F-4, W.Nr. 7205, marked with 'White 1' carried Priller's personal emblem, the 'Ace of Hearts'.

my fire since I wanted to recognize its type. When the distance between the two of us had diminished to some 150-200 metres, the rear gunner opened up at me with his twin machine guns. Owing to my accumulated speed I rapidly reduced the gap to a mere 50-80 metres. I saw British roundels on the fuselage and wings; I fired my cannon at the rear gunner. I flew past the enemy machine, barely missing it, and broke to port. At the same moment I saw the flashes of my cannon rounds as they hit the rear turret, fuselage and cockpit, located on top of the fuselage. Only then did I realize that it was a four-engined bomber. Both inboard engines, mounted slightly lower, were hardly visible from the rear. My wingman and the other *Rotte* of our *Schwarm* also carried out attacks with the advantage of speed and altitude. As soon as they broke off their attacks, I again swung into a firing position behind the bomber. Levelling off at the same altitude I noticed that it was jettisoning its bombs into the water and that its left landing gear had dropped down. During my second pass I noticed that the rear turret remained silent (the gunner was most probably shot dead). The attacked machine turned around and now was flying at 2 metres to the northwest, back towards Dover. It was evidently damaged, for there was a distinct oil sheen on the surface of the water behind the aircraft. I again closed in and, hovering at the same altitude, opened fire with my machine guns and cannon. As I pulled up, I saw my rounds raking all over the bomber's fuselage and wings. I made two more firing passes (and my wingman one), while the other *Rotte* covered us against the pursuing Spitfires. When I bored in for my fifth attack (from the rear, at the same height), the bomber had reached a point 3-5 kilometres to the south west of Deal. This time I fired from point-blank range - about 20 metres distant. Moments later, as I was getting set for another pass, I saw the bomber trip over the surface of the water with its extended undercarriage. The aircraft momentarily bounced back into the air before slamming into the sea. On observing this, I pulled up. Then I saw a British rescue launch racing for the scene of the crash. As I circled once more at an altitude of 100 metres, I saw the launch stop. However, the enemy bomber was gone, with only an oily blotch floating on the water. Since by that time my fuel reserve was getting low, I turned straight for home".[34]

Five days later, on 23rd July 1941, in the course of two big aerial engagements, JG 2 claimed 27 victories: six each by Oblt. Erich Leie and Oblt. Rudolf Pflanz, and three by Ofw. Günther Seeger. JG 26 contributed a further 11, including three by *Kommodore* Obstlt. Adolf Galland (his 71st, 72nd and 73rd victories). In fact, on that day the RAF lost only 11 Spitfires in action (five more returned with combat damage), together with 3 Hurricanes and one Short Stirling bomber of No 15 Sqn RAF.

On 9th August 1941 pilots of JG 26 put an end to the combat career of the RAF's famed ace Douglas Bader, who was shot down near St. Omer and captured. Overall, JG 26 claimed 11 victories on that day for the loss of only one machine. On the other hand, the RAF's pilots were credited with the destruction of 18 Bf 109s plus 12 'probables' and a further nine damaged. The RAF's actual losses on that day amounted to 10 Spitfires destroyed and six damaged. Curiously, the Luftwaffe lost only one aircraft – a Bf 109 F-4, W.Nr. 8350 of 3./JG 26 (its pilot, Uffz. Albert Schlager, was killed).

The following day, 10th August 1941, Maj. Walter Oesau recorded his first victory since taking command of JG 2. Two days later he added four Spitfires to his tally. On the very same day three more Spitfires fell prey to the *Gruppenkommandeur* of III./JG 2 Hptm. Hans 'Assi' Hahn, which increased his score to 46 and earned him the Oak Leaves to his Knight's Cross.

In the late summer of 1941, II./JG 26 converted to a new aircraft, the Focke Wulf Fw 190 A. This formidable, radial-engined fighter was earmarked to replace the Messerschmitt Bf 109

A 6./JG 2's pilot climbing out of cockpit of his Messerschmitt Bf 109 F-2, marked with 'Yellow 15', upon return from a combat mission; Abeville-Drucat, December 1941. Of note is the C3 fuel triangle, which indicates that the aircraft was powered by DB 601 N engine.

MONOGRAFIE MONOGRAPHS SPECIAL EDITION

Fs in the remaining *Gruppen* of both JG 2 and JG 26.

On 4th September 1941 two more JG 2 pilots received Knight Crosses: Ofw. Kurt Bühlingen and Ofw. Josef 'Sepp' Wurmheller. On the same day, Uffz. Karl Novak of 9./JG 2 shot down a highly unusual opponent – a twin-engined Westland Whirlwind of No 263 Sqn RAF (flown by Sgt. G.L. Buckwell).

Another massive air battle broke out on 13th October 1941 during the RAF's Circus 108A and 108B operations. Galland himself recalled:

"On that fateful November 13th, I flew with Peter Göring[35] as my wingman against a formation of Blenheims, which were heavily protected by fighters. Still climbing, we headed straight for the *Möbelwagen*[36], overtaking British fighters to our right and left. Although this was so incredibly impertinent, it succeeded. This young, enthusiastic pilot had never seen so many Spitfires at such close range. When we were about 200 yards from the bombers, I called out to him, 'Let them have it, Peter!'

He was flying about 50 yards to my left. After the first burst of fire, his machine suddenly dived vertically. There was no one behind him. I followed him down and saw a flame shoot up, marking his crash. He died in the knowledge of his first victory, probably shot through his head."[37]

During this engagement the Germans claimed eight victories, including two by Galland himself. The RAF's actual losses were 13 aircraft destroyed and two damaged.

On 23rd October 1941 the RAF sent out five Fighter Wings for a sweep over Pas-de-Calais. German observation posts erroneously identified some of the aircraft in this massive formation as bombers. Hence, JG 26's 'Friedrichs' scrambled to intercept this apparent bombing raid. Fortunately for the Germans, they managed to sneak in above and behind the fleet of Spitfires; after a lightning attack, they claimed nine shot down. Three of those were attributed to the *Geschwaderkommodore,* Obstlt. Adolf Galland (his victories 90th through 92nd) and two to the *Staffelkapitän* of 1./JG 26, Hptm. Josef Priller (his 54th and 55th victories). The German's own losses amounted to three Bf 109 F-4s. All of them belonged to the 8th *Staffel*, which had been bounced from above by a gaggle of Spitfires. As a result, Uffz. Werner Korte was killed, while Lt. Hans Ragotzi suffered injuries.

October 1941 proved particularly successful for JG 2's pilots, who claimed a total of 33 Spitfires throughout the month. Nine fell to the guns of the *Kommodore's Stabsschwarm*. Walter Oesau himself scored his 100th victory on 26th October 1941, a Spitfire Mk VB, AB822 of No 72

Messerschmitt Bf 109 F-4 of Stab III./JG 2 parked in a wooden hangar at Theville; December 1941.

Reichsmarschall Hermann Göring curiously peeking into the cockpit of Messerschmitt Bf 109 F-2, W.Nr. 6750, during his visit on 5th December 1941 at Audembert, where JG 26 was stationed. Seen in the foreground is the barrel of 20 mm MG FF/M cannon mounted in the aircraft's wing.

Sqn flown by Sgt. L. Stock, thereby becoming the Luftwaffe's third pilot (after Mölders and Lützow) to reach the 'century-mark'.

However, there were others who rose to fame in the latter part of 1941. When, in July 1941, Hptm. Johann Schmid was posted to III./ JG 26, his score stood at a modest nine 'kills'. Only a month later he had racked up 25, which earned him the Knight's Cross, awarded to him on 21st August 1941. On the same day he was promoted to become *Staffelkapitän* of 8./JG 26. Schmid scored his 45th and last victory on 6th November 1941, when he shot down a Spitfire Mk VB of No 452 Sqn RAF (flown by Sgt. B.M. Geissman) over the Channel. While Schmid was circling the crash site, the wing of his Bf 109 F-4 (W.Nr. 7211) coded 'Black 1' struck the water and broke off. Schmid went down to the bottom trapped inside the cockpit of his mount.

On 8th November 1941 the British launched their last operations of the so-called 'non-stop offensive'. Two squadrons of Hurribombers (Hawker Hurricanes adapted to the fighter-bomber role), escorted by five Spitfire squadrons, targeted a distillery at St. Pol. Concurrently, a dozen Blenheims assisted by eleven squadrons of Spitfires, carried out Circus No 110, attacking marshalling yards at Lille.

The Luftwaffe's defensive actions on that day were nothing short of exemplary. German radars plotted the British formation well in advance of its arrival, giving the interceptors ample opportunity to position themselves favourably. While the Germans used the sun - their usual hideout - in a cloudless sky, a sheet of white fog hung low over the ground making the RAF machines perfectly visible from above. The Germans were also helped by a strong, easterly wind, which notably stretched the Spitfire formation and slowed down the Hurricanes - so much, in fact, that their escorts had to circle south of Le Touquet, waiting for their charges to arrive. However, before they could rendezvous with the fighter-bombers, they were jumped by several gaggles of I. and III./JG 2's Bf 109 Fs. The British quickly lost five Spitfires (the Germans claimed seven) and the Hurribombers were forced to abandon their mission.

The Circus 110 fared no better. One of the Spitfire Wings tasked with providing rear cover for the bombers was grounded by fog. Worse still, a considerable part of the remaining escort scattered en-route in a vicious running battle with some Focke Wulf Fw 190 As of I./JG 26. When the main chunk of the British formation arrived at the target area they were attacked by JG 26's *Stabsschwarm*, led by Obstlt. Galland. The *Kommodore* himself claimed two Spitfires. The RAF's losses on that day totalled 17 Spitfires that failed to return.

On 18th November 1941, Obstlt. Galland scored his last 'kill' as commander of JG 26. Interestingly, during this mission he flew a special Bf 109 F-2 equipped with wing-mounted cannons. Afterwards he reported:

"I led my *Staffel* towards the puffs of bursting anti-aircraft shells in the vicinity of Boulogne. Suddenly, I spotted two Spitfires at

Göring, accompanied by *Kommodore* of JG 26 Obstlt. Galland, admiring the latter's scoreboard painted on the rudder of the Bf 109 F-2, W.Nr. 6750, which shows a total of 94 victories (and the Oak Leaves with Swords of the Knight's Cross).

a height of 500 metres, passing below on a reciprocal course. I 'split-essed' to place myself directly behind them and moved in to attack. In that instant I saw six more Spitfires. A wild melee ensued. The Spitfire pilots were aggressive and evidently expert at their trade. In the meantime, 15 Bf 109s butted in, turning the dogfight into utter chaos and getting in the way of other fighters. After several attempts at lining up an opponent in my sights I violently veered to starboard and snapped out a burst, giving a lot of deflection. A well-placed cannon shell punctured the Spitfire's right tailplane, which nearly broke in half and fell off. The Spitfire went into a tumbling spiral. I followed it down; the British pilot failed to regain control over his machine and plummeted into the water. The pilot either attempted to bail out at the last moment or was thrown out of the cockpit on impact. A half-deployed parachute could be seen floating at the crash site for a long time."[38]

In the latter half of 1941, in the period between 22nd June and 31st December 1941, both *Jagdgeschwadern* operating in the West (JG 2 and JG 26) claimed 838 victories over enemy aircraft for the loss of 100 of their own pilots - together with one captured and 48 injured. German equipment losses amounted to 168 destroyed fighters, of which 110 were lost in combat.

In the same period, the RAF's losses amounted to 1036 aircraft destroyed (Cat. E) and 464 heavily damaged (Cat.B, i.e. repairable). In the light of this report the *Jagdwaffe*'s claims appear credible. On the other hand, the RAF

claimed 731 German aircraft shot down, while the Luftwaffe's actual losses boiled down to 110 machines. This glaring disparity speaks for itself.

In the latter part of 1941 the air war in the West was undoubtedly overshadowed by the titanic clash on the eastern front. Strategically, the cross-Channel air campaign during that period proved of little relevance; tactically, the Luftwaffe's pilots won the battle. However, stripping the western Europe of the Luftwaffe's fighter units and rushing them to Russia (where they were needed so badly), meant that the RAF's already overwhelming numerical superiority would only increase with time. Hence, the German tactical victory in countering the British non-stop offensive could not be exploited – there were far too few German fighters in the West to sustain a prolonged campaign of resistance, not to mention establish dominance in the air over the English Channel. As the Allied air forces steadily grew in numbers, they could afford to intrude ever deeper and with more impetus into the airspace over Occupied Europe, while the German defenders' attempts to 'hold the line' were all in vain. By the time the United States of America joined the Allied coalition, bringing forward its huge fleet of heavy bombers and long-range escort fighters, all hope for the Luftwaffe was lost.

During the winter of 1941/42, French-based Messerschmitt Bf 109 Fs had many skirmishes with British fighters but the intensity of the air war slackened due to the seasonal conditions. At this time, both of the *Jagdgeschwadern* sta-tioned in France were transitioning to Focke-Wulf Fw 190 As. Before the conversion was complete, the 'Friedrichs' of the *Stabsschwarm* of JG 2 took part in countering a British raid against the MAN engine factory at Augsburg, on 17th April 1942. The British plan called for a daring, cavalry-charge type of operation. Twelve brand-new four-engined Avro Lancasters of Nos 44 and 97 Sqns were to take off in the afternoon and fly along at low level, in broad daylight, all the way to their target in Augsburg - a distance of 725 kilometres. They would then drop their bombs and return. Initially, the British formation, led by a South African, Sqn/Ldr J.D. Nettleton, caught the German defences off-guard. JG 2's personnel became aware of the raid only as the first six Lancasters roared over their airbase at Beaumont le Roger. Otto Happel, one of JG 2's personnel, reminisced:

"It was late in the afternoon of 17 April at Beaumont le Roger. Our fighters had been up on their last operation of the day, and the first of them were just returning and coming in to land when somebody yelled: *Viermots flying low over the field!*

I immediately warned our incoming fighters of the danger over the R/T. Major Walter Oesau shot past me like greased lightning, heading for his Me 109 - which was always held at instant readiness. Without further ado he set off after the departing bombers."[39]

The German fighters immediately scrambled and sped off, chasing the Lancasters. The feverish pursuit lasted for 30 minutes. Again, Otto Happel:

Geschwader Adjutant, Oblt. Rottenberg reporting to the Reichsmarschall. In the middle, holding a briefcase, is Uffz. Johannes Kirches. Galland's Bf 109 F-2, W.Nr. 6570 is visible in the background.

Another personal aircraft flown by Galland was a Messerschmitt Bf 109 F-2/U1. This machine had its 7.92 mm MG 17 cowl-mounted machine guns replaced by 13 mm MG 131 guns. Since the protruding breeches of these guns didn't fit into the standard cowling, they were covered with special bulges.

"We later learned that four of the bombers had been shot down. Unteroffizier Pohl's victim was the *Geschwader*'s 1000th kill, and Major Oesau's was his 101st (the latter, No 44 Sqn's L7536, KM•H, which was only the tenth production Lancaster to be built, came down near Bernay, taking Oesau's score to 101).

It was common knowledge that *Kommodore* Oesau had received a *Startverbot* (i.e. had been banned from operational flying after achieving his 'century' the previous October), but his excuse was a classic. He immediately informed his superiors that he had been up on a routine test flight when these monsters suddenly appeared out of nowhere and he had been forced to shoot down a Lancaster purely out of self-defence. A perfectly believable story to anybody who did not know the true facts."[40]

In spring 1942 the Messerschmitt Bf 109 F-4s deployed in the West were required to take on yet another role. On 10th March 1942 Gen. Hugo Sperrle, the commander of the *Luftflotte 3*, ordered the creation of *Jabo* (*Jagdbomber* – fighter-bomber) *Staffeln*, one apiece attached to JG 2 and JG 26. They received the designation 10.(Jabo)/JG 2 and 10.(Jabo)/JG 26. The fighter-bomber *Staffel* subordinated to JG 2, led by Hptm. Frank Liesendahl, was stationed at forward landing grounds near Evreux and Caen. Their main task was hunting down British coastal shipping between Brighton and Torquay.

During the following three months (until 26th June 1942) the pilots of the *Jabo Staffel*

scored impressive successes, claiming to have sunk 20 ships amounting to a total of 63,000 GRT. The Bf 109 F-4/Bs' main asset was its considerable speed, which very much facilitated hit & run attacks, as well as the fact that it didn't have to be escorted to the target – as soon as its bomb was dropped it became, in essence, a 'pure bred' fighter once more. The other *Jabo Staffel* – 10. (Jabo)/JG 26 – under Hptm. Karl Plunser, focused more on ground coastline targets such as railway stations, gasworks, barracks, factories and sports facilities. The Jabos bombed and strafed their targets. In April 1942 British intelligence recorded 37 such forays, carried out by a total of 106 fighter-bombers. 17 of these attacks were directed against gasworks and their ancillary installations.

A typical such raid occurred on 20th April 1942 at 07:10 hrs, when five Bf 109 F-4/Bs, flying at an altitude of 800 metres, made landfall over St. Alban's Head and dashed for Swanage. Both the town and Poole Harbour were bombed and strafed; three people were killed and 14 injured. Weather conditions over the area were very bad, a factor that prevented RAF fighters from intercepting the elusive intruders; the cloud base was down to just 200-300 metres.

On 24th April 1942, 10.(Jabo)/JG 26 registered its first combat loss during an attack on a gasworks at Folkestone, when anti-aircraft batteries shot down Bf 109 F-4/B, W.Nr. 7196, flown by Fw. Hans-Jürgen Fröhlich. The aircraft crashed into the Channel, killing the pilot on the spot. In May 1942 the *Jabo* units flew 57 missions, carried out by a total of 136 aircraft. Despite strengthening their anti-aircraft defences in the most threatened coastal regions, the British managed to shoot down only one more aircraft, Bf 109 F-4, W.Nr. 7232, 'White 11', shot down by the Royal Navy on 20th May 1942. The aircraft was flown by Uffz. Oswald Fisher, who had taken off from St. Omer/Fort Rouge along with another 'Friedrich'. Both machines carried single 250 kg bombs under their bellies and were ordered to harass shipping in and around the port of Newhaven. At the approaches to the harbour the two Germans detected a small convoy escorted by corvettes. Fisher decided to attack one of them. In such instances he usually fired his guns first in order to force the crews manning the AA guns to duck for cover. This time, however, he decided that it wasn't worth wasting his ammunition on such a small vessel. Fischer released his bomb while skimming over the wave tops. To his dismay, the bomb bounced off the surface of the water and, instead of slamming into the ship's side, hopped over it. As Fischer was passing over the deck, he was hit by a burst of machine gun fire. His engine temperature immediately soared to 160°C. With no chance whatsoever of making it back to France, Fischer radioed his wingman to advise that he was going to ditch near Beachy Head. He managed to put his shot-up machine down on the beach and was promptly captured. His aircraft was later restored to flying condition and issued to an RAF experimental unit, where it was flight-tested (for a total of 1.5 h flying time).

Atrocious weather conditions over the Channel and southeast England in June 1942 curtailed the *Jabos'* operations and they carried out just 68 sorties. In the same month the fighter-bomber *Staffeln* began to convert onto the Fw 190 A-3/U3. It was in this manner that the Messerschmitt Bf 109 F's combat service in the West came to an end.

Messerschmitt Bf 109 F over North Africa and Malta

After II./JG 27 had been withdrawn from the Eastern Front, the OKL (*Oberkommando der Luftwaffe*) decided to transfer the *Gruppe* to North Africa. The *Gruppenkommandeur* of II./JG 27 at that time was Hptm. Wolfgang Lippert, a recipient of the Knight's Cross and 25-victory *Experte* (this number including four victories won over Spain). His *Gruppe* was comprised of three *Staffeln*: 4. (under Oblt. Gustav Rödel, a Knight's Cross winner, with 20 victories to his credit), 5. (Oblt. Ernst Düllberg, credited with seven victories, commanding), and 6./JG 27 (led by Oblt. Rolf Strößer). The *Gruppe's* collective tally stood at 142 aerial 'kills'. The top scorers were Ofw. Erwin Sawallisch (19) and Ofw. Otto Schulz (nine).

First to arrive, on 14th September 1941, was 4./JG 27. By the end of the month the remaining two *Staffeln* were also in Africa. Meanwhile, on 26th September 1941 the 4. *Staffel* began operations with an uneventful first mission. It was followed by several days of sandstorms,

Messerschmitt Bf 109 F-2/U1 of Obstlt. Galland viewed from the other side. Note start crank below the cowl 'bulge' housing the breech of the MG 131 machine gun.

which grounded the Germans. On 3rd October 1941 - when the skies finally cleared - the Messerschmitts took to the air. In the morning, near Buq Buq seven Bf 109 Fs of 5./JG 27 jumped six Hurricanes of No 33 Sqn RAF, which were flying escort to a reconnaissance machine of No 451 Sqn RAF. Uffz. Horst Reuter bagged a Hurricane flown by Sgt. Lowry, who bailed out of his flaming fighter. In the afternoon the British sent out a 'recce' Hurricane with close cover of five Hurricanes of No 33 Sqn, and top cover provided by several Curtiss P-40 Tomahawks. The formation was already heading home when they were bounced by four Bf 109 Fs of 4./JG 27.

The Tomahawks struggled to keep the attackers at bay but paid dearly for the action, as two of them went down in flames. Oblt. Rödel and Lt. Schacht scored one apiece.

Two days later, on 5th October, three Bf 109 Fs of II./JG 27 sweeping the area of Sidi Omar again set upon four Hurricanes of No 33 Sqn RAF escorting a reconnaissance aircraft. Two Hurricanes, one apiece, fell to the guns of Oblt. Düllberg and Uffz. Reuter: the two British pilots, P/O Lush and Sgt. Seamer, were captured. The following day, 6th October, the Messerschmitt pilots raked up more quick victories. Over Sidi Omar Bf 109 Fs of 4./JG 27 surprised 12 Toma-

A scrambling *Schwarm* of Messerschmitts Bf 109 F-4 trops of I./JG 27. Note white theatre markings: fuselage band, nose and wingtips.

This Messerschmitt Bf 109 F-4 trop was flown by *Adjutant* of I./JG 27. The whole nose of the aircraft is painted in RLM 04 *Gelb*, indicating that the photo was taken during the early period of war over North Africa.

The engine of Messerschmitt Bf 109 F-4 trop coded 'White 2' of 1./JG 27 was just started by a mechanic who carries an *Andrehkurbel* (start crank) in his left hand.

hawks of No 2 Sqn SAAF; Oblt. Rödel and Ofw. Schulz knocked down one apiece. Barely ten minutes later the Germans chanced upon several Hurricanes. Again the victors were Oblt. Rödel (one 'kill') and Ofw. Schulz (two 'kills').

The first Messerschmitt Bf 109 F lost in combat over Africa was Bf 109 F-4 trop, W.Nr. 8440. It was shot down by the rear gunners of a flight of Maryland bombers belonging to No 12 Sqn SAAF. The German pilot, Lt. Gustav Langanke of 5./JG 27, was posted missing.

On 17th October, II./JG 27 lost its second pilot in Africa. British anti-aircraft fire brought down Bf 109 F-4 trop, W.Nr. 8471, flown by Oblt. Franz Schulz, who was killed. During freelance fighter sweeps carried out on 20th, 22nd and 23rd October, II./JG 27 accounted for a total of three British aircraft (claimed by Oblt. Rolf Strössner, Oblt. Ernst Düllberg and Hptm. Wolfgang Lippert).

No Toms.

On 30 October the Germans ran into 11 Hurricanes and a similar number of Tomahawks of Nos 238 and 250 RAF, which were patrolling the area between Gambut and Bardia. Not for the first time the Bf 109 Fs proved their superiority over the Allied fighters. The Germans laid claim to four Hurricanes (three by Ofw. Otto Schulz and one by Lt. Arthur Schacht) for no loss of their own.

On 10th November the pilots of Stab and 1./JG 27 returned from Germany to Gazala airfield, bringing with them their new Bf 109 F-4 trop fighters. Two days later, near Sollum and Bardia, three pilots of II./JG 27, Oblt. Düllberg, Ofw. Krenzke and Uffz. Reuter, each shot down one British fighter. On the same day 1./JG 27 recorded its first victory since converting onto the Bf 109 F. The victim was a P-40 Tomahawk

of No 4 Sqn SAAF. No single victor could be determined; hence it was filed as a *Staffelabschuß* (a squadron victory).

No such doubts were to be found on 15th November when the pilots of 1./JG 27 put their Bf 109 Fs to good use and tallied three more. Ofw. Espenlaub nailed a Hurricane of No 33 Sqn RAF (its pilot, Sgt. Price, was killed in action) in the early hours whilst flying escort to a mixed formation of Bf 110s and Ju 88s bound for a British airbase at Giarabub. As the day wore on, Oblt. Schneider and Fw. Hillert each notched up a Maryland of No 21 Sqn SAAF.

On the morning of 17th November, German observation posts reported a lone Bristol Bombay transport passing in the vicinity of Gazala airfield. Ofw. Otto Schulz of 4./JG 27, who happened to be on readiness duty at that time, immediately scrambled in his Bf 109 F. Hardly three minutes passed before he returned to the ground with a victory. This action earned him the fitting nickname "Eins-zwei-drei-Schulze". The Bombay he had shot down had been carrying 16 soldiers of the Special Air Service (SAS) led by Capt. Thompson. The British commandos had been on a mission to sabotage Luftwaffe aircraft at Gazala airfield, but were taken prisoner instead.

On the night of 17th/18th November 1941 a sandstorm, followed by heavy rainfall, raged over Cyrenaica. Luftwaffe airfields in the area were flooded. Most unfortunately for the Germans, at dawn, on 18th November, the British launched their massive offensive code-named "Crusader". Only a few German fighters managed to get airborne from their waterlogged airfields. Hptm. Redlich and Ofw. Espenlaub of I./JG 27 shot down a Maryland bomber apiece.

Hptm. Wolfgang Redlich, the *Gruppenkommandeur* of I./JG 27, in the cockpit of Bf 109 F-4 trop marked with 'White 1'.

X

Details of 1,350 hp Daimler Benz DB 601 E and related accessories. This engine powered the Bf 109 F-4.

On 19th November, the second day of the British offensive, two victories were scored by Uffz. Reuter of II./JG 27. It was not until the following day that the Luftwaffe airfields dried up sufficiently to allow bigger formations of Bf 109 Fs get back into action. During one of the ensuing scraps Lt. Hans-Arnold Stahlschmidt of I./JG 27 engaged nine unescorted Marylands of No 21 Sqn SAAF and knocked down three of them. The bomber squadron's diarist recorded:

"The South Africans hardly knew what hit them. They had the impression of being raked from stem to stern by a withering hail of cannon and machine gun fire. The Germans, a gunner lat-er noted, had been led by a master pilot who carried out his attack 'with faultless precision'. The Marylands jettisoned their bombs, closed formation and dived to gain speed, but to no avail. Lt. Stahlschmidt came in at them like a fury, attacking the rear sub-flight. The middle Maryland bore the brunt. Stahlschmidt next attacked the leading flight. One went down but the formation held together and the gunners fired back. The Marylands were now fleeing at zero feet, and Lt. Stahlschmidt bored in for his third kill, bringing down Maj. Steward's aircraft."[41]

On 22nd November 1941 some fierce skirmishes took place in the air. Pilots of I. and II./

Messerschmitt Bf 109 F-4 trop, W.Nr. 8477, coded 'White 11' of 1./JG 27, flown by Ofw. Albert Espenlaub (credited with 14 victories) surrounded by British soldiers after it had bellied in on 13th December 1941.

Messerschmitt Bf 109 F-4 trop, coded 'White 5' of 1./JG 27 captured by the British in December 1941.

JG 27 claimed a total of 13 allied fighters and eight bombers, albeit for the loss of six Bf 109 Fs. Two pilots were captured and a further two injured. Among the latter was the *Staffelkapitän* of 5./JG 27 Hptm. Ernst Düllberg.

The following day II./JG 27 bagged nine fighters and one bomber, but it was a bittersweet victory. One of the two pilots lost on that day was none other than the unit's CO, *Gruppenkommandeur* Hptm. Wolfgang Lippert. His Messerschmitt Bf 109 F-4 trop, W.Nr. 8469, was knocked out by a well-aimed burst fired by a Tomahawk pilot. Lippert took to his parachute but failed to clear the aircraft and collided with its empennage, breaking both his legs. Several hours later he was found by a British patrol and rushed to hospital in Cairo. By the time he arrived his wounds were hopelessly infected.

Initially, Lippert refused to have his legs amputated, but his condition steadily deteriorated and he was finally operated on. Ten minutes after the operation, he died. He was buried with full military honours. Both British and Italian officers attended the ceremony – the Italians as POWs.

On 24th November 1941 Rommel mounted a counteroffensive supported from the air by Bf 109 Fs of JG 27. The Germans claimed five enemy aircraft for no loss. Three days later, on 27th, Rommel halted his advance and regrouped for a strike against the fortress of Tobruk. Pilots of JG 27 added three more British aircraft (Lt. Remmer, Lt. Stahlschmidt and Oblt. Schneider, one apiece) to their mounting score.

Despite the recent successes of the *Deutsches Afrika Korps*, both in the air and on the ground,

Messerschmitt Bf 109 F-2s of II./JG 53 arriving at Comiso airfield in Sicily. In the foreground 'White 12' of 4. Staffel.

Rommel was still very limited by the quantity of supplies at his disposal. On 7th December 1941 his reserves were exhausted, forcing him to fall back. JG 27 personnel abandoned the airfield at Gazala and withdrew to Tmimi. Whilst retreating, the German fighters took every opportunity to fight back against their numerically superior enemy. The good news for the Germans was that III./JG 27 had also relocated to Africa under the command of Hptm. Erhard Braune.

On 9th December 1941, at 10:35 hrs, 19 Tomahawks of No 112 Sqn RAF and No 3 Sqn RAAF took off for a sweep in the area of Tobruk/ El Adem. As they passed El Adem and turned south, six Bf 109 Fs of I./JG 27 swooped down from out of the sun and tore through their ranks. In their first pass the Germans killed Sgt. Rex Wilson, an eight-victory ace. The three victors after this scrap were Oblt. Homuth, Uffz. Grimm and Oblt. Schneider.

Around midday the same area witnessed another skirmish between fighters. This time Hurricanes of No 238 Sqn RAF were battered by a *Schwarm* of II./JG 27's Bf 109 Fs. Two Hurricanes fell prey to Uffz. Niederhöfer and Uffz. Reuter. Five hours later, Uffz. Niederhöfer gunned

Another shot of the same aircraft. Standard white theatre markings, used by the Luftwaffe in the MTO, are yet to be applied. A ground control tower is visible in the background.

The *Gruppenkommandeur* of I./JG 27 Hptm. Eduard Neumann in the cockpit of a Bf 109 F-4 trop, December 1941. The pilot wears a life jacket of old type, at that time used only in bomber and *Zerstörer* units.

This Messerschmitt Bf 109 F-4/Z, W.Nr. 7343, coded 'Black 10' of 5./JG 53, was written off on take-off from Comiso on 14th February 1942. The unfortunate pilot, Uffz. Gerhard Kitzenmaier, lost control of his fighter and skidded into a parked Dornier Do 17 Z of KG 77.

Ofw. Otto Schultz in the cockpit of his Bf 109 F-4 trop. Note markings and the emblem of Stab II./JG 27.

down another British aircraft, a reconnaissance Westland Lysander.

The following day, 10th December 1941, at 10:45 hrs six Bf 109 Fs of 2./JG 27 headed out to escort a group of *Stuka* dive bombers. The weather was marginal, it was drizzling and banks of dark cloud hung low above the ground. The German aircraft quickly topped the cloud layer. Fw. Elles spotted six Douglas Boston bombers of No 24 Sqn SAAF through a break in the cloud. Their crews, oblivious to the danger, droned on in two 'vics' of three aircraft. The Messerschmitts closed in at full bore and blazed away at the rear flight. Lt. Kothmann shot down the bomber on the right flank, which went down streaming flames and crash-landed on the desert floor. However, the attacking German fighter was raked by return fire. One bullet hit Kothmann in his stomach. Although seriously injured, he returned to Tmimi and made a smooth landing. His squadron comrades immediately lifted him from the cockpit so that medical personnel could attend to his wound.

Meanwhile, Hptm. Gerlitz hammered away at the leading bomber of the rear flight. The Boston took the full force of his well-aimed burst and plummeted to the ground. The bomber on the left flank fell to Ofw. Förster. It exploded in a ball of fire. Fw. Elles lined up the machine flying on the left flank of the leading flight. As his gun burst hit home, the Boston quickly caught fire and dived through the cloudbank, later slamming into the ground. Lt. Körner latched onto the tail of the bomber on the right flank. His adversary took three full bursts before it began to belch flames. It dived earthward, leaving a trail of dark, thickening smoke. Lt. Sinner zeroed in on the last bomber, piloted by the squadron CO, Maj. Donnelly. Sinner closed the gap and opened up from point-blank range, knocking out the bomber's rear gunner with his first burst. Then he chopped the throttle back

Lt. Hans-Joachim Marseille in the cockpit of his Messerschmitt Bf 109 F-4/Z trop, W.Nr. 8693. Martuba, mid-February 1942.

and again thumbed down the trigger. The guns remained silent. Saved by the jammed guns of the German pilot, the badly shot-up bomber limped back to the nearest allied airfield. This event in the history of No 24 Sqn SAAF was soon christened the "Boston Tea Party". The South African outfit lost 12 crewmembers; most of them were due for rotation home after their eight-month combat tour. The Commonwealth Air Force commanders learned their lesson from this incident and from then on Bostons never flew unescorted.

11th December 1941 saw the conspicuous debut of III./JG 53 in Africa. On the first day of their operational activity JG 53 pilots scored three victories, followed by seven more the following day. III./JG 27 also opened its scoring in Africa on 12th December, as the *Kapitän* of 9.

Messerschmitt Bf 109 F-4/Z/B of 10.(Jabo)/JG 53 in a revetment at San Pietro airfield. Note ETC 50/VIIId underbelly bomb rack loaded with four SC 50 bombs.

An excellent shot showing the emblem of 10.(Jabo)/JG 53 – a bomb crashing into silhouetted Malta.

Staffel, Oblt. Erbo Graf von Kageneck, chalked up a Hurricane and a P-40. On 13th December intense clashes in the air produced four victories for JG 27 and two more for JG 53, but they had to be offset against another tragic loss. Messerschmitt Bf 109 F-4 trop, W.Nr. 8477 flown by Ofw. Albert Espenlaub of 1./JG 27 was hit in the radiator and forced down behind the lines. The German ace, credited with 14 victories, was captured. Before the day was out, he attempted to escape and was promptly shot dead. Of JG 53's roster of pilots, Lt. Vockelmann was badly injured and hospitalised in Gazala.

The following day I./JG 27 was dealt another disheartening blow. During a melee with some Australian P-40 Tomahawks, Ofw. Hermann Förster, one of the *Gruppe*'s most experienced pilots (287 combat sorties, 13 aerial victories) was shot down. He bailed out but was reportedly killed by a machine gun burst as he hung in his harness. Seven bullets were found in his body[42].

On 16th December the *Staffelkapitän* of 7./JG 53, Oblt. Heinz Altendorf, was lost, shot down by allied ack-ack and taken prisoner. The next day, Commonwealth forces launched a series of air raids against retreating columns of Axis troops. One of the allied formations was intercepted by a dozen of JG 27's Bf 109 Fs. The

Germans claimed five Hurricanes (Lt. Marseille two, another two by Lt. Franzisket and one by Lt. Sinner). In the afternoon another Hurricane fell prey to Lt. Friedrich Hoffmann.

On Christmas Eve, 24th December 1941, a *Schwarm* of III./JG 27's Bf 109 Fs forced some Hurricanes into a defensive Lufbery circle. The Germans, although outnumbered by five-to-one odds, began to orbit above, waiting for an opportunity to strike. One of the British pilots, P/O Thompson of No 94 Sqn RAF, pulled up steeply and loosed off a long burst at a Messerschmitt passing him some 300 meters above. By pure luck, a couple of bullets punctured the undersides of the German fighter. One lodged itself in the abdomen of the unfortunate pilot, the *Staffelkapitän* of 9./JG 27, Oblt. Erbo Graf von Kageneck (a 67-victory ace). Critically injured, von Kageneck made an emergency landing and was hurried to hospital in Naples. Nevertheless, the infection of his wound proved fatal and on 12th January 1942, he died. His successor at the head of 9./JG 27 was Lt. Klaus Faber.

The major threat to the shipping routes, which the Axis used to supply their armies in North Africa, was the allied stronghold and air base on Malta. In December 1941, in an attempt to finally pound the troublesome island

into submission, the Germans moved *Luftflotte 2* from the Eastern Front to Mediterranean bases. Among the units relocated to Sicily was JG 53, recently strengthened by a newly formed (in February 1942) fighter-bomber *Staffel* designated 10.(Jabo)/JG 53. The unit was equipped with the Messerschmitt Bf 109 F-4/B variant and led by Oblt. Werner Langemann. The aircraft were capable of carrying a single 250 kg bomb slung beneath their bellies or, alternatively, four 50 kg bombs.

On 19th December 1941, the *Geschwaderkommodore* of JG 53, Maj. Günther Frhr. von Maltzahn, scored the unit's first aerial victory (a Hurricane) in the new theatre of operations. On the following day, three more Hurricanes were shot down by pilots of I./JG 53 (Oblt. Friedrich-Karl Müller, Hptm. Herbert Kaminski

Messerschmitt Bf 109 F-4/Z/B, coded 'White 10' of 10.(Jabo)/ JG 53, flown by Uffz. Felix Sauer.

Rigging up SC 50 bombs. Of interest is the improvised bomb lift. San Pietro airfield, March 1942.

This Messerschmitt Bf 109 F-4/Z/B, W.Nr. 7473, coded 'White 3' of 10.(Jabo)/JG 53 was forced by engine malfunction to belly in near Donnalucata, on 27th March 1942. The pilot, Uffz. Felix Sauer, walked away unscathed.

and Lt. Werner Schöw claiming one each). On 23rd December, II./JG 53 opened its scoring: at 11:20 hrs Lt. Hans Möller of 6. *Staffel* knocked down a Hurricane to the southeast of the island. The Hurricane fighters - which at that time were the workhorse of the Malta air defences - stood little chance against the then latest version of the Messerschmitt Bf 109. The first recorded loss of a Bf 109 F over Malta occurred on 3rd January 1942 when Bf 109 F-4/Z, W.Nr. 7091, was downed by anti-aircraft fire; its pilot, Uffz. Werner Mirschinka, was killed.

In mid-February 1942, the Bf 109 Fs of II./JG3, commanded by Hptm. Karl-Heinz Krahl, also made their presence felt over Malta. The *Gruppe* opened its victory tally on 15th February 1941 when, at 13:15 hrs, five kilometres southeast of the island, Uffz. Wolfgang Vogel of 6. *Staffel* claimed a solitary Beaufighter. The first loss of a Bf 109 F in air-to-air combat did not occur until 22nd February 1942. By that time the pilots of JG 53 and II./JG 3 had amassed over 60 victories! On that day, seven Hurricanes of No 185 Sqn RAF scrambled to intercept a big

formation of Ju 88s shepherded by some Bf 109 Fs. Over Hal Far, Sgt. J. R. Sutherland sneaked up on a Bf 109 F-4/Z, W.Nr. 7541, flown by Uffz. Walter Schwarz of 9./JG 53, and 'gave him the works'. The German perished in the wreckage of his mount.

The next day 10.(Jabo)/JG 53 recorded its first loss; Bf 109 F-4/Z, W.Nr. 7159, flown by Gefr. Otto Butschek was lost in a duel with a Hurricane. The damaged Messerschmitt ditched some ten kilometres to the northeast of Malta but the pilot did not survive. On 3rd March 1942 it was II./JG 3's turn to sustain its first loss. A Bf 109 F-4 trop, W.Nr. 8649, was knocked out of the sky by an anti-aircraft shell and crashed into the sea. The pilot, Uffz. Benedikt Wegmann of 5. *Staffel*, bailed out and was taken prisoner.

By early March 1942 the superiority of the Bf 109 Fs over the island was so complete that British fighters hardly ever rose to challenge them. However, the plight of the Malta defenders was to improve when, on 7th March, 16 Spitfire Mk VBs arrived, followed shortly afterwards by another batch of 16. The pace of

Another shot of the same aircraft. It was damaged beyond repair and duly written off. Of note is the unit's emblem in the rear fuselage.

The nose of a Messerschmitt Bf 109 F-4/Z. The black 'Ace of Spades' emblem superimposed on a white diamond unmistakably identifies it as a machine belonging to JG 53.

operations quickened daily. III./JG 53 lost one of its best pilots, the *Staffelkapitän* of 7./JG 53, Lt. Hermann Neuhoff. He reminisced:

"On 10th April, I led a *Schwarm* over Malta. The other *Schwarm* of my *Staffel* unexpectedly drifted off and was nowhere to be found. We ran into three Spitfires and I opened fire at the machine crossing my flight path. Suddenly something thudded into my aircraft. Lt. Schöw called out his first victory – unfortunately, it was me. He mistook me for a Hurricane!

I resolved to stay in the cockpit since I knew that ditching the aircraft would increase my chances of survival. However, when the flames began to sear into the cockpit, I jettisoned the canopy. Seconds later my '109 blew up. Luck-

Messerschmitt Bf 109 F-4/Z of 6./JG 53 parked in a revetment at San Pietro airfield, spring 1942.

Ground crews cleaning and polishing Bf 109 F-4/Z coded 'Yellow 8' of 6./JG 53. Comiso, spring 1942.

ily, I had undone my seat belts and got rid of the canopy. I was thrown clear of the aircraft at a height of 2,500 meters. At 400 meters I pulled the ripcord and landed safely near Luqa".[43]

Lt. Hermann Neuhoff was promptly taken prisoner. At the time of his capture his tally stood at 40 victories, including 21 over Russia. He was a recipient of the German Cross in Gold and a veteran of over 400 combat missions. Four days later II./JG 53 mourned the death of its *Gruppenkommandeur*, Hptm. Karl-Heinz Krahl, shot down by ground fire in the vicinity of Hal Far airfield. Hptm. Kurt Brändle succeeded him.

The intensity of the air battle in that period is testified by the fact that between 20th and 28th March 1942, Messerschmitt Bf 109 Fs carried out 5,667 sorties over Malta, practically neutralizing the British air units stationed on the island. Due to the Luftwaffe's effort, the Axis forces in Africa received large quantities of supplies in April 1942. Losses in shipping between Italy and Tripoli dropped below 1%. Nonetheless, the Germans failed to take advantage of this rare opportunity to storm the nearly defenceless island. Sowing the seeds of his own demise, Hitler decided not to launch operation "Hercules", an airborne assault on Malta. Since the Germans

Messerschmitt Bf 109 F-4/Z trop, W.Nr. 8580, coded 'Yellow 1', a regular mount of the *Staffelkapitän* of 3./ JG 27 Hptm. Gerhard Homuth. Note 47 yellow-colored *Abschussbalken* (victory bars) on the rudder.

Messerschmitt Bf 109 F-4 coded 'Yellow 9' of 9./JG 53 taxiing in billows of dust at Gazala airfield, June 1942.

soon had to withdraw most of *Luftflotte 2*, the situation on the island steadily turned in the defenders' favour from mid-May 1942.

Meanwhile in North Africa, the British offensive had lost momentum by mid-January 1942. Faced with staunch resistance from the Axis ground forces and hindered by a shortage of supplies, it promptly 'ran out of steam'. Most reinforcements earmarked for the British troops in Egypt were hurriedly diverted to the Far East, to counter the Japanese invasion of the Malay Peninsula.

On 21st January Rommel decided to take the initiative and quickly regained lost territory. At first, the reaction of the Commonwealth air force to the German counteroffensive was half-hearted. The first major clashes in the air did not take place until 8th February 1942. That morning, Lt. Hans-Joachim Marseille shot down two Hurricanes of No 274 Sqn RAF near his home base at Martuba. About 10:30 hrs, a *Rotte* of Bf 109 Fs of II./JG 27 came across four Hurricanes of No 1 Sqn SAAF some 700 meters below. The *Rotteführer* (element leader), Ofw. Otto Schulz,

A group of 10.(Jabo)/JG 53 pilots clad in tropical gear posing for a photo by a Messerschmitt Bf 109 F-4/B. Comiso, Sicily, spring 1942.

Messerschmitt Bf 109 F-4 coded 'Yellow 1' of 9./JG 53 on a patrol, May 1942. Of interest are white MTO markings added to the standard ETO camouflage scheme and lack of tropical filter.

wasted no time and plunged into a dive. He took aim at the leader of the first pair, snapped out a short burst and zoomed back up to the sun, trading speed for height. One of the British fighters attempted to chase him but, due to his poor rate of climb, was quickly left far behind. Meanwhile, Schulz turned around and made one more firing pass. This time his slugs found their mark and the damaged Hurricane was forced to belly-in. The German easily regained altitude and from a height of 2,700 meters he bored in for an attack on the other pair of Hurricanes. The burst he fired was exceptionally well aimed. One Hurricane was hit in the engine and promptly crash-landed; the other, with its stabilizer shot to ribbons, staggered back to base.

At noon, Oblt. Keller of I./JG 27 shot down two Kittyhawks of No 3 Sqn RAAF, and in the afternoon, in a skirmish over Bomba Bay, Lt. Marseille got two Curtiss fighters, while Oblt. Homuth and Lt. Körner contributed one apiece. Having scored four on that day, for a total of 40, Lt. Marseille emerged as the premier Luftwaffe ace in Africa, overtaking Oblt. Homuth with 39 and Ofw. Schulz with 37.

On 10th February 1942 Rommel seized Tmimi and halted his counteroffensive. In the air, the Bf 109 F pilots fully enjoyed their supremacy. Pilots of JG 27 claimed 57 victories in February, 35 in March and 43 in April.

On 26th May 1942, the Axis launched another offensive along the North African coast.

Oblt. Hans-Joachim Marseille in the cockpit of his Bf 109 F-4/Z trop, W.Nr. 10059, coded with 'Yellow 14'. Martuba airfield, 16th May 1942.

A mechanic painting the emblem of JG 27 on the yellow engine cowling of a Bf 109 F-4 trop.

This time, JG 27 was assisted by Bf 109 Fs of III./JG 53. In the early morning of 27th May, the second day of the Axis' renewed drive west, Ofw. Krenzke of II./JG 27 shot down a Kittyhawk of No 2 Sqn SAAF. In the early afternoon, JG 27 lost one of its aces. During an escort mission for some Bf 109 E 'Jabos', Fw. Reuter (20 victories) was shot down. He bailed out and was captured. Before the day was out, the Germans' sweeps over the frontline had yielded another four Kittyhawk victories; the claimants were Lt. Körner of I./JG 27, Lt. Jenisch and Ofw. Krenzke (both of II./JG 27), and Ofw. Stumpf of III./JG 53.

The following day the British strove to provide some air support for their hard-pressed ground troops. In the ensuing clashes they lost eight aircraft at the hands of JG 27 pilots. On the morning of 29th May 1942, Hurricanes of No 80 Sqn RAF and Kittyhawks of No 2 Sqn SAAF engaged – and lost – in a shoot-out with 13 Bf 109 Fs of II./JG 27 and III./JG 53. The Germans knocked down five of their opponents. Shortly afterwards, over Acroma, Bf 109 Fs of III./JG 27 covering a bunch of Ju 87s were jumped by Kittyhawks of No 450 Sqn RAAF. The Australians paid for their victories – two *Stukas*

Lt. Werner Schroer, *Adjutant* Stab I./JG 27, climbing out of his Bf 109 F-4 trop (note the distinctive marking identifying his function in the *Gruppe*).

Re-fuelling Bf 109 F-4 trop, W.Nr. 8747, coded 'Yellow 8' of 3./JG 27. In the summer of 1942 this aircraft was usually flown by Fw. Rainer Pöttgen, Oblt. Marseille's wingman.

A servicing team working to make a Bf 109 F-4 trop serviceable again after a forced landing on the desert.

and one Bf 109 F (its pilot, Lt. Erik von Fritsch was taken prisoner) – with three losses.

On 30th May 1942 both sides stepped up their activities. Throughout the day formations of Bostons and fighter-bombers targeted German positions around the British stronghold known as the 'Knightsbridge Box'. At 07:00 hrs four Bf 109 Fs of I./JG 27 attacked a group of 20 Kittyhawks of No 250 Sqn RAF from out of the sun. One of the Kittyhawks fell to the guns of Oblt. Hans-Joachim Marseille. Three hours later a *Schwarm* of I./JG 27's Bf 109 Fs jumped nine bombers escorted by 15 Curtiss fighters. Fw. Keppler shot down one of the latter, but the machine piloted by Uffz. Zimmermann was forced to belly-land, crippled by combat damage.

In the afternoon Stab I./JG 27 and 4./JG 53 encountered another group of Bostons escorted by P-40s. The Germans claimed five enemy aircraft. Shortly after 16:00 hrs, Oblt. Vögl of 4./JG 27 claimed a Hurricane and two P-40s; Ofw. Bendert claimed one P-40. The last scrap of that eventful day occurred at 17:20 hrs. Near the front, ten Bf 109 Fs of I. and II./JG 27 jumped 11 Bostons protected by 25 Kittyhawks; Lt. von Lieres, Hptm. Maak and Oblt. Börngen claimed one apiece.

On the last day of May 1942, despite occasional heavy sandstorms, activity in the air hardly slackened. I./JG 27 tallied seven (Oblt. Marseille three, Fw. Steinhausen two, Lt. von Lieres and Ofw. Mentnich one each), II./JG 27 six (Oblt. Vögel and Oblt. Schulz two each, Fw.

Heider and Fw. Stiegler one apiece), and III./JG 53 six (Lt. Müller two, and Hptm. Belser, Oblt. Pufahl, Lt. Harder and Maj. Gerlitz, one apiece). The Luftwaffe lost two pilots – Ofw. Krenzke (credited with five victories) was killed in action, whilst Oblt. Emmerich Fluder (four victories) went missing. Fw. Gromotka, the third pilot to have gone down, walked back across the desert and reached his unit the following day.

In the first ten days of June 1942 air combat was concentrated around the fortress of Bir Hakeim. During this period, Oblt. Hans-Joachim Marseille – a pilot who had increased his already impressive tally of victories on an almost daily basis – became something of a celebrity among the Luftwaffe's fighter pilots. On 3rd June 1942 he entered into a lone attack against a group of P-40s from No 5 Sqn SAAF. His engine-mounted cannon jammed after the very first burst, having fired only ten rounds. Marseille chose to press on, and over the course of the next 11 minutes shot down six Curtisses. He achieved this feat using only the two cowl-mounted machine guns and expending 360 rounds of ammunition. His wingman, Fw. Rainer Pöttgen, described this action in the following words:

"All the enemy fighters were brought down in a turning engagement. Marseille was a master of deflection shooting and he instinctively knew when to press the triggers. When he

This heavily weathered nose marked with 'Berlin Bear' emblem of II./JG 27 belonged to Bf 109 F-4 trop, W.Nr. 8438, 'White 12', which was captured by British troops at Ain El Gazala airfield in December 1941. Two RAF officers are visible in the background

The 'souvenir' hunters have already started cutting off the emblem of 4./JG 27 from the fuselage.

This Messerschmitt Bf 109 F-4 trop, W.Nr. 13136, coded 'White 7' of 7./JG 27, was battle-damaged and forced to belly-land behind British lines on 26th October 1942.

opened up, one could simply watch and enjoy the fireworks as the slugs impacted against an enemy aircraft. The hits he scored could be seen flashing over the engine cowling, running down the fuselage, and disappearing around the cockpit area. Marseille could not explain how he managed to lay off the right deflection with such ease. Watching him at work, I noticed that during dogfights he used to throttle back, which enabled him to outturn his opponent. Then one burst was enough to send the enemy crashing down in flames".[44]

On 17th June 1942 four Bf 109 Fs of II./JG 27 bounced nine Bostons guarded by some 30 fighters. Oblt. Otto Schulz shot down a Hurricane of No 274 Sqn RAF for his 51st and last

victory. Shortly thereafter he was himself shot down by a Kittyhawk and crashed to his death. He was the first of the great Luftwaffe aces killed over the African deserts. Meanwhile, Oblt. Marseille piled up his victories at an unprecedented rate. At 12:02 hrs he brought down two P-40s. As he pulled up to regain height advantage, his confused adversaries formed a Lufbery circle. Marseille slashed through, taking down two more. They were his 98th and 99th victories. His squadron mates began to prompt him over the R/T: 'And now the hundredth, Jochen!'

Marseille continued the patrol, looking for an opportunity to hit the 100 mark. Over Gambut airfield he spotted a lone Hurricane flying at 100 meters. He instantly dropped down on

Another shot of the same machine. Its pilot, Lt. Helmuth Fenzl of 9./JG 27, was taken prisoner.

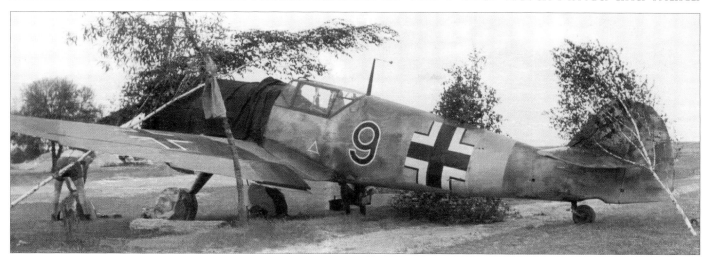

the latter's tail and let go with all barrels. The Hurricane crashed at the edge of the airfield, near some anti-aircraft gun emplacements. The Messerschmitt *Schwarm* reformed and headed home. A few minutes later the Germans spotted above them a brace of Spitfires on a reconnaissance mission. Marseille pitched up into a vertical climb and knocked down one of them. He thus became the 11th Luftwaffe pilot to surpass the 100 victories mark.

After the capture of Tobruk on 21st June 1942, Rommel resolved to continue his advance towards Cairo. The following day, I. and III./

JG 27 along with III./JG 53 moved to airfields around Gambut. 26th June turned out to be a day of particularly heavy fighting in the air. The Germans claimed 28 victories: 13 by I./JG 27, eight by II./JG 27, five by III./JG 27, and two by III./JG 53. Top individual scorers were Lt. Körner (five), Lt. Stahlschmidt (four), and Lt. Schroer (three).

The operations flown by the German fighters began to be curtailed by dwindling fuel reserves. Nevertheless, on 1st July 1942, Rommel decided to launch an assault against the new British defence line, and the first battle

Camouflaged Messerschmitt Bf 109 F-2 coded 'Black 9' of 2./JG 51 at a forward landing ground at Starawieś (Poland) on the eve of the operation 'Barbarossa'.

Messerschmitt Bf 109 F-2s of I./JG 51 at Starawieś airfield in the first days of the war in the Soviet Union.

of El Alamein broke out. On that day, pilots of JG 27 shot down six enemy aircraft and seven more the following day. On the afternoon of 9th July 1942, eight Bf 109 Fs of I./JG 27 were pitted against a new adversary – five American four-engined B-24 Liberator bombers. Despite numerous attacks, only one of them was eventually brought down; it was credited to Fw. Steinhausen.

By 19th July 1942 Rommel had only 28 serviceable tanks left, a force far too meagre to advance any further. Two days later, the British counter-attacked and the air battle flared up again. On 22nd July 1942, Lt. Stahlschmidt of 2./JG 27 shot down three enemy aircraft. These victories pushed his total tally to 40. Five days later the *Gruppenkommandeur* of I./JG 27, Hptm. Gerhard Homuth, won his 50th through 52nd victories. Over the next few days the British counteroffensive lost its momentum and died down. Losses in men and equipment were staggering. Both sides needed time to recuperate in preparation for the next round, which started on 31st August 1942. There were relatively few

On 24th June 1941 five aircraft were damaged on landing at Pruzana airfield, including this Messerschmitt Bf 109 F-2 'Yellow 5' of 12./JG 51. Note the 'Falcon's head' emblem of JG 51 on the cowling. The sides and bottom of the cowling were painted yellow.

A tired-looking pilot of 9./JG 51 clambers out of the cockpit of a Messerschmitt Bf 109 F-2 after a skirmish which took place in Boruysk area on 20th June 1941, during which *9. Staffel* claimed seven Russian bombers.

encounters in the air during that period. On 7th August 1942, Uffz. Bernhard Schneider of 5./JG 27 shot down a Bristol Bombay transport aircraft of No 216 Sqn RAF with Gen. Gott on-board. The newly appointed commander of the British Eighth Army perished in the crash. His appointed successor was Gen. Bernard Mont-gomery. *There goes the bridge at Arnhem!*

In August 1942 I./JG 27 tallied a total of 22 victories, this number including 19 fight-ers as well as Beaufighter, Blenheim and Bos-ton apiece. On 31st August Oblt. Hans-Joachim

Marseille, who just returned from a few weeks' leave in Germany, scored a triple. Of note is the fact that I./JG 27 scored all its August victories without losses of its own. Also in August 1942 notably active was II./JG 27, which claimed no fewer than 83 aerial victories, including the aforementioned Bristol Bombay transport. Top scorers in the *Gruppe* were pilots of *4. Staffel*, who racked up 65 'kills'. At that time the rank-ing ace of 4./JG 27 was Condor Legion veteran Ofw. Erwin Sawallisch with 33 victories to his credit, half of which he scored in the first two

The pilot of this Messerschmitt Bf 109 F-2 of 2./JG 51 was indeed lucky to return to base. The shot-up cockpit testifies to the ferocity of the air war fought on the Eastern Front in the summer of 1941.

Ground crews servicing the engine of a Messerschmitt Bf 109 F-2. Eastern Front, summer 1941.

weeks of August 1942. However, before the month was out, on 19th August 1942 Ofw. Sawallisch went missing over the sea while on a routine test flight. Two other II./JG 27 pilots ended up in British captivity before the end of the month.

Meanwhile, in the same period III./JG 27 could lay claim to only three P-40 fighters, for the loss of two pilots. One of the latter was *Kapitän* of 7. *Staffel* and 11-victory ace Oblt. Hermann Tangerding, who on 31st August, south of El-Alamein, was brought down by ground fire. III./JG 53 fared no better. The *Gruppe* claimed seven (five fighters and two Beaufighters), but at the same time lost four pilots (two killed in action and two captured).

At dawn of 31st August 1942 Rommel launched yet another offensive. The first victory of that day was notched up by Lt. Kaiser of I./JG 27, who shot down a Douglas Boston bomber over Burg el Arab. Later on Oblt. Marseille added two Hurricanes to his score (one of the British pilots managed to bail out). At 11:30 hrs Oblt. Sinner of II./JG 27 knocked down another Hurricane. In the evening, at 18:50 hrs, Oblt. Marseille, Oblt. Rödel and Oblt. Sinner each shot down a Spitfire of No 601 Sqn RAF. In the scrap with Spitfires only one Bf 109 F, with Fw. Niederhöfer at the controls, was battle-damaged and forced to belly-land in friendly territory. The following day saw the greatest success in the brilliant com-

Messerschmitt Bf 109 F-2 coded 'White 13' of 7./JG 51 at Bobruysk-Süd airfield, July 1941. The pilot is wearing a mosquito net over his head.

bat career of Oblt. Hans-Joachim Marseille, who claimed no fewer than 17 British fighters, most of them P-40s. On 2nd September 1942 the same pilot scored five, and on 3rd September a further five. Despite such successes, the German fighter pilots could do little to help their helplessly outnumbered ground troops. The offensive, faced with determined resistance, stalled.

In September 1942 I./JG 27 claimed 87 victories, of which, amazingly, 54 were credited to one man, Oblt. Marseille. The *Gruppe*'s own losses amounted to 11 aircraft. During the same stint of time II./JG 27 shot down 15, but lost 10. The highest-scoring pilots of the *II. Gruppe* in September 1942 were *Gruppenkommandeur* Hptm. Gustav Rödel and Oblt. Rudolf Sinner, each with five victories. Pilots of III./JG 27 overcame their bad luck and laid claim to 34 enemy aircraft destroyed. The *Gruppe*'s top claimant in September was Lt. Werner Schroer of *8. Staffel* with 13 victories. Own losses were

A line-up of partially camouflaged Bf 109 F-2s of II./JG 51 at Siedlce airfield, late June 1941. The *Geschwader* emblem can be seen on the engine cowlings.

Oblt. Hans Knauth, the *Staffelkapitän* of 10./JG 51, in the cockpit of his Bf 109 F-2 coded 'White 1'.

A moment of relaxation for a crew chief of JG 51. Siedlce, late June 1941.

It was not until the arrival of Spitfire Mk V, that the Allies attained qualitative parity with the German fighters. The Luftwaffe also held the advantage of more experienced flying personnel. Pilots such as Marseille, Stahlschmidt or Schulz scored multiple victories vastly against inexperienced novices on their first combat sorties.

Oblt. Friedrich Körner of I./JG 27 appraised the fighter he flew in the African skies in the following words: "The Bf 109 F was an excellent aircraft, and I flew it with enthusiasm. It was superior in operational height to Hurricane, Curtiss and Spitfire. Our tactics were the results of its performance: dive from height out of the sun, climb, renewed attack – no dogfight, if possible. The MG 151 cannon was very good, and mostly I did not need to use the machine guns in the fuselage, all the more because loading them on the ground took too much time, and their effect on the target was negligible. (...)

The British tactics corresponded with the performance of their aircraft – low wing loading, tight turning radius, good stunt flying abilities. The Bf 109 was devised for speed and therefore it is impossible to call a type good or bad. If the pilot was able to fly his aircraft to the limit of its performance, he could obtain maximum results".[45]

Oblt. Werner Schroer, who served with I. and III./JG 27, and was second-highest scoring pilot in the Desert with 61 victories, recalled: "I believe that our armament (a combination of heavy machine guns and cannons) was better than the armament of the Hurricanes (eight or twelve machine guns). Our Bf 109s were often able to return with forty or fifty hits. Over and above this, our ammunition was superb. Of-

limited to five machines and two pilots, who were taken prisoners.

In late September 1942 German fighter outfits in the MTO began to convert to the successor of the 'Fritz', the Bf 109 G-2. Throughout its over a year long tenure in Africa, the Messerschmitt Bf 109 F proved its superiority over allied fighters deployed in that theatre of war.

The commander of IV./JG 51 Maj. Friedrich Beckh leaving the cockpit of his Bf 109 F-2 upon return from a sortie. Note the double chevron of the *Gruppenkommandeur* partially visible on the fuselage.

ten the pilots would arrange the sequence of loading the belts: tracer, explosive, and armour piercing bullets. But first you must hit your opponent – and that was the problem.

How often I have missed, because accurate deflection shooting was not taught at training schools or during practice flights. My unforgettable *Staffelkapitän* 'Vati' Redlisch, who was a wonderful person and a great leader, taught me shooting at the expense of many hours of his flying allowance for months, because I missed again and again. Maybe in fear or in haste, I started to fire on fighters from 1,000 to 500 meters. Then one day I was alone and sat behind a Curtiss (merely by chance) – and from then on it was all right. However, there is no doubt that my true teacher was Marseille. I studied his tactics for attacking the British defensive circles for a long time, tried it myself often without success – and finally, I learned the lesson".[46]

Messerschmitt Bf 109 F over Russia

By 21st June 1941, the eve of Operation 'Barbarossa', the Luftwaffe had amassed 858 fighter aircraft in 20 *Gruppen* along the border with the Soviet Union, of which 657 were combat-ready. The majority of them were Bf 109 Fs (a total of 680, of which 555 were serviceable). The remaining 179 (including 102 serviceable) were the older E models.

The main role for the *Jagdwaffe* – the fighter arm of the Luftwaffe – in the forthcoming battle was to win and maintain air supremacy over the front lines, which stretched for an incredible 1,600 kilometers. *Luftflotte 2* (2nd Air Fleet), which operated in the crucial central sector of the front, controlled 11 *Gruppen*, along with three *Geschwader Stab* (Fighter Wing HQ) flights. In the south, *Luftflotte 4* included three *Geschwader Stab* flights and seven *Grup-*

Sweltering heat of summer 1941 turned airfields into sun-scorched wasteland. Every landing and take-off invariably kicked up billows of dust. In the foreground a Bf 109 F-2 of 1./JG 51 taxiing at Słuck airfield on 30th June 1941. A white ring on the propeller's spinner is visible.

Messerschmitt Bf 109 F-2 of JG 52. In the summer and autumn of 1941 the *Geschwader* operated on the southern sector of the Eastern Front.

Oblt. Horst Walther (eventually credited with 35 victories) of 6./JG 51 exits the cockpit of his Bf 109 F-2 'Yellow 11' on landing at Staraya Bychow. On that day, 26th July 1941, Walther shot down a Soviet Pe-2 bomber for his second victory.

Messerschmitt Bf 109 F-2 'Yellow 10' of 6./JG 51 photographed at Staraya Bychow in late July 1941.

pen. In the northern sector of the front, *Luftflotte 1* had only one *Geschwader Stab* and *four Gruppen* on strength, whilst in the Far North, *Luftflotte 5 (Ost)* was supported by a single, incomplete *Gruppe*. Because this force was required to cover an enormous stretch of land, German fighters usually operated in no more than *Schwarm* or even *Rotte* strength. Only rarely, when tasked with escorting their own bombers, would a force of two *Schwärme*, or a whole *Staffel*, fly together.

Shortly after the outbreak of war with the Soviet Union it became clear that, unlike in the West, most air combat in the East would take place below 3,000 meters. Light Flak and small-arms fire posed an additional threat to German fighters, especially to the Messerschmitt Bf 109 F with its vulnerable liquid-cooled engine. One chance hit by a piece of shrapnel, or a single stray bullet, in the radiator would usually lead to a rapid loss of engine coolant and, eventually, the aircraft. Furthermore, the sheer vastness of

On 23rd July 1941 Gefr. Günther Schack scored his first victory in the air, a Soviet SB-2 bomber.

the terrain - and the scarcity of roads, rail tracks and other landmarks - made it very difficult for a pilot to maintain orientation as he flew over the monotonous, nearly featureless land. Practically every Luftwaffe pilot who served on the Eastern Front lost his bearings at least once and was forced to land at some other airfield.

On the other hand, the campaign in the East gave German fight pilots an unparalleled opportunity to tangle at will with a vastly inferior (both technically and tactically) opponent. Their individual victory tallies duly soared. Both seasoned veterans and novices racked up relatively easy 'kills', especially in the first days of the conflict, against large groups of unescorted medium bombers. The Soviet bomber pilots never attempted any defensive maneuvers; for the most part they simply flew on, until they were all chopped down. However, the *Jagdwaffe* failed in its priority task, as it never won complete command of the skies. The enemy possessed seemingly inexhaustible reserves of men and aircraft. By the late summer and autumn

of 1941 the VVS (*Voyenno-Vozdushnye Sily* – the Soviet Air Force) had recovered from the initial shock and managed to gain local air superiority over the Dnieper crossings and the Crimea.

At the beginning of the war there were as many as 9,917 Russian combat aircraft in the western military districts of the Soviet empire. Of those, 1,139 were long-range bombers and 1,145 were naval aircraft. The most numerous were fighters (4,989) and bombers (3,888).[47] The grand total of Red Air Force aircraft, dispersed all over the Soviet Union, was close to 20,000! The hasty modernization of the Russian air fleet, which had commenced in the late thirties, allowed it to deliver 3,719 aircraft of new types by 22nd June 1941. Nearly half of them were issued to operational units located in the western military districts. Widespread propaganda campaigns had been launched in the thirties to promote the Red Air Force amongst *Comsomol* (Communist Union of Youth) members and this had triggered massive voluntary enlistment. Nevertheless, the quality of the basic training,

Gefr. Günther Schack sitting by the cockpit of his Bf 109 F-2 'White 2' of 7./JG 51.

Oblt. Karl-Heinz Schnell was awarded the Knight's Cross on 1st August 1941 after scoring his 31st victory.

Messerschmitt Bf 109 F-2 flown by the *Staffelkapitän* of 9./JG 51 Oblt. Karl-Heinz Schnell.

perhaps due to the scale of enlistment, was poor. Most of the flight school graduates sent to operational units were simply not prepared for combat service. They had not been taught to navigate, or even shoot! This situation led to a high accident rate on operational training flights. The first three months of 1941 saw 71 crashes and 156 minor accidents, resulting in 141 fatalities among pilots and the destruction of 138 aircraft.[48]

At the same time the VVS badly lacked experienced cadres of both senior and junior commanders. They had perished in Stalin's purges of 1937-1939 (which affected 5,616 airmen).

Messerschmitt Bf 109 F-2 coded 'White 10' of 7./JG 51 at Orsha, late July 1941.

Lt. Heinz Schumann is being assisted by his crew chief into his Messerschmitt Bf 109 F-2/B 'Black 1' of 2./JG 51. Schumann joined the Stab I./ JG 51 in February 1941. He scored six victories in the Channel front, whereupon he became an expert in fighter-bomber missions. On 18th March 1943 he was presented with the Knight's Cross. He perished in a flying accident on 8th November 1943 as the *Geschwaderkommmodore* of SG 10.

The same aircraft in full view. Note two emblems: of the *Geschwader* on the engine cowling, and of the *Gruppe* below and just ahead of the cockpit. The aircraft is in standard RLM 74/75/76 finish.

Increased activity of the Russian ground-attack aircraft made it necessary for the Germans to camouflage dispersal areas at their forward landing grounds. Seen in the photo is Messerschmitt Bf 109 F-2 'Yellow 4' of 9./JG 51.

Beside camouflage netting, freshly cut branches were used to hide aircraft from the enemy.

The second wave of purges started in April 1941 and was in full swing when the war in the East broke out. Hence, in June 1941 a staggering 91% of commanders at the head of Russian air units had held their posts for no longer than six months.[49]

Worse still, the purges discouraged the surviving commanders from showing the same kind of initiative to be found amongst their German counterparts. Fear of the NKVD (The People's Commissariat of Internal Affairs) and the omnipresent political commissars led to every order being carried out blindly, regardless of the current tactical situation.

German pilots who flew the Messerschmitt Bf 109 F in the East enjoyed a tremendous technical advantage over their opponents. By 22nd June 1941, around 39% of Russian fighter aircraft were bi-planes, mostly of the Polikarpov I-153 Chaika, Polikarpov I-15 and I-152 (I-15bis) types. Those aircraft, with their meager top speed ranging from 346 to 415 kph, had great difficulty catching up with German bombers, not to mention engaging German fighters on even terms.

The most popular Russian fighter design of that period was the Polikarpov I-16, which could attain a top speed of 448 kph (Type 10). Its armament consisted of four 7.62 mm machine guns or, alternatively, two 20 mm cannons and two 7.62 mm machine guns. The stubby I-16 was not an easy aircraft to fly, being rather unforgiving and unstable in the air. Unbelievably, its main landing gear was manually operated, and it took 18 full turns with a hand crank, fitted in the cockpit, to retract it.

Shortly before the war, Soviet units stationed in the western military districts were re-equipped with 886 relatively modern MiG-1 and MiG-3 fighters. They had been designed as high-altitude interceptors. The MiG-1 was by no means a pilot's dream; it was difficult to fly and lacked stability even in level flight. Moreover, because of the cockpit's location far to the rear of the fuselage, it had a very limited forward view, which made take-offs and landings at best risky. Canopies frequently jammed in the closed position, which inspired MiG-1 pilots, undoubtedly concerned about their own safety, to fly with open cockpits. Besides, the poor quality of the canopy's glazing seriously hampered visibility from the cockpit. Some of those shortcomings were corrected in the MiG-3. It featured a sliding canopy and a redesigned undercarriage. Also its overall performance was vastly improved. Of special note was its top speed of 640 kph.

Another advanced, new-generation Russian fighter was the Yakovlev Yak-1. A total of 105 were hurried into service before the start of the

Starboard side of Bf 109 F-2 coded 'Yellow 4' of 9./JG 51.

Messerschmitt Bf 109 F-2/B 'Black 1' of 2./JG 51, latter part of August 1941. The aircraft is armed with four SC 50 bombs rigged on the ventral rack.

war (of which 92 were serviceable). The Yak-1 had a remarkably good performance. It was fast (top speed of 580 kph) in level flight, had a decent rate of climb and was very maneuverable. Unfortunately for the Russians, due to poor craftsmanship and the use of low-grade construction materials, the aircraft's in-service performance was less impressive (for example, the top speed of most serial production machines did not exceed 540 kph).

The third and last new fighter type in the Red Air Force inventory was the LaGG-3. It was skinned with so-called "delta wood", which was a heavily compressed pine plywood soaked in phenolic resins. Since the impregnants necessary for production of the plywood had to be imported, local substitutes of inferior quality were developed. In order to maintain the structural strength of the aircraft, the plywood

actually used was several times thicker than the "delta wood" used on the prototypes, which increased the aircraft's weight and drastically affected its handling and performance. It became a standing joke among Russian pilots that, rather than being an acronym of the designers' names (Lavochkin, Gorbunov, and Godkov), "LaGG" stood for *lakirovanny garantirovanny grob* ("guaranteed varnished coffin").

On Sunday 22nd June 1941, at 02:50 hrs, the first German aircraft ventured into the airspace of the Soviet Union. A Messerschmitt Bf 109 F-2 pilot, the *Staffelkapitän* of 4./JG 3, Oblt. Robert Olejnik, scored the first victory over Russia:

"On 19th June the pilots of II./JG 3 flew their Bf 109 F-2s to the airstrip at Dub, some eight km from the Polish town of Zamość, which lay 80 km south-east of Lublin, and

Engine cowl close-up of a Messerschmitt Bf 109 F-2 belonging to JG 3. Of note are distinctive round main landing gear wheel wells.

Messerschmitt Bf 109 F-2 of JG 53 parked in a camouflaged revetment at a forward landing ground somewhere in Russia in summer 1941.

Cheering groundcrews welcome a pilot, who waggles the wings of his Messerschmitt Bf 109 F-2 to announce that he just scored yet another victory for JG 51.

about 50 km from the nearest Russian soil. On the occasion of the Midsummer Night celebrations we lit a huge bonfire and had the usual cold drinks. Then, around midnight, there came a telephone call from the *Geschwader*: 'All unit commanders immediately to the command post!' There, each received an envelope with a mission order, but it was only to be opened when the code word 'Barbarossa' was given. It was impossible to think about sleep; though we all lay down in our tents to rest, we were excited and full of tension. On 22nd June 1941, at about 02:30 hrs, the password came through. I opened my envelope and found that

Ofw. Edmund Wagner (credited with 55 victories) of 9./JG 51 back from another combat sortie in August 1941. Note 'Mädi' (Wagner's wife's nickname) in white script under the cockpit.

an attack against the Soviet Union was about to begin.

Everybody in the *Geschwader* knew that I was an early riser and that I liked to fly the first missions at dawn, so I made the first take-off. About 03:30 hours I took off with my *Rottenflieger* to reconnoiter the Russians' airfields near the border, watching for enemy fighters. While doing so I discovered that on every Russian airfield two or three fighters were stood at readiness. After flying over several airfields, I flew over the first airfield I'd seen on the way back.

As I got nearer I saw that two of the aircraft already had pilots sitting in them. At a height of 700-800 metres I flew a wide turn around the airfield and watched closely. After one and a half circuits, I saw the Russians start their engines and taxi out, then take off immediately. As they were obviously looking for a fight, I attacked the first 'Rata' with a height advantage of 300-400 metres, and succeeded in shooting it down with only a few rounds in my first attack. Comparing times with my *Rottenflieger* later, this happened at 03:58 hrs. The second fighter

Ofw. Edmund Wagner was killed in a clash with a Pe-2 several months later, on 13th November 1941, while flying Bf 109 F-2, W.Nr. 9693 coded 'Yellow 1'.

Another shot of Ofw. Wagner's Bf 109 F-2, with the *Geschwader* emblem clearly visible on the engine cowling.

was probably shocked to see one of his unit go down burning and must have flown away, because I could no longer find him. Returning to our own airfield, I waggled my wings three times. Unbelieving, my comrades shook their heads – most of them had only just woken up and were peering sleepily from their tents."[50]

At 03:40 hrs 23 machines of I./JG 3 scrambled from the airfield at Dub. They were tasked with bombing and strafing Russian aircraft at airfields in and around the city of Lvov. *Gruppenkommandeur* Hptm. Hans von Hahn reminisced:

"We set upon the Russian airfields in the Lvov area. The early morning was drab and hazy, and we could easily have got lost over the unfamiliar terrain. Down below everything was as calm and peaceful as it could be, no anti-aircraft

artillery fire, not a single aircraft took off to challenge us. Soon, the first airfields came into view. We couldn't believe our eyes. The enemy landing grounds were crammed with all sorts of aircraft, some reconnaissance machines, lots of fighters and bombers. They were not camouflaged or dispersed; actually, they were lined up wingtip to wingtip, as if on parade, in long, neat rows. We dropped our 50 kg bomblets into this mass and strafed it. A great number of Russian aircraft were painted in a silvery-gray color and marked with prominent red stars. They burst into flames one after another. We came back for more and wreaked havoc on those airfields until dusk. We were truly amazed at the incredible concentration of airfields and aircraft, which the Russians had prepared along our border!"[51]

Messerschmitt Bf 109 F-2/ Bs, 'Black 1' and 'Black 12' (in the background), of 2./JG 51 taxiing out. Schatalovka airfield, August 1941.

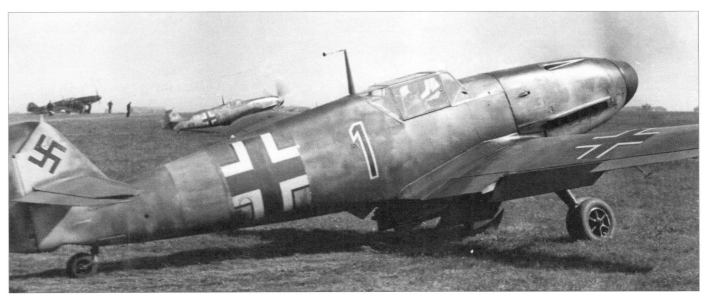

Messerschmitt Bf 109 F-2s of 10./JG 51 readied for action.

Fitting a new engine to a Bf 109 F-2 of I./JG 51. Poniatovka airfield, 21st August 1941.

On the first day of the war in the East I./JG 3 tallied eight aerial victories and a further 36 aircraft destroyed on the ground. The *Gruppe* lost one pilot – at 08:30 hrs, during a take-off for the second mission of that day, Lt. Theodor Ritter of 3./JG 3 flying Bf 109 F-2, W.Nr. 8173, crashed at the end of the runway. He succumbed to his wounds the following day in hospital at Zamość.

The pilots of II./JG 3 were also in the air before 04:00 hrs. The *Gruppe*'s first victory over Russia was scored by Oblt. Walter Dahl, flying with the *Gruppenstab*: at 04:30 hrs he shot down a MiG-3. Two hours later II./JG 3 ran into a large

gaggle of Russian fighters. The Germans bagged seven of them for no losses of their own. Overall, on the first day of hostilities II./JG 3 shot down 16 enemy aircraft. The only loss was a Bf 109 F-2, W.Nr. 12658, coded 'Black 9' of *5. Staffel*, shot down during air combat in the area of Lvov-Brody. Its pilot, Fw. Hermann Freitag, was posted missing but on 2nd July 1941 he returned to his parent unit. Four machines of the *Gruppe* were slightly damaged.

For III./JG 3, the first day of the war with the Russians proved remarkably unlucky. In the early morning, as ground crews were shackling up a 50 kg bomb under the belly of a Bf 109 F of 7./JG 3, the bomb exploded, killing four mechanics and injuring another. The *Gruppe* scored only one victory in the air (at 08:10 hrs Uffz. Rüffler of *7. Staffel* bagged an I-15 fighter) and

12 aircraft destroyed on the ground. Then, during the unit's first mission over the Dniester river, Russian anti-aircraft artillery brought down the Bf 109 F-2, W.Nr. 8244, coded 'Black 10', flown by the *Staffelkapitän* of 8./JG 3, Oblt. Willi Stange. The German pilot successfully bellied in, but was promptly captured and executed by Russian soldiers. During the second mission of the day, Bf 109 F-2, W.Nr. 8238, coded 'Yellow 6' flown by Fw. Richard Bock of the 9th *Staffel* was shot down in an aerial skirmish. Bock was listed as MIA. Hence, the day cost III./JG 3 two aircraft destroyed and another five damaged.

Stab/JG 51, commanded by Maj. Werner Mölders, was at that time stationed at Siedlce. On 22nd June 1941 it carried out 34 sorties. The *Geschwaderkommodore* himself opened the unit's victory tally – at 05:00 hrs Maj. Mölders

A factory-fresh Bf 109 F-2, just delivered from Germany, with the 'addressee' – in this case IV./JG 51 – painted on propeller's blade.

Messerschmitt Bf 109 F-2 of II./JG 51 photographed at Schatalovka in early September. The spinner is painted with RLM 70, with one third segment of white.

Messerschmitt Bf 109 F-2 of an unidentified Luftwaffe fighter unit, Eastern Front, late summer 1941.

shot down an I-153 bi-plane. The *Stabsschwarm* (HQ flight), which operated along with II./JG 51, scored a total of five victories (four by Maj. Mölders, one by Oblt. Grasser) for no losses.

During I./JG 51's first outing of the day - an escort mission - dogfight with a big group of enemy fighters developed. Two were shot down (one each by Oblt. Heinrich Kraft and Lt. Heinz Bär) for the loss of one machine – Bf 109 F-2, W.Nr. 5678, coded 'Brown 9' of 3./JG 51. Its pilot, Fw. Theodor Stebner, made a forced landing behind the Russian lines but was fortunate enough to evade capture and returned six days later.

About 09:30 hrs Lt. Heinz Bär of 1./JG 51 and his wingman Ofw. Heinrich Höfemeier, detected an unescorted formation of some 30 SB-2 bombers near Siedlce, while escorting a damaged Heinkel He 111 back to its base. The two Germans called over the radio for reinforcements and then engaged the Russians. Lt. Bär flamed two for his 19th and 20th victories: Ofw. Höfemeier notched up four – the first victories of this young pilot. As he latched onto the tail of the fifth, he was hit by return fire. Slightly injured, he broke off the attack and returned to base. Meanwhile, pilots of 3./JG 51, roused by Lt. Bär's radio call, arrived at the scene and knocked down nine more bombers. In the afternoon, at 17:45 hrs, Oblt. Heinrich Krafft scored his fourth victory of the day, a DB-3.

For II./JG 51 the initial missions against unescorted Russian bombers turned into a regular hunting spree. The day yielded 23 victories over

Messerschmitt Bf 109 F-2 of Stab IV./JG 51, flown by the *Gruppenkommandeur* Hptm. Karl-Gottfried Nordmann, crash-landed after a rough combat sortie.

bombers and five over fighters without a single loss being incurred. Besides this, 63 red-starred aircraft had been destroyed on the ground. The *Gruppenkommandeur* of II./JG 51, Hptm. Josef Fözö, recorded:

"We have barely left our cockpits. On the first day of the campaign in the east our aircraft were out five times. Each time we returned with our eyes almost glued shut by sweat and dust, lips parched and our tongues thick and sticky with thirst. As soon as we touched down, we rushed to a creek running nearby and dipped our faces in its ice-cold water. Then, still dripping with water, we walked back to our mounts.

Mölders seems to be everywhere one looks. He went up with one of the *Gruppen*, and after what seemed like just a few moments he was back on the ground, strolling towards his command post. He exchanges information with the minimum of words, only quick questions and answers. He has already devised another attack in his mind. Now he words it in a clear, easily comprehensible form. He comes up to me and says:

'Go for a sweep behind the lines. Take Hannes with you!' – he meant Kolbow, the best *Staffelkapitän* in my *Gruppe*[52].

We quickly took to the air. The landscape rolled below as we flew on. We stayed alert. Where are the Ratas? Where are those damned bumblebees hiding? Looks like the lads from the Red Air Force haven't noticed there's a war going on... Where's the Flak? It's either non-existent, or just too lazy to shoot at us. Either way, not a single burst could be seen in the sky throughout our mission.

The sky is crystal clear. I can see rising currents of air trembling with heat. Not a cloud, wherever I look. We race over forests and lakes, which twinkle like tiny blobs of silver. That grayish, twisting ribbon down below is a river. Ahead, a dark patch looms in the distance. This must be the town we are looking for. Mölders' instructions during his short briefing were: 'if

Messerschmitt Bf 109 F-2 with gear and flaps lowered, coming down to land. Note yellow wingtip undersides, which were Luftwaffe theatre markings on the Eastern Front.

Uffz. Franz-Josef Beerenbrock being congratulated by his squadron comrades after scoring his 41st and 42nd victories on 23rd September 1941, for which on 6th October 1941 he was awarded the Knight's Cross. Note that Beerenbrock's Bf 109 F-2 is fitted with additional armoured-glass screen mounted on top of the windshield.

Messerschmitt Bf 109 F-4 'Black 1' flown by the *Staffelkapitän* of 2./JG 51 Oblt. Friedhelm Höschen. Staraya Russa, winter of 1941/42. Noteworthy aspects include an interesting dapple camouflage and starboard wingtip painted in yellow.

Bf 109 F-4 'Black 11' of 2./JG 51 wrecked in an emergency landing. Winter of 1941/42.

you don't find anything in the air, check out the ground. There are two airfields, one to the north and the other to the south of the town.'

Here we go! Banking our machines, we head down for the first of the two airfields. Did they camouflage their aircraft so well, or is the airfield empty? Damn, indeed the airfield seems abandoned. Hopefully we will come across them on our way back. Perhaps this forward landing ground was never occupied. How about the other airfield?

Horrido![53] Enemy aircraft are parked close to one another. Are they Ratas by any chance? Yes, indeed they are! Welcome! We'd like to renew our acquaintance, if you will![54]

I count 40 machines. No, there are more... 45 in all. Pity they didn't get off the ground to try their hand with us, we'd accept the chal-

lenge with pleasure. Not that we were utterly disappointed to see them defenseless on the ground - all the worse for them!

How could it be that no alarm spurred them to come rushing down the runway? Isn't there anyone brave enough to jump into the cockpit of his fighter and take off to tangle with us? There's nothing going on down there. The airfield looks deserted, as if some mysterious plague has wiped out its former occupants. Let us bring some life into this place.

The show is on. Spurts of dirt kicked up by our slugs cross the airfield, dust billows up. The first bursts find their mark. We're hitting them hard! Our rounds tear into fuel tanks, engines... Up we go, only to turn around and swoop down again. We are loosing off burst after burst... Every single machine down there gets plastered

- even those on the far ends are riddled with bullets. Taking stock of the situation, we can see that the destruction is complete.

At the edge of the airfield I spot a forlorn fuel bowser. How could I leave it like that, all alone..? There are no longer any aircraft to refuel anyway! A short burst slams into the bowser and immediately tongues of flame lap hungrily from its bowels. It may go off any moment now, such a load of fuel won't simply burn out. Indeed, an internal explosion rips apart metal sheets, which lob into the air in fiery arches. The remaining fuel spills onto the ground, turning everything around into a raging furnace.

Time to bid our farewell, there's nothing left for us to do here! We are making one more orbit over the Ratas' cemetery to pay our disrespects. A pall of smoke drifts skywards and gets into our cockpits. Thank you very much, we are almost cooked now! We are sweating profusely through physical effort and excitement. A quick look at my wristwatch: we've been here for 40 minutes. Let's get back home quickly. Perhaps another important task is awaiting us.

Casting a final look around, I reassess the situation. Columns of heavy smoke boiling up testify to what we have done here. Well done! Wherever we manage to start a fire like that, we save time and effort for other pilots, who can see from far away that this place has already been thoroughly worked over.

We land, taxi to our revetments, unbuckle our seat belts... There's so much to report.

One exciting piece of news follows another. We had just been debriefed when the second *Staffel* of our *Gruppe* returned:

'We ran into twenty Martin bombers!'

'You lucky devils! How many did you get?'

'All twenty of them!'[55]

We gather at the command post. Here all victory claims made in the morning are summed up. They amount to 27 air kills and 22 aircraft confirmed destroyed on the ground. Then comes our turn to report:

'Forty five Ratas, one fuel bowser, all destroyed north of Biała Podlaska'

Mölders peers at me disbelievingly. For the first time I see him get excited:

'Joschko[56], Kolbow! What are you trying to tell me? Forty five in one go? With no resistance, no air combat, just like that? You just went there and knocked out all of them by yourselves?'

Other pilots report the same figure – forty five.

'I'll be damned!' – I could hear growing respect in our commander's voice – 'Then it's all true!'

I look at him. His face is beaming with pride. He heartily shakes Kolbow's hand, then mine, and pats our backs.

'Men – he said – twenty two plus forty five plus twenty seven... we got ninety four!'[57]

The first day of the war against the Soviet Union was also well remembered by Oblt. Walter Stengel of 6./JG 51:

"On the eve of 'Barbarossa', the *Staffel*'s kills, listed on our victory board, showed that

Fw. Otto Tange of 5./JG 51, the holder of the Knight's Cross, posing in front of his Messerschmitt Bf 109 F-2 coded 'Black 3'. Tange tallied a total of 68 victories. He was shot down and killed by Soviet antiaircraft fire on 30th July 1943.

I had only two victories. Our *Kommodore*, Werner Mölders, said that that would soon change...

At 04.30 hrs, on 22nd June 1941, I took off with my 6./JG 51 on our first mission against Russia. We still saw trains heading east and west across the Russian border but the airfields near the front were filled with Russian aircraft, which leads me to believe that the Russians were going to attack us. On this occasion, we had no encounter with enemy aircraft and landed nearly two hours later.

We had a quick breakfast while our machines were refueled and re-armed. The whole of II./JG 51 had landed after the first sorties without any victories, so when we took again, we hoped for better luck. This time, at about 07.30 hrs, my 6th *Staffel* encountered a flight of enemy aircraft. I shot down a 'Rata', as did at least two other pilots, thus winning for II./JG 51 the first victories on the new front. We landed and as soon as possible took off again on another mission. The first day was typical of those that followed, though we often had to move to a new airfield in order to keep pace with the advance of the ground troops".[58]

Pilots of III./JG 51 claimed 19 enemy aircraft, including 15 SB-2s, and a further 23 destroyed on the ground. The unit's own losses were limited to one aircraft lost in air combat near Brest-Litovsk. Its pilot, Oblt. Gottfried

Schlitzer, made it back to his unit on foot the following day. Four more aircraft of III./JG 51 were damaged.

Meanwhile, IV./JG 51 commenced its war in the East in the early hours of 22nd June 1941 by flying escort to a group of *Stuka* dive bombers bound for the Russian fortifications at Brest-Litovsk. Before the day was out, the *Gruppe* had performed several more escort missions and freelance fighter sweeps on the eastern bank of the Bug river, especially in the Kobryń area. The result was 23 Russian aircraft shot down against the loss of one Bf 109 F-2, W.Nr. 6656, which suffered an engine malfunction and was forced to belly-in at an airfield in Krzewica. The pilot walked away unscathed.

For II./JG 52 the war with Russia started at 02:50 hrs, with an escort flight for some *Stukas* which were sent to bomb Russian barracks near the border. During the ensuing missions the *Gruppe* scrapped several times with enemy aircraft, and claimed 16 of them for the loss of one of their own (Bf 109 F-2, W.Nr. 5780) and an injured pilot; Gefr. Walter Köhne was hit by shrapnel from an anti-aircraft shell near Augustów.

JG 53 was particularly active on 22nd June 1941. First to get into the air, at 02:50 hrs, were the machines of II./JG 53. Half an hour later they chanced upon a gaggle of I-16 fighters but the ensuing skirmish proved inconclusive, without loss on either side.

At 03:40 hrs machines of III./JG 53 took off for their first action of the day. The Stab and 7. *Staffel* targeted airfields at Alytys and Oranji, whilst 8./JG 53 struck at Ossow airfield. A total of seven Soviet bombers were destroyed on the ground. Returning to their base at Suwałki, the Germans encountered a dozen or so I-15 biplanes. Although the little, nimble fighters were much slower than the Messerschmitt 109s, they were exceptionally maneuverable and hence difficult to hit. During this fracas the Germans experienced for the first time the tactics that were later frequently employed by I-15 and I-153 pilots against Bf 109s. A Russian pilot would allow a Bf 109 to close in from behind and then, when the German had almost got within range, flip his machine on its back in a tight half-loop to reverse his heading. Still upside down, he would then engage a very surprised Bf 109 pilot in a headlong attack. However, on this occasion the technical and tactical advantage held by the Germans was so great that the pilots of III./JG 53 shot down four Russians for no losses of their own. Three of them were credited to Hptm. Wolf-Dietrich Wilcke, and one to Fw. Werner Stumpf. At 03:40 hrs it was time for I./JG 53 to join the campaign in the East. Its task was to escort *Stukas*; the mission was uneventful and after 70 minutes all machines returned safely to their base at Krzewicza.

Despite the heavy blows received in the opening hours of 'Barbarossa' the Soviet Air Force was far from neutralized. At 05:38 hrs Bf 109 Fs of II./JG 53 were scrambled to intercept an approaching formation of twin-engined SB-2 bombers. The German fighters bounced them before the bombers could cross the frontline. The first two fell to the guns of Hptm. Walter Spies, two more to Ofw. Stefan Litjens, a fifth to Uffz. Herbert Rollwage, and a sixth to the CO of II./JG 53, *Gruppenkommandeur* Hptm. Heinz Bretnütz (for his 32nd victory). Moments later the pilots of II./JG 53 heard in their headsets the voice of their commander:

'I've been hit in the engine, I'm injured!'

They watched his Bf 109 F-2, W.Nr. 6674 marked with "black <<+−", belly-land between Erzvilkas and Nemaksciai. Some Lithuanian peasants found the injured Bretnütz and hid him from the searching Russians. Four days later he was handed over to advancing German troops. However, by that time his injured leg had been infected with gangrene. Although immediately hospitalized, Bretnütz had to have his leg amputated and died the following day.

At 06:00 hrs pilots of III./JG 53 took off for their second mission of the day. They were to cover some *Stukas* heading for Grodno. In the ensuing scrap with I-16s and I-153s they shot down six enemy fighters. Ofw. Josef Kronschnabel was one of the victors:

"I got one of the Ratas in a head-on pass. It fell off towards the ground streaming flames and smoke. I had no other choice but to blast him out of the sky. It came charging at me with all guns ablaze".[59]

Ofw. Eduard Koslowski shot down an I-153 but was then forced down behind the lines in his damaged Bf 109 F-2, W.Nr. 5523, coded 'Black 2'. He evaded capture and the following day returned to his unit. The second mission flown by I./JG 53 began at 06:30 hrs. The objective was to carry out a fighter sweep north of Brest-Litovsk. By the end of the patrol, Uffz. Ludwig Reibel of 1./JG 53 had bagged an I-153.

The *Stabsschwarm* took off for its second mission of the day at 06:40 hrs. Lt. Franz Schiess recorded the following:

"Once our machines have been refueled and re-armed, we go back into the air. I am piloting a reserve machine. We are passing over burning Brest, heading for Kobryn. There we mix it up with a bunch of Russian fighters. They are Curtiss[60] fighters, small bi-planes with retractable landing gear and huge radial engines. Our *Kommandeur* quickly shoots one down in flames and the enemy fighter spins to the ground. Then he jumps another and rakes him with gunfire. The Russian breaks away and makes a run for it, going at full bore close to the ground. Our CO gives chase but overshoots

Messerschmitt Bf 109 F-2 'White 4' of 4./JG 51, camouflaged with white distemper, at Briansk airfield in February 1942. It was flown by Lt. Horst Wunderlich (credited with 10 victories), who was killed in action over Tunisia on 30th November 1942.

Messerschmitt Bf 109 F-2's pilot was protected from the front by an additional armour glass mounted on top of the windshield, and from the rear by an armour plate installed inside canopy hood.

Messerschmitt Bf 109 F-2 'White 12' of 4./JG 51 readied for action. Briansk, winter of 1941/42.

and has to pull up. This is the moment I've been waiting for! I go flat out after the Russian and, as he pulls up to hop over a line of trees, I am some 60 meters behind his tail. I press the triggers and pump lead into the Curtiss until I have to pull up to avoid collision. A flurry of burning pieces flashes below as I speed past, then from the corner of my eye I can see an explosion on the ground. It marks the point of impact and the final resting place of my adversary. Scratch one Russian fighter! I wish I could enjoy this sight for a little bit longer but the air is still full of Russians. Oblt. Pufahl got another, so all in all our *Schwarm* has bagged four. Passing over our airfield, we waggled our wings. As soon as we got back on the ground, our ground crews rushed to meet us. They were overjoyed at our successes. They were their victories as much as ours".[61]

At 09:10 hrs the aircraft of I./JG 53 were already heading back for the frontline. It was another escort mission for some *Stukas*. Again

Refuelling a Messerschmitt Bf 109 F-4 of Stab I./JG 51 at Staraya Russa, winter of 1941/42. The machine bears markings of the *Gruppe's* Technical Officer (< ○).

they slugged it out with I-16s. One of the Russian fighters was gunned down by Lt. Walter Zellot of *1. Staffel*, another – by Lt. Walter Seiz of 3./JG 53 – on the return leg. At 09:35 hrs the *Stabsschwarm* took off for the third time. Shortly afterwards the four Stab pilots got to grips with some 20 I-16s. Although the enemy were five times as numerous, they failed to inflict any losses and the *Schwarm* returned safely to base. The third operation by III./JG 53, a strafing attack on some airfields in the Vilnius area, got underway at 10:45 hrs. After 85 minutes all the *Gruppe*'s aircraft were back at their base.

Shortly after 11:00 hrs, elements of I./JG 53 were scrambled to deal with a group of SB-2 and SB-2bis bombers, which were reported to be approaching the airfield. Again, the Russians suffered dearly at the hands of the German pilots. Five bombers crashed in flames, three of them the victims of Lt. Ernst-Albrecht Schultz; the remaining two fell to Uffz. Ludwig Reibel.

An hour later, at 12:18 hrs, I./JG 53 was again rushed into the air to handle an oncoming wave of Soviet bombers. Oblt. Hans Ohly, the *Staffelkapitän* of 1./JG 53, claimed two SB-2s, his wingman, Fw. Eckhard Wenzel, another.

At 15:25 hrs, Fw. Kurt Sauer of 9./JG 53 claimed an "I-17" (in fact a MiG-1 or -3). Twenty minutes later the *Stabsschwarm* of JG 53 flew its fourth mission of that hectic day, a sweep over the frontline. Lt. Franz Schiess duly joined in:

"During my third mission[62], over Biala Podlaska I spotted three twin-engined aircraft, which were fired upon by our Flak. I orbited to the left, swung into a firing position behind the bomber on the right flank and opened up. The SB-2 instantly began to shed pieces, and its starboard engine burst into flames. The next moment the bomber turned into a ball of fire and hurtled towards the ground. Second victory! From there we headed for Kobryn, where

we strafed an airfield. I managed to set one Curtiss on fire".[63] During the same mission the *Geschwaderkommodore* Maj. Günter Freiherr von Maltzahn and Lt. Karlheinz Preu shot down one bomber apiece.

At 16:10 hrs, III./JG 53 mounted another mission, a strafing attack against an enemy airfield. The Germans ran into some Russian bombers and a group of MiG-3s, and in a furious furball shot down 11. Hptm. Wolf-Dietrich Wilcke nailed his fifth that day.

Harsh winter conditions in Russia at the turn of 1941/42 were particularly tough for groundcrews. Seen in the background is 1,350 hp Daimler-Benz DB 601 E engine which powered the Bf 109 F-4.

The same aircraft with its tail jacked up for gun boresighting. Visible markings include *Geschwader* emblem on the engine cowling, *Gruppe* emblem under cockpit, yellow fuselage band aft of the cross, as well as yellow lower cowl, rudder and lower wingtips.

A hangar at Staraya Russa
airfield crammed with
various types of Luftwaffe
aircraft. In the foreground
a Messerschmitt Bf 109 F-4,
in the background an Arado Ar
66 and a Henschel Hs 126.

Meanwhile, Ofw. Josef Kronschnabel had a close call:

"In the afternoon, during my third sortie, I was some 20 kilometers behind the lines when my engine suddenly packed up. I immediately feathered the propeller and glided back. Fortunately, our troops in this sector were rapidly advancing and I managed to belly-in on the German side of the frontline. I picked up a ride in a Kübelwagen, which transported the wounded to the rear, and by the evening I was back at my home base".[64]

At 16:30 hrs I./JG 53 staged another escort mission for some *Stukas*. On their way back the pilots were alerted to the presence of two bombers north of Biała Podlaska. After a brief chase the two DB-3s were shot down by Fw.

Eckhard Wenzel and Lt. Udo Padior. Only eight minutes later, the returning Messerschmitts waded into a group of Russian bombers and quickly dispatched five of them.

In the meantime, Russian DB-3s once again attempted to break through the German fighter umbrella in order to bomb their airfields. This time they were met by a patrolling *Schwarm* of 7./JG 53. In a matter of just three minutes (from 17:20 to 17:23 hrs) the Germans claimed three of them.

The relentless Russian incursions continued well into the late afternoon. Half an hour later the *Alarm-Schwarm* of 5./JG 53 was scrambled to intercept another wave. A few minutes later they jumped a group of SB-2 and SB-2bis bombers, and shot down three of them. At 18:25 hrs

a *Schwarm* of 9./JG 53 swept the nearby frontline sector and returned with two victories over Russian fighters.

At 19:15 hrs the JG 53 *Stabsschwarm* flew its fifth and final mission of the day. Lt. Franz Schiess described the event:

"An overwhelming feeling of tiredness slowly gets into my bones, but I have no choice. There's one more mission, my fourth today, to be flown. Since we encounter no opposition in the air, we strafe Russian columns. The roads are so jammed with traffic that we don't even need to aim precisely. As we swoop down, an indescribable panic breaks out on the ground".[65]

Shortly before nightfall, III./JG 53 flew its last mission of the day, and at 20:45 hrs tangled with some Russian fighters, claiming three of them. Overall, on 22nd June JG 53 claimed 71 aircraft destroyed in the air and a further 30 on the ground. The unit's own losses were limited to three machines and one pilot (Hptm. Bretnütz).

At dawn on 22nd June 1941, in the northern sector, JG 54 participated in the first wave of German attacks against Russian airfields located along the border. The *Geschwaderstab* and II./JG 54 laid on an escort for the bombers of KG 1, KG 76 and KG 77. The target of the first raid, carried out shortly before 03:00 hrs, was an air-

Messerschmitt Bf 109 F-2 coded 'Red 9' of 5./JG 51 at Briansk airfield, February 1942. The horizontal bar denoting *II. Gruppe*, located between the tactical number and fuselage cross, was overpainted with white distemper.

The Knight's Cross winner Lt. Hans Strelow getting strapped in the cockpit of his Messerschmitt Bf 109 F-2 at Briansk, February 1942.

Messerschmitt Bf 109 F-4 'Black 8' of 5./JG 51 in front of a hangar at Briansk, February 1942.

field at Kovno. The *Geschwaderkommodore* Maj. Hannes Trautloft related:

"At 2:30 hrs, when I arrived at the airfield, the stars overhead still twinkled against the dark night sky. My flying boots were wet with dew, which covered the clover on the taxiways. The airfield had woken up a long time ago. Aircraft were being warmed up in their revetments by our mechanics. I was greeted by reverberating din of 45 engines being simultaneously revved up to maximum power. Bright yellow and bluish flames shot back from their exhaust stacks. The air was filled with a curious mixture of smells: soil, flowers, grass, gasoline and oil. I could hear birds start to chirp. The first hint of dawn brightened the sky in the east, and the darkness and deep shadows were quickly retreating. Everybody at the airfield shared the common sensation that the breaking day was to determine our fates. Chilled by the cold

Pilot of this battle-damaged Bf 109 F-4 of 5./JG 51 was lucky to make it back to base.

of night, we climbed into our cockpits. The metal of my seat, and the seat belts were damp and cold. My crew chief tightened my harness. 'Good hunting!' he shouted at me before I shut the canopy. The engine roared into life. As always prior to a combat sortie, my throat felt dry. Today also, my heart was perhaps beating a little faster.

We took off at 02:30 hrs. All the units of *I. Fliegerkorps*[66] had been ordered to cross the border at 03:00 hrs sharp. As we were passing above, the hitherto silent landscape suddenly burst into life. At 03:05 hrs our artillery batteries along the entire front opened up with a formidable barrage. Everywhere I looked, I could see muzzle flashes. A truly fascinating sight. In

Results of a head-on collision which occurred on 10th April 1942. During an alarm scramble Lt. Ernst Weismann of 12./JG 51 (at the controls of Bf 109 F-4, W.Nr. 8266 coded 'Yellow 5') slammed into a landing Bf 110. Weismann was seriously injured but returned to active duty.

A camouflaged Messerschmitt Bf 109 F-2 of III./JG 51. Dugino, May 1942.

Uffz. Otto Würfel of 9./JG 51 greeted by groundcrews at Dugino upon returning from a sortie in his Bf 109 F-2.

Pilots of 9./JG 51 at Dugino airfield, spring 1942. From left to right: Uffz. Helmut Brunke (+ 13.03.1943), Oblt. Hermann Lücke (+ 08.11.1943), Ofw. Bernhard Lausch (+ 04.07.1942), Fw. Walter Brake, unknown, Uffz. Erich Holbein (+ 29.01.1943) and Fw. Siegfried Schwaneberg.

that instant war on the eastern front became a reality. From our altitude one could see far to the north, beyond the Neman River, whilst away to the south the Rominter Heide[67] loomed in the distance. Watching the gigantic drama unfold beneath us, we all realized that a new chapter in history was being written in front of our very eyes, and that our own destiny was being forged then and there.

We were heading towards Kovno. The pilots were jittery, I could tell that from the way they flew. I knew that distinctive nervousness from other theaters of war, the anxious expectation of the unknown. So many questions troubled our minds: What are the Russians going to do? Will we achieve surprise? Will the Russian fighters come up and fight? Are their aircraft better than ours? The progress of our first mis-

sion quickly brought along the answers. The Russians were caught completely off-guard. At most airfields we attacked there was no opposition whatsoever.

Far below, still barely discernible against the dark background, lay the town and the airfield of Kovno. At that very moment the sun rose above the horizon, its rays glinting off our aircraft in the crystal-clear air of the early morning. Our bombers dropped their loads on Kovno airfield. Their bombs were bursting among parked aircraft. All of a sudden we spotted two enemy fighters ahead of us, but as quickly as they turned up, they disappeared in the distance. During our return we saw numerous fires along the frontline. Large plumes of smoke billowed high up into the sky. Our first combat mission resulted in two air victories. The Russians didn't even know what hit them. However, during the day this was to change.

Messerschmitt Bf 109 F-4, W.Nr. 13051, 'Black <·+·' flown by the *Geschwaderkommodore* of JG 51 Maj. Karl-Gottfried Nordmann. Smolensk, May 1942.

Maj. Karl-Gottfried Nordmann climbing out of the cockpit of his Messerschmitt Bf 109 F-2, W.Nr. 12825. Dugino airfield, June 1942.

Petsamo, July 1942. In the foreground Messerschmitt Bf 109 F-4 coded 'Yellow 12' of 6./JG 5, flown by the Knight's Holder Lt. Heinrich Ehrler (credited with 208 victories). Of note is the emblem of *6. Staffel* – a green four-leaf clover.

Members of the *Reichsarbeitsdienst* (Reich Labour Service) pushing a Messerschmitt Bf 109 F-4 of IV./JG 51 to its dispersal pen. Seschtschinskaya airfield, 19th July 1942.

Our airfields at Gerlinden and Lindental reported bombers passing above. The *Staffeln* held at combat readiness immediately took off to prevent the enemy from entering the airspace of Eastern Prussia. Of 26 SB-2 type Martin bombers, 17 were shot down. The survivors retreated in a hurry. Everywhere one looked, there were wrecks burning on the ground, and parachutes floating in the air. The fleeing enemy was chased as far as Schaulen[68]. We were in the air all day long. Every pilot flew five to seven sorties. Our spines and backsides hurt. We carried out, alternately, bomber escorts, freelance sweeps and strafing attacks against ground targets. By the afternoon we had gained air supremacy in our assigned sector. Russian fighters were conspicuously absent.

In the late afternoon, during one of the sweeps, near Kovno we came across a group of some 50-60 Martin SB-2 bombers. Unfortunately, our fuel reserve was running low, so we could only afford two passes. Our first attack failed. During our second pass the engine of one of the bombers caught fire. The bomber jettisoned its load and then exploded in mid-air. As we wheeled around, we were caught in a heavy crossfire from the rear gunners. The enemy formation turned south. Low on fuel,

Messerschmitt Bf 109 F-4 of II./JG 5 landing at Petsamo (Finland) in the summer of 1942.

we had to break off the attack. However, over the radio we called in reinforcements, which later shot down 11 bombers from that group. One of our Me 109s, damaged by the return fire, failed to lower its undercarriage and had to make a wheels-up landing. All went smoothly and not much damage was done. Most fortunately, a brand-new machine was delivered to us that day. It was fitted with a gun camera. An hour later we flew another mission. One of our pilots got completely lost and in the evening he reported himself at Litzmannstadt (Łódź).

In the evening once again we headed towards Schaulen but encountered no opposition in the air. We flew at low level, passing our ground troops, who were mid-way between Kovno and Schaulen. Huge clouds of dust – just like previously in Poland – gave away the position of our advancing columns. Fires raged all around. Entire villages were burning. A cloud of black smoke, visible from far away, shrouded

Tauragė. After our last mission we reported our successes to the Corps headquarters. For only one loss, the *Geschwader* had tallied 45 victories in the air and 35 on the ground.

The effects of the strain and tension endured throughout the day began to show. We were dead tired and craved for a bit of sleep. We finally hit the sack after midnight. We were supposed to be at combat readiness just two hours later!" [69]

Throughout the day the Stab flight and II./JG 54 flew two more missions - which were bomber escorts - and a dozen or so sweeps in *Staffel* or *Schwarm* strength, mounted in response to the ever increasing number of forays by Russian bombers.

At 09:50 hrs Lt. Hans Beißwenger of 6./JG 54 claimed an I-16 for the first victory of II./JG 54 over Russia. In the afternoon, between 16:45 and 17:40 hrs, the *Gruppe* countered attacks by twin-engined Russian bombers, which

Fw. Kurt Knappe of 5./JG 51 taxiing out in his Messerschmitt Bf 109 F-2 coded 'Red 4', Orel, August 1942. Knappe received his Knight's Cross on 3rd November 1942. He was subsequently killed in action in the West with JG 2, on 3rd September 1943. By the time of his death he was credited with 56 victories.

Although of low quality, this photo is exceptional as it shows a Messerschmitt Bf 109 F-4 of 3./JG 52 which sports the rarely applied 'umbrella' emblem of the *Staffel* on the rear fuselage, aft the cross. The emblem of I./JG 52 may be seen on the engine cowling.

Messerschmitt Bf 109 F-4 of 7./JG 5 at Petsamo airfield.

stubbornly pressed on, wave after wave. The result was 14 SB-2s shot down for no loss. The CO of JG 54, Maj. Hannes Trautloft, had an opportunity to score his ninth victory. On the first day of the war with Russia II./JG 54 lost two pilots. Uffz. Walter Puregger of 5./JG 54, while at the controls of Bf 109 F-2, W.Nr. 5790, perished in a dogfight north-east of Ukmergė (Lithuania), whilst Lt. Günther Schreiterer of 6./JG 54 (flying Bf 109 F-2, W.Nr. 8908) was killed over Lindieken near Ebenrode[70], in a mid-air collision with another Bf 109, of I./JG 54. More lucky was the pilot of 5./JG 54, who after sustaining battle damage safely belly-landed his Bf 109 F-2, W.Nr. 9542 near Tauragė.

Pilots of I./JG 54 commenced operations at 03:00 hrs with a sweep in the Kovno area. There they mixed it up with a group of Russian fighters. Two of them fell to the *Staffelkapitän* of 1./JG 54, Oblt. Adolf Kinzinger. During the second mission of the day, shortly before 06:00 hrs, the *Gruppe* ran into some unescorted SB-2 bombers bound for German airfields in Eastern Prussia.

Nine of them were brought down. In the afternoon I./JG 54 escorted small groups of Ju 88s as they bombed forward landing grounds near Kovno and Schaulen. At 13:45 hrs, Oblt. Adolf Kinziger shot down an I-16 for his 13th victory - his third on that day. The *Gruppe* lost one pilot: Uffz. Robert Brock of 3./JG 54, who flew Bf 109 F-2, W.Nr. 5733, was killed in the collision with a machine of II./JG 54. Another Bf 109 F-2 (W.Nr. 12638) was forced down near Altenburg after running out of fuel and sustained 50% damage.

For the flying personnel of III./JG 54 the campaign in Russia started at 03:10 hrs with an escort mission for some bombers tasked with knocking out an airfield at Pojewitsch. Since there was little to do for the escorting fighters in the air, on their way back they strafed a Russian column heading for the border. The second and the third mission of III./JG 54 followed suit: they were escorts for Ju 88s which bombed the airfield at Kédainiai, located some 35 km north of Kovno. During the first of those two missions the pilots of III./JG 54 recorded their first

Ofw. Heinz Klöpper of 11./JG 51, who on 4th September 1942 was awarded the Knight's Cross in recognition of his 64 victories, exits the cockpit of his Bf 109 F-2 coded 'Red 12'.

aerial combat on the Eastern Front. Lt. Waldemar Wübke of 9./JG 54 shot down two SB-3s, whilst Uffz. Rudolf Damoser of the same *Staffel* claimed another. From noon and throughout the rest of the day III./JG 54 stood at readiness, scrambling several times to intercept groups of enemy aircraft reported in the vicinity. In the course of those missions two Soviet fighters and one bomber were claimed. Overall, on 22nd June 1941 the pilots of JG 54 were credited with 34 victories for the loss of three pilots.

On the first day of Operation 'Barbarossa' Luftwaffe pilots flying Messerschmitt Bf 109 Fs accounted for no fewer than 194 Russian aircraft, against the loss of 14 machines. Over the next few days they struggled to establish air superiority. The Red Air Force, despite losing 1,811 aircraft in one day, was still very active. The Russians' losses continued to mount on an unprecedented scale. On 23rd and 24th June 1941 the Germans destroyed a further 1,357 Soviet aircraft.

The Bf 109 Fs of *Luftflotte 1* and JG 51, which operated in the north, were involved in particularly heavy fighting. On the morning of 23rd June 1941 ten SB-2 bombers set out to strike Königsberg, whilst another 16 struck off for Gumbinnen airfield in Eastern Prussia. Fighters of JG 54 intercepted both raids. Between 10:07 and 10:25 hrs they claimed 22 bombers. At 11:47 hrs pilots of III./JG 54 jumped another group of SB-2s and downed 12. The leader of the bomber formation was shot down by the *Staffelkapitän* of 9./JG 54, Oblt. Hans-Ekkehard Bob, whose aircraft was in turn damaged by return fire and forced down behind the lines (as

related by him in the opening passages of this book). Oblt. Bob evaded capture and returned to his unit two days later. On 24th June, pilots of JG 51 wreaked havoc among formations of poorly-armed and unescorted SB-2s and SB-3s, shooting down no fewer than 57 of them.

On 25th June 1941, due to the collapse of the Russian defenses and the speedy advance of German armored units spearheading Army Group 'Center', III./JG 53 moved to a recently captured airfield at Vilnius. There the Russians attempted to knock out the German fighters on the ground, but their successive raids were swiftly countered by Bf 109 Fs. As a result, Stab and III./JG 53 claimed 30 bombers, including four by the *Geschwaderkommodore,* Maj. Günther Freiherr von Maltzahn. JG 51, which operated further south, claimed as many as 68 Soviet bombers, including six by the *Staffelkapitän* of 5./JG 51, Oblt. Hans Kolbow.

Despite such hitherto unheard of successes and hundreds of destroyed Russian aircraft, the situation of German fighter units was steadily deteriorating. The Russian airmen fought with unbelievable determination. Rear gunners often chose to stay in their already doomed bombers and fight back to the very end, rather than bail out. The poor defensive armament of the SB-2 and SB-3 bombers was hardly adequate to shoot down an attacking Messerschmitt. However, the notorious shortage of spare parts experienced by the German forward units meant that any damage inflicted by the bombers' return fire could easily ground a fighter for a long time. Consequently, more and more German fighters became unserviceable.

The Knight's Cross holder Hptm. Hans-Ekkehard Bob was born on 24th January 1917 in Freiburg. He scored a total of 59 aerial victories, including 21 in the West. Presently he's one of the eldest active pilots in Europe.

On 30th June 1941 Russian bombers undertook a desperate but futile attempt to neutralize a German troop concentration at Berezina bridgehead near Babruysk. While providing a fighter screen over the area, pilots of JG 51 bagged a staggering 113 enemy aircraft for the loss of seven of their own (one pilot was killed and another injured). Each of the following pilots shot down five enemy bombers on that day: the *Geschwaderkommodore* of JG 51 Obstlt. Werner Mölders (his 78th to 82nd victories), the *Gruppenkommandeur* of I./JG 51 Hptm. Hermann-Friedrich Joppien (his 48th to 52nd victories) and Lt. Heinz Bär of 1./JG 51 (victories 23 through to 27th).

On 12th July 1941 Hptm. Leppla scored 500th victory over Russia for JG 51, which also happened to be 1,200th victory of the *Geschwader* in the Second World War. On the other hand, for the first time in its history the unit was seriously affected by serviceability problems. On 15th July 1941 Hptm. Becht, TO (Technical Officer) with Stab JG 51, reported that the *Geschwader* was at 47% of its original operational strength. As many as 26 machines were grounded due to lack of spare parts. Of 58 airworthy aircraft, in 22 engines worked for more than 50 hours without overhauls. Since 22nd June 1941 the *Geschwader* wrote off a total of 89 aircraft and received only 49 as replacements.

Between 4th and 6th July 1941 the VVS launched a series of air raids over the Baltic states in order to slow down the advance of German armoured spearheads in this region. Bf 109 F pilots of JG 54 kept the Russians at bay. Of 121 victories the former claimed in that period, majority fell to *II. Gruppe* commanded by Hptm. Dietrich Hrabak. On 5th July the victory tally of his II./JG 54 surpassed the 300 mark.

While unescorted formations of SB-2 and DB-3 bombers continued to be butchered, Soviet fighters concentrated their efforts on gaining local air superiority over key sectors of the front. In the period between 22nd June and 13th July 1941 pilots of *I. Fliegerkorps* claimed 487 Russian aircraft destroyed in the air and a further 1,698 on the ground.

Despite such heavy losses the Red Air Force maintained numerical superiority. The breathtaking intensity of operations, combined with scarcity of spare parts, seriously hampered the German fighter arm in Russia in performing their tasks. As reported by II./JG 54's quartermaster, as of 9th July 1941 the *Gruppe* had only five serviceable Bf 109 Fs on strength!

On 14th July 1941, in the vicinity of Lake Ilmen, the Soviet Eleventh Army, supported by 235 aircraft, staged a major counterattack against the German Fourth Panzer Group. Once again the Luftwaffe in northern Russia summoned all available strength for a maximum effort to beat off the enemy in the air – this time successfully.

Meanwhile, over Ukraine the Bf 109 Fs of JG 3 also achieved considerable successes. The most distinguished pilot was Hptm. Walter Oesau, the *Gruppenkommandeur* of III./JG 3, who in the period between 22nd and 30th June 1941 raised his tally from 42 to 50 enemy aircraft destroyed in the air, and on 26th July 1941 he scored his 86th victory. However, two days later he was transferred out of Russia to assume command of JG 2, stationed in France. On 15th July 1941 Ofw. Hans Stechman of 9./JG 3 shot down three I-153 fighters to claim 1,000th aerial victory of his *Geschwader*.

On the same day the individual tally of Maj. Werner Mölders, the *Geschwaderkommodore* of JG 51, surpassed 100 victories. The following day the OKW (*Oberkommando der Wehrmacht*) issued a special communiqué announcing that Maj. Mölders, as the first soldier of the German armed forces, was to be decorated with the Reich's highest military award, the Knight's Cross

This Messerschmitt Bf 109 F-2 of 15.(span)/JG 51 bears the name of *Capitán* Antonio Noriega Labat, who was killed in action on 1st July 1942.

Uffz. Otto Gaiser of 10./JG 51 sitting on the wing of a Bf 109 F-2. Vitebsk, December 1942.

with Oak Leaves, Swords and Diamonds. Concurrently, an order issued directly by Führer's headquarters banned Mölders from any further combat flying. He was also promoted to the rank of Oberstleutnant (Lieutenant Colonel) and appointed *Inspekteur der Jagdflieger* (the Inspector General of Fighters). Mölders turned the command of JG 51 to Maj. Friedrich Beckh.

By the end of July 1941 several Bf 109 F pilots won Knight's Crosses. Among them were Maj. Günther Lützow, the *Kommodore* of JG 3, Maj. Günther von Maltzahn, the *Kommodore* of JG 53, Maj. Hannes Trautloft, the *Kommodore* of JG 54, as well as Oblt. Robert Olejnik of JG 3, Lt. Heinz Bär of JG 51 and Lt. Erich Schmidt of JG 53.

On 1st August 1941 Lt. Max-Hellmuth Ostermann claimed 1,000th victory for JG 54. At that time the *Geschwader* was tasked with covering a front sector stretching for nearly 400 kilometres, from Finland to Latvia. The Russians were up in force, as proved by the fact that only on 10th August 1941 the 'Grünherz' pilots ('Green Heart' was JG 54's emblem) claimed 54 victories. One of the top claimants was Oblt. Hans 'Fips' Philipp, the *Kapitän* of 4. *Staffel*, who on 24th August 1941, in recognition of his 62 victories (of which 40 were scored over Russia), was awarded the Oak Leaves to his Knight's Cross. The first JG 54 ace killed in action on the Eastern Front was Ofw. Georg Braunshirn (13 victories), shot down in an aerial combat on 16th August 1941.

In early September 1941 the component *Staffeln* of JG 54 were relocated to Sivierskaya and Krasnogwardiejsk in Leningrad area, where they were to spans the 900-day siege of the city. Before the month was out, the *Geschwader* suffered two painful losses. On the 9th Oblt.

Hubert Mütherich (credited with 43 victories) was killed in a failed emergency landing. On the 30th September another Knight's Cross holder, *the Gruppenkommandeur* of III./JG 54 Hptm. Arnold Lignitz was shot down in a dogfight with I-153s over Leningrad. Lignitz successfully bailed out and landed in the city's centre, but was later murdered by Russians.

In the meantime, in the southern sector of the front, III./JG 52 began its rise to fame. On 4th August 1941 Oblt. Günther Rall, the *Staffelkapitän* of 8./JG 52 and the future third-ranking Luftwaffe ace with 275 victories, bagged three I-16s for his fourth through sixth 'kills'. On the same day another future top ace of the Luftwaffe (eventually with 220 victories to his credit) Lt. Hermann Graf of 9./JG 52, claimed his first. Three days later III./JG 52 recorded its 100th victory.

Nevertheless, the first part of August 1941 saw the heaviest fighting in the air over the front sector in the vicinity of Yelna. There, during the first 16 days of the month, pilots of JG 51 and III./JG 53 claimed 169 Soviet aircraft for the loss of 11 own machines. In such conditions pilots' individual tallies soared up. On 14th August Lt. Heinz Bär scored his 62nd, whilst Hptm. Joppien surpassed 60, Ofw. Hoffmann 40, and Oblt. Gallowitsch, Uffz. Beerenbrock and Oblt Hohagen 20 victory marks. In the latter part of August 1941 successes had to be offset by the loss of several distinguished pilots. On 25th August 1941, after scoring his 70th 'kill', Hptm. Hermann-Friedrich Joppien, the *Gruppenkommandeur* of I./JG 51, was killed in a shoot-out with a group of bombers escorted by MiG-3s. Six days later Lt. Erich Schmidt of III./JG 53, victor in 47 aerial combats, was shot down by antiaircraft fire. He was seen to bale out of his stricken machine near a Soviet airfield but remained missing ever since.

In early September 1941 the main effort of the German army in the southern sector of the front concentrated around the city of Kiev in Ukraine, where a huge encirclement battle was fought. On 8th September Maj. Friedrich Beckh, the *Kommodore* of JG 51, scored 2,000th victory for his *Geschwader* (of which nearly 1,300 were racked up over Russia). On 13th September, 25 Russian aircraft fell to the guns of JG 3 over Kremenchuk bridgehead (on the bank of Dnieper River). Of this bag, 20 were credited to *II. Gruppe*. The *Geschwaderkommodore* Maj. Günther Lützow himself shot down two DB-3 bombers for his 69th and 70th victories. The Germans' own losses were limited to one Bf 109 F. On 16th September 1941 Russian troops at Kiev were completely surrounded. Ten days later a staggering 440,000 Red Army soldiers marched into German captivity. During that ten-day, final phase of the battle for Kiev the Bf 109 Fs gained the air supremacy over the battlefield. During that period JG 3 claimed 35 victories, JG 51 another 41, whilst III./JG 53 contributed with 14 more. On the last day of September 1941 the Wehrmacht launched operation 'Typhoon', with its objective of seizing Moscow before the impending winter. However, the depleted *Jagdwaffe* was hardly capable of furnishing protective cover over German ground troops, which often suffered from attacks by Russian bombers and ground attack aircraft.

At that time I./JG 52, which hitherto had been stationed in the Netherlands, was hurried to the Eastern Front to help tip the balance in favour of the Germans. On 2nd October Oblt. Karl-Heinz Leesmann, one of the new arrivals, bagged four Russian aircraft. The following day pilots of JG 51 shot down two, but the *Geschwader* lost two of it own. Among them was Ofw. Heinrich Hoffmann (63-victory *Experte*) of 12./JG 51. He most probably fell victim to Star-shiy Leytenant Sergeyev of 233 IAP (Fighter Air Regiment). Hoffman was posthumously awarded the Oak Leaves to his Knight's Cross (he was the first NCO so honoured). On 5th October 1941 pilots of JG 51 took revenge, shooting 20 Russian aircraft for no losses of their own. On 10th October 1941 the top scorers were I./JG 52, with 58 claims against seven losses.

The first five weeks of the German operation 'Typhoon' cost the Red Army devastating losses, which amounted to 650,000 soldiers. During that period JG 51 alone claimed 289 victories against combat losses of 13 Bf 109 Fs. Among the *Geschwader*'s top scorers of that time Ofw. Edmund Wagner (with 22 claims) was in the lead. On 24th October 1941 Maj. Günther Lützow, the *Geschwaderkommodore* of JG 3, scored his 100th victory.

Early November 1941 brought along a sudden deterioration of weather conditions. Persistent downpours turned roads into a sea of churned dirt and the German offensive literally bogged down. Due to urgent needs elsewhere, some Luftwaffe fighter units were transferred to the Mediterranean theatre. From then on the Army Group Centre could only count on Bf 109 Fs of JG 51 as well as I. and II./JG 52 to provide some respite from ever-present Soviet Sturmoviks and bombers. On 4th November JG 51 ac-

Pilots of the Spanish 15.(span)/JG 51 at Orel-West airfield on 13th November 1942. In the background Messerschmitt Bf 109 F-4 'Black 7', with the unit's emblem visible on the engine cowling.

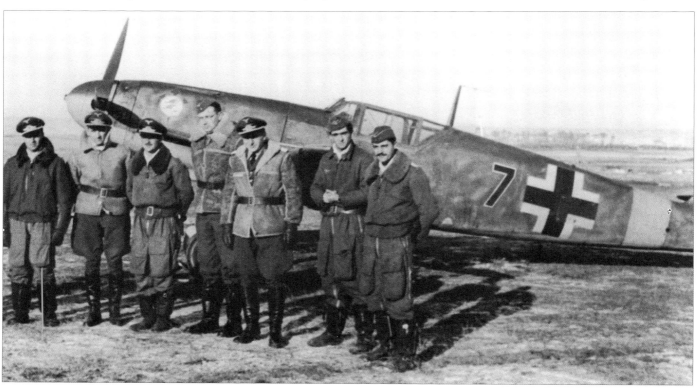

counted for 18 Russian aircraft for the loss of two of its own. On 13th of the same month the *Geschwader* lost one of its aces. During a shoot-out with rear gunners of Pe-2 bombers Ofw. Edmund Wagner of *9. Staffel*, credited with 57 victories, was hit and crashed to his death.

Between 4th and 15th November I./JG 52 added 35 victories to its previous score but lost its *Gruppenkommandeur* Oblt. Karl-Heinz Leesmann (credited with 32 'kills'), who on 6th November 1941 suffered serious combat injuries. On 27th November 1941 temperature in Moscow area dropped to -40°C. When five days later it rose to -15°C, German troops mounted a desperate, last-chance thrust against Moscow. Pilots of II./JG 51, taking advantage of fair, sunny weather, knocked down 18 Russian aircraft. Their *Gruppenkommandeur* Hptm. Hartmann Grasser scored his 40th. However, these turned out to be the last major successes of the Bf 109 F pilots in 1941.

Two days later, on 6th December 1941, the Russians launched their massive counteroffensive. Overwhelmed by numerically superior enemy and worn out by extreme weather, the Wehrmacht began to fall back. After the *Luft-flotte 2* and *II. Fliegerkorps* had relocated to the Mediterranean theatre, the entire central sector of the Eastern Front was to be covered by a woefully inadequate force of 69 serviceable Bf 109 Fs (as of 10th January 1942) divided among Stab, II., III. and IV./JG 51 as well as I. and II./JG

52. Worse still, their pilots were by then often tasked with fighter-bomber missions, which were understandably unpopular due to withering enemy antiaircraft fire. For the first time morale in some German fighter outfits slumped. The *Gruppenkommandeur* of II./JG 52 Hptm. Erich Woitke was relived of his command, whilst 7./ JG 51 was entirely disbanded and its personnel pressed into service as infantry with the Luftwaffe field divisions.

In January III./JG 51, entrusted with unrewarding fighter-bomber missions, failed to score a single air-to-air victory. At the same time II./JG 51, apparently tasked with other assignments, knocked down no fewer than 46 Russian aircraft. Two pilots of *II. Gruppe*, Lt. Hans Strelow and Ofw. Wilhelm Mink, proved particularly successful. On 4th January 1942 they shot down five MiG-3s of 16 IAP between them (Ofw. Mink three, and Lt. Strelow two). Ten days later Mink downed a Pe-2 bomber, whilst Strelow notched up two R-Z biplanes (for his 30th and 31st victories). On 24th January 1942 Ofw. Mink again bagged a Pe-2, and on 27th a R-Z biplane. On the same day Strelow claimed an 'I-26' fighter (most probably a Yak-1), but the *Gruppe* temporarily lost it *Kommandeur*. After downing his 45th opponent Oblt. Hartmann Grasser was himself shot down. He baled out behind enemy lines but was able to make his way back to German lines. He returned to his unit only after a lengthy stay in hospital.

During its tenure on the Eastern Front, from July to December 1942, the second contingent of the Spanish squadron scored 16 victories.

Messerschmitt Bf 109 F-4 of the Spanish squadron 15.(span.)/JG 51 on the Eastern Front.

some engines reached 50 hrs.

In February 1942 the long overdue deliveries of spare parts and aircraft finally improved somewhat the plight Bf 109 F outfits in Russia. This was when the star of Lt. Hans Strelow of 5./JG 51 shone at its brightest. Four 'kills' claimed by him on 4th February brought his total to 36. By 28th February he ran his personal tally up to 40. When it reached 52, on 18th March 1942 he was awarded the Knight's Cross. Only a week later, after his score had risen to 66, on 24th March 1942 he was presented with the Oak Leaves to his Knight's Cross.

Meanwhile the situation of JG 54, which operated from their perennial and well-equipped bases around Leningrad, was much better. Spacious, partially heated hangars (courtesy of the Russian Air Force!) offered German ground crews relatively comfortable conditions. Despite many attempts, only once did the Russians manage to catch JG 54 off-guard and successfully bomb the airfield at Sivierskaya. It occurred on 2nd January 1942 when five Pe-2s escorted by eight I-16s destroyed ten German aircraft on the ground. In the ensuing and immediate counterattack III./JG 54 shot down six Russian aircraft, including five by Ofw. Karl-Heinz Kempf of *7. Staffel.*

Throughout the first winter on the Leningrad front the most successful pilot was Oblt. Max-Hellmuth Ostermann of 3./JG 54, who by the end of 1941 racked up 46 victories. On the New Year's Day he downed a Yak-1, followed by two more on 8th January, and another the next day. By 28th January 1942 his score stood at 60. Overall, in the first month of 1942 'Grünherz' pilots claimed a total of 99 enemy aircraft against the combat loss of eight Bf 109 Fs.

Late January 1942 saw the return, after a leave in Germany, of Hptm. Hans Philipp of *4. Staffel,* the then ranking ace of JG 54 with 72 victories. On 2nd February he claimed his 73rd 'kill', a MiG-3 flown by Starshiy Leytenant Ivan Chulkov of 41 IAP, a Rusian ace credited with nine individual victories and two shared. On 14th February 1942, south of Lake Ladoga, Hptm. Franz Eckerle, the *Gruppenkommandeur* of I./JG 54, and his wingman Uffz. Proske, tackled

'Fips'

with four I-16 and four I-15bis fighters of 71 IAP. In the ensuing dogfight Eckerle shot down one I-15bis, flown by Serzhant Aleksey Baranowsky, for his 59th individual victory. Coincidentally, it was also JG 54's 1700th. However, moments later Eckerle's Messerschmitt Bf 109 F-2, WNr. 9728, *Stammkennzeichen* CH+OP, was boxed in by three Russian fighters and raked with gunfire. The German pilot bailed out. He was promptly captured and shot dead by Russian soldiers. He was succeeded at the head of I./JG 54 by Hptm. Hans Philipp.

In the latter half of February 1942 heavy fighting in the air broke out in the areas of Demiansk and Cholm. There, between 18th February and 18th March 1942, pilots of III./JG 3 claimed 81 victories for the loss of only three own machines. I./JG 51 contributed with another 20, against no loss of their won.

Concurrently, in the southern sector I. and II./JG 77 excelled. By far the highest scorers were Hptm. Herbert Ihlefeld, the *Gruppenkommandeur* of I./JG 77, and his wingman Oblt. Friedrich Geißhardt. On 22nd 1942 Ihlefeld claimed his 100th 'kill', whilst Geißhardt his 60th.

In April 1942, as soon as III./JG 52 relocated to the Crimea, the *Gruppe* began to wreak havoc among local VVS units. On 30th April Lt. Hermann Graf shot down six, Fw. Alfred Grislawski two more, and remaining pilots another 12. The following day the *Gruppe* tallied 13 enemy aircraft destroyed, and on 2nd May as many as 25.

Messerschmitt Bf 109 Fs also saw extensive service in the Far North, in Murmansk area. Initially they were issued to II./JG 5, and beginning with May 1942, also to III./JG 5. In May 1942 the two *Gruppen* combined victory tally was 149 Russian aircraft destroyed in the air for the loss of 11 own pilots. On 12th June II./JG 5 recorded its 500th victory, fittingly scored by the *Gruppe*'s ranking ace Fw. Rudolf Müller. At that time II./JG 5 was commanded by Hptm. Horst Carganico, credited with 50 'kills'.

Along with the start of German operation 'Blau', which was launched on 28th June 1942, the main air battle shifted in the area of Voronezh. There the Russians despatched its newly formed 1st Fighter Army (*Istribitelnaya Armiya* – 1 IA), which was tasked with winning local air superiority and hence allow Soviet ground-attack aircraft and bombers to interdict German spearheads heading east. The first clash occurred on 5th July 1942 and the 1 IA came out of it badly battered – the Germans claimed 48 Russian aircraft for the loss of only two of its own. On that day the following three pilots – the *Staffelkapitän* of 9./JG 3 Oblt. Victor Bauer, Oblt. Erwin Clausen of II./JG 77 and the *Gruppenkommandeur* of I./JG 3 Hptm. Georg Michalek – each added four victories to their individual scores. Overall, between 29th June and 9th July 1942 *Luftflotte 4* recorded claims of 540 Russian aircraft destroyed in the air. Only in July 1942 the *II. Gruppe* of JG 77, which secured the southern flank of the front, amassed a staggering 332 victories. The top scorers were Hptm. Heinrich Setz (with 50), Oblt. Anton Hackl (37), Fw. Ernst-Wilhelm Reinert (26) and Lt. Lutz-Wilhelm Burkhardt (24). The German air supremacy over the area between the Don and Donets rivers was complete.

In July 1942 the Luftwaffe fighter units in the Eastern Front began to convert onto the then latest Bf 109 G-2 model and their trusty Bf 109 Fs gradually phased out. Throughout its operational service in Russia the Bf 109 F held the advantage over any and all types of fighters in the VVS inventory. Theoretically, the performance of Yak-1 and LaGG-3 fighters was not vastly inferior to that of the Bf 109 F. Nevertheless, poor Russian craftsmanship resulted in multiple, drag-increasing protrusions and fissures in airframes, as well as numerous in-service failures of hastily and crudely assembled aircraft. Moreover, frequent cases of canopies getting oiled over or jammed shut made Soviet pilots fly with open cockpits, which further decreased their aircraft's speed. Russian fighters were prone to catch fire, their fireproof bulkheads were ineffective and, due to flying with open cockpits, fires quickly spread out.

Another reason for superiority of the German fighter arm in Russia was its carefully honed and well-rehearsed tactics of aerial combat. Whereas Russians usually attacked en masse and went for escorting fighters, Germans always attempted to lure escorts away before pouncing on defenceless bombers or Sturmoviks. German pilots always tried to knock down leaders of Russian formations, which invariably led to utter confusion among the remaining aircraft. The Messerschmitts nearly always carried out their slashing attacks with the advantage of surprise, bouncing from high above and out of the sun. Then they used the speed built up in the dive to zoom up and out of reach of the Russian fighters, without giving the latter an opportunity to engage in a turning fight.

Besides, the Germans always aimed at maintaining the basic *Rotte* formation of two aircraft for mutual protection. Meanwhile, lack of discipline in the air among Russian fighter pilots, of whom each seemed to fight its own battle, often cost them losses disproportionate to successes. With the advantage of speed in climb, dive and level flight, Bf 109 F pilots could engage (or prudently disangage, if the odds appeared too heavy) their opponents at will. All these factors, combined with vast combat experience of most Luftwaffe pilots serving on the Eastern Front between June 1941 and June 1942, made the Bf 109 F such a potent weapon.

Messerschmitt Bf 109 F-4 of the Italian 150. *Grupo Autonomo CT* **.**

Messerschmitt Bf 109 F-4 designated EB-1 undergoing tests at the USA in the Wright Field base.

X

Messerschmitt Bf 109 F-4 trop captured by the British in North Africa bearing the RAF markings and number HK849.

Foreign users

Spain

On 21st June 1942, 2. *Escuadrilla Azul* (Blue Squadron) equipped with 13 Bf 109 F-2 aircraft, commanded by Maj. Julio Salvador Diaz-Benjumea, arrived at the Orel airfield at the Eastern Front. The squadron was attached to JG 51 with designation 15.(span.)/JG 51. After over five months spent in Russia the unit was withdrawn to Spain where it was officially dissolved on 23rd December 1942. Its pilots flew 1312 combat missions over the Eastern Front. They took part in 117 engagements claiming 16 enemy aircraft shot down. Two pilots were killed and two wounded. The unit's best pilot was Hptm. Manuel Bengoechea Menchaca who shot down three enemy aircraft.

On 1st December 1942, the third tour of Spanish airmen, Tercea Escuadrilla Expedicion-ara commanded by Maj. Carlos Ferrandiz-Arjonilla, arrived at the Orel airfield. The unit was also designated 15.(span.)/JG 51. In April 1943, the squadron was rearmed with Focke-Wulf Fw 190 A-3/A-4 aircraft. The third tour of Spanish pilots flew a total of 1716 combat missions. They took part in 112 engagements claiming 62 enemy aircraft shot down (including 33 on Messerschmitt Bf 109s). The unit lost two pilots killed.

In spring of 1943 Spain purchased 15 Messerschmitt Bf 109 aircraft from Germany. The planes were to be used mainly for training pilots who were later sent to the Eastern Front as part of 15.(span.)/JG 51. Germany delivered 14

Bf 109 Fs in the F-2 and F-4 variants. They were the following aircraft:

1. Bf 109 F-2, W.Nr. 7237
2. Bf 109 F-2, W.Nr. 7341
3. Bf 109 F-2, W.Nr. 7486
4. Bf 109 F-2, W.Nr. 7539
5. Bf 109 F-2, W.Nr. 8172
6. Bf 109 F-2, W.Nr. 8205
7. Bf 109 F-2, W.Nr. 8328
8. Bf 109 F-2, W.Nr. 12638
9. Bf 109 F-2, W.Nr. 12906
10. Bf 109 F-4, W.Nr. 10062
11. Bf 109 F-4, W.Nr. 13106
12. Bf 109 F-4, W.Nr. 13110
13. Bf 109 F-4, W.Nr. 13210
14. Bf 109 F-4, W.Nr. 13329

The machines reached Spain in May 1943 and began their service in the *Escuela de Caza*. At the end of 1943 they were transferred to *23. Regimento de Caza*. The planes were given designations from 6●132 to 6●145 which were later changed to C.4F-132 to C.4F-145 and dubbed "*Zacuto*" (knapsack). The last Bf 109 F was decommissioned in 1951.

Italy

In spring of 1943 the Italian air force received 12 Messerschmitt Bf 109 F-4 aircraft which were to be used for pilot training since delivery of new Messerschmitt Bf 109 Gs was expected. The Messerschmitt Bf 109 F-4s were sent to *150. Grupo Autonomo CT*. They flew their first missions on 17th April 1943. Over six Bf 109 F-4 aircraft were destroyed during training.

Messerschmitt Bf 109 F painted in the Soviet air force colours.

Messerschmitt Bf 109 F-4 in tri-colour, experimental camouflage and national markings of the Hungarian Air Force.

Hungary

The first Messerschmitt Bf 109 F-4 fighters were delivered by the Luftwaffe to the Hungarian air force in November 1942. Twelve planes from III./JG 52 were sent to 1./1 Fighter Squadron. The aircraft flew fighter-bomber missions. In March 1943 the unit received further 8 Bf 109 F-4s. On 31st May 1943 Hungary received another batch of 19 Bf 109 F-4 fighters.

Switzerland

On 25th July 1942 two Messerschmitt Bf 109 F-4/R1 aircraft, flying from Paris to Friedrichshafen, landed by mistake in the area of Bern on the Swiss territory. They were W.Nr. 7197, NW+KU and W.Nr. 7605, PC+JY equipped with the ETC type launchers mounted under the fuselage. Both fighters received designations J-715 and J-716 respectively and became part of the Swiss air force where they served until 1948.

Japan

In January 1943 Japan received two Messerschmitt Bf 109 F-4 fighters.

Slovakia

The Slovak squadron designated 13.(slov.)/JG 52, fighting as part of JG 52, received the first Messerschmitt Bf 109 F-4 aircraft on December 18, 1942. The fighters were flown by the Slovak pilots until the end of February 1943. The unit scored 16 aerial victories and lost four aircraft.

Soviet Union

In October 1941, one Messerschmitt Bf 109 F-2 of JG 51 was captured by the Russians after an emergency landing in the central sector of the Eastern Front. After repairs made by mechanics of 47th Fighter Regiment stationed in Tushino the aircraft was tested by specialists of the Air Force Experimental Institute. In spring of 1942 the Russian air force captured another three Bf 109 F fighters. In the area of Stalingrad, in the winter of 1942, at least two more Bf 109 F-4s of JG 3 fell into the hands of the Russians.

Sweden

On 9th October 1943 two Messerschmitt Bf 109 Fs emergency landed in the area of Sövde in Sweden as a result of navigation mistake. One of them was Messerschmitt Bf 109 F-1, W.Nr. 6741, coded DJ+JW, piloted Lt. Karl Materleitner from the *Schießschule* (aerial gunnery school) in Værløse, Denmark. The pilot returned to Germany after two weeks. The aircraft was used for flight tests. It was scrapped in 1945. The other machine was coded DR+ZM.

Great Britain

The first Messerschmitt Bf 109 F-2 was captured by the British on July 10, 1941 after emergency landing in Kent County. The aircraft was W.Nr. 12764 flown at that time by the commanding officer of I./JG 26, Hptm. Rolf Pingel. After overhaul, the plane was tested in flight. On 20th October 1941 it crashed near Fowlmere. In spring of 1942, Messerschmitt Bf 109 F-4, W.Nr. 7232 of 10.(Jabo)/JG 26, piloted by Uffz. Oswald Fischer emergency landed near Beachy Head in England. In the course of the war in Europe and Africa, the British captured a few more Bf 109 Fs that were used by 112 and 250 RAF squadrons as liaison aircraft.

Republic of South Africa

One of the aircraft captured in North Africa, Messerschmitt Bf 109 F-4 trop, 'White 6' of II./JG 27, was sent to the RSA and is now on display in the National Museum of Military History in Johannesburg.

United States of America

The first two Messerschmitt Bf 109 F-4 aircraft were sent to the USA from the Soviet Union. They were machines from 9./JG 3 that had landed on one of the Russian airfields. After be-

ing fitted with American instruments and radios, one of the aircraft was designated EB-1 and the other one EB-100. The latter was tested at the Wright Field base and later, on 21st March 1944, transferred to the Elgin base on Florida.

Messerschmitt Bf 109 F camouflage and markings

Standard Messerschmitt Bf 109 F camouflage was described in *Oberflächenschutzliste 8 Os 109 F and G*. Upper surfaces were covered with irregular, sharp splinter RLM 74 *Graugrün* and RLM 75 *Grauviolett* blotches. Colour division lines were usually soft. Lower surfaces and sides were painted RLM 76 *Lichtblau*. Additionally, there were small, irregular RLM 74 *Graugrün*, RLM 02 *Grau* and RLM 70 *Schwarzgrün* spots and blotches painted on the sides. Propeller blades were painted RLM 22 *Schwarz*, wheel wells and cockpit interior were RLM 02 *Grau*. The instrument panel was painted RLM 66 *Schwarzgrau*.

The spinner was usually painted entirely with RLM 70 *Schwarzgrün*, but is some cases one third of its surface was painted RLM 21 *Weiß*. The front section of the spinner was often painted RLM 76 *Lichtblau* or RLM 21 *Weiß*.

Standard Luftwaffe markings were applied to Messerschmitt 109 F aircraft. These were 900 mm high, B2 type *Balken* crosses on the sides of the fuselage and on lower surfaces and 1000 mm high, B1 type *Balken* crosses on the upper wing surfaces and 300 mm side, H2 type swastika of the tail fin.

Immediately after leaving the production line, the aircraft were given a *Werknummer* (series number), stencilled in black at the base of the vertical stabilizer. Additionally, the aircraft had a four letter factory radio code known as *Stammkennzeichen*, painted on the sides of the fuselage (two letter on each side of the cross, e.g. DP+VB)

Messerschmitt Bf 109 F-4/Z trop coded 'White 1' of 1./JG 27. The aircraft sports 'desert tan' of RLM 79 *Sandgelb* on the upper surfaces and RLM 78 *Hellblau* on the lower surfaces and fuselage sides. Lower cowling yellow, fuselage band, propeller's spinner and front part of the engine cowl, as well as wingtips, are white.

The painter was obviously creative while camouflaging Messerschmitt Bf 109 F-4, W.Nr. 13169, 'Black 4' of 8./JG 5. The dark uppersurfaces of the plane were supplemented with an attractive white squiggle pattern.

This Messerschmitt Bf 109 F-4 of Stab III./JG 3 is a good example of additional camouflaging performed at the unit level.

An old Messerschmitt Bf 109 F-4, W.Nr. 7510, coded 'Black 11', still in service at Crete in early 1943. At the time the aircraft probably served with 8./JG 27. Note the worn appearance of the plane, unusual fuselage cross, as well as the starboard wing which may possibly come from another aircraft as it sports a national marking of different type than the one on the port wing and seems to be camouflaged in greys in contrast to the rest of the planes' uppersurfaces painted in RLM 79 *Sandgelb*.

and on the lower wing surfaces (one letter on each side of the cross, e.g. D+P V+B). *Stammkenzeichen* was usually painted with RLM 22 *Schwarz*.

Aircrafts used in Northern Africa were painted RLM 79 *Sandgelb* on the upper surfaces and partially on the sides. The under surfaces and lower part of the fuselage was painted with RLM 78 *Hellblau* (in some documents also named *Himmelblau*).

In the winter months, especially on the Eastern Front, standard camouflage on the aircraft's upper surfaces and sides was covered by easily removable white paint or lime.

Many units, operating on various fronts, replaced standard camouflage with their own schemes. In JG 54, operating on the northern sector of the Eastern Front, sides of the fuselage were covered with RLM 70 *Schwarzgrün* wavy lines which formed an irregular web. Spaces between the lines were filled with RLM 02 *Grau* or RLM 75 *Grauviolett* blotches. In such cases the back of the fuselage was usually painted with RLM 70 *Schwarzgrün*. Sometimes, the upper wing and elevator surfaces were painted with irregular RLM 70 *Schwarzgrün* patches.

Another field JG 54 scheme variation was applying irregular RLM 70 *Schwarzgrün* and earth-brown patches of unknown paint mixture to upper surfaces and sides of the fuselage. Lower surfaces were then painted with RLM 76 *Lichtblau*.

Numerous Bf 109 F-4/Z Trop with standard African camouflage were delivered to JG 5, stationed in the Far North. There, RLM 79 *Sandgelb* was supplemented with additional large RLM 70 *Schwarzgrün* and RLM 75 *Grauviolett* blotches.

It was a common practice at JG 77 to paint the upper and side aircraft surfaces with uniform RLM 70 *Schwarzgrün*, occasionally with irregular patches, smudges or blotches. Similar practice was employed by JG 51, but there usually the upper and side surfaces were painted RLM 70 *Schwarzgrün* and RLM 71 *Dunkelgrün*. The same system was also used by JG 52.

Camouflage was supplemented by quick aerial identification markings painted in white (in the Mediterranean) or yellow (the Eastern Front). These comprised a band around the rear section of the fuselage, round the cross or behind it and lower or both sides of the wing tips.

The engine cowling or its lower part were also often painted in the quick identification colour.

Individual aircraft markings were painted on the sides of the fuselage. Function symbol of the unit's staff or single/double digit tactical number painted in the units colour was located in front of the cross. Behind it was the unit's tactical marking. The units' emblems were painted on the nose section of the fuselage or under the cockpit. Sometimes, also the wing's, squadron's and even flight's emblems were painted. Often, all these markings were supplemented by pilot's personal markings. It was a standard practice to paint vertical bars symbolizing aerial victories on the rudder or the entire vertical stabilizer.

Bibliography

Bob Hans-Ekkehard: *Verratener Idealismus. Errinerungen eines Jagdfliegers*, Freiburg 2003

Caldwell Donald L.: *JG 26, Top Guns oft he Luftwaffe*, New York 1993

Chazanow Dmitrij: *Nad Stalingradem*, Warszawa 1995

Fernandez J., Ledet M., Kulikov V.: *Operation Barbarossa (1 partie), 22 juin 1941: l'URSS pour cible. Batailles Aeriennes n 12*, Outreau 2000

Fernandez-Sommerau M., Van Mol J.P., Mombeek E.: *Messerschmitt Bf 109 Recognition Manual, A Guide to Variants, Weapons and Equipment*, Hersham 2004

Forell Fritz von, Maj.: *Mölders und seine Männer*, Berlin 1941

Foreman John: *Air War 1941: The Turning Point, Part 1 – From the Battle of Britain to the Blitz*, London 1993

Fözö Josef: *Freie Jagd von Madrid bis Moskau, Ein Fliegerleben mit Mölders*, Berlin 1943

Galland Adolf: *Die Ersten und die Letzten*, München 1984

Green William: *The Augsburg Eagle, A Documentary History, Messerschmitt Bf 109*, London 1980

Hitchcock Thomas H.: *Bf 109 F, Monogram Close-Up 9*, Sturbridge 1990

Ishoven Armand van: *Messerschmitt Bf 109 at War*, London 1977

Król Wacław: *Wielka Brytania 1940*, Warszawa 1990

Michulec Robert: *Messerschmitt Me 109, cz. 2*, Gdańsk 1998

Mombeek Eric, Bergström Christer, Pegg Martin: *Jagdwaffe, Barbarossa, the Invasion of Russia, June-December 1941, Luftwaffe Colours, Volume Three Section 2*, Hersham 2003,

Mombeek Eric, Waldman David, Pegg Martin: *Jagdwaffe, Battle of Britain, Phase Four November 1940 – June 1941, Luftwaffe Colours, Volume Two Section 4*, Hersham 2003,

Murawski Marek J.: *JG 27 w akcji, vol. III*, Lublin 2002,

Nowarra Heinz J.: *Die 109, Gesamtentwicklung eines legendären Flugzeugs*, Stuttgart 1979

Nowarra Heinz J.: *Luftkrieg über Großbritanien, die letzte Phase der „Schlacht um England"*, Rastatt 1978

Paterson Michael: *Podniebne bitwy*, Warszawa 2006

Prien Jochen, Rodeike Peter: *Messerschmitt Bf 109 F, G, & K Series, An Illustrated Study*, Atglen 1995

Prien Jochen: *Pik-As, Geschichte des Jagdgeschwaders 53, Teil 1*, Illertissen b.r.w.

Prien Jochen, Stemmer Gerhard, Rodeike Peter, Bock Winfried: *Die Jagdfliegerverbände der Deutschen Luftwaffe 1934 bis 1945, Teil 6/I, 6/II, 7, 8/I, 8/II, 9/I, 9/II & 9/III*, Eutin b.r.w.

Prien Jochen, Stemmer Gerhard: *Messerschmitt Bf 109 im Einsatz bei der Stab und I./Jagdgeschwader 3*, Eutin b.r.w.

Priller Josef: *JG 26, Geschichte eines Jagdgeschwaders*, Stuttgart 1980

Ring Hans, Shores Christopher: *Luftkampf zwischen Sand und Sonne*, Stuttgart 1972

Ritger Lynn: *The Messerschmitt Bf 109 Part 2: 'F' to 'K' Variants*, Bedford 2007

Scutts Jerry: *Bf 109 Aces of North Africa and the Mediterranean*, Oxford 2003

Šnajdr Miroslav: *Operace „Barbarossa", Letecká válka 22. června 1941*, Praha 2003

Toliver Raymond F., Constable Trevor J.: *Das waren die deutschen Jagdflieger-Asse 1939-1945*, Stuttgart 1975

Weal John: *Bf 109 F/G/K Aces of the Western Front*, Oxford 1999

Endnotes

[1] Maj. Günther von Maltzahn, the CO of JG 53 (author's note).

[2] This action, described by the adjutant of Stab/JG 53, Oblt. Wilfried Pufahl, took place on 16th April 1941. At 18:40 hrs Maj. Günther von Maltzahn shot down a Spitfire for his 14th victory. Story taken from: Nowarra Heinz J.: *Luftkrieg über Großbritanien, die letzte Phase der „Schlacht um England"*, Rastatt 1978, pp. 21-22

[3] 1,350 hp, as compared to 1,100 hp of the DB 601A.

[4] The commonly held belief that the prototypes designated V21 through V24 were the aircraft serial-numbered W.Nr. 5601 through 5604 is neither supported by the LC2-IA report of the RLM Technical Department (Aufstellung des Technischen Amtes des RLM), dated to 1st March 1941, nor by the following reports.

[5] At that time Hitler was convinced that he would easily conquer France (which he did), and then sign a peace treaty with Great Britain to end the war in Western Europe. Hence, he deemed it unnecessary to devote resources to developing new types of armament.

[6] Some sources claim that only 11 or 19, not 25 aircraft of the F-0 variant were actually manufactured.

[7] Steig- und Kampfleistung – the Luftwaffe's term describing the maximum power output.

[8] Some sources mention 49 Erla produced F-1s.

[9] For more details see: Michulec Robert: *Messerschmitt Me 109, vol. 2*, Gdańsk 1998, p. 17.

[10] Ishoven Armand van: *Messerschmitt Bf 109 at War*, Surrey 1977, p. 107.

[11] Robert Michulec mentions 1380 aircraft.

[12] According to a loss report mentioned in Prien Jochen, Rodeike Peter: *Messerschmitt Bf 109 F, G & K, An Illustrated Study*, Atglen 1995, p.23, 9./JG 51 listed a Bf 109 F-3 W.Nr. 4796 as damaged on 24th June 1941, while Stab/JG 51 lost a Bf 109 F-3 W.Nr. 4791 on 28th June 1941.

[13] Perhaps there were several more. An analysis of the lost aircraft lists suggests that at least three more F-5s were in active service. These were: Bf 109 F-5, W.Nr. 8754, coded 'F6+YH' of 1.(F)/122, lost on 30th May 1942; Bf 109 F-5, W.Nr. 15556 of 1./JGr. 50 lost at Lachen-Speyerdorf on 7th September 1943 (its pilot, Uffz. Mielsen, was injured) and Bf 109 F-5, W.Nr. 8142 of Flugzeugüberführungsgeschwader 1, lost in 1943 with Ofw. Heinz Pelter at the controls. However, in the author's opinion, these are merely cases of erroneously recorded data.

[14] OKL - Airforce High Command of the Third Reich.

[15] Code name for the ground control station (author's note).

[16] Król Wacław: *Wielka Brytania 1940*, Warszawa 1990, pp. 244-245. F/Lt Franciszek Jastrzębski managed to belly-in at the French coast, but in so doing suffered serious injuries and died later in hospital.

[17] Forell Fritz von, Maj.: *Mölders und seine Männer*, Berlin 1941, pp. 125-126.

[18] Mombeek Eric, Waldman David & Pegg Martin: *Jagdwaffe, Battle of Britain, Phase Four November 1940 – June 1941, Luftwaffe Colours*, Volume Two, Section 4, Hersham 2003, p. 353.

[19] Here we go again! (author's note).

[20] Foreman John: *Air War 1941: The Turning Point, Part 1 – From the Battle of Britain to the Blitz*, London 1993, p. 176.

21 Bach (Ger.) – in the Luftwaffe's vernacular the Straits of Dover, sometimes the English Channel itself (author's note).

22 An Englishman in the Luftwaffe's jargon (author's note).

23 Schwarze Männer (Ger.), slang name for the Luftwaffe's ground crews, in reference to their characteristic black-coloured overalls (author's note).

24 Prien Jochen: *PIK-AS, Geschichte des Jagdgeschwaders 53*, Teil 1, Illertissen, pp. 291-296.

25 Foreman John, op. cit. p. 297.

26 Jagdflieger Führer (author's note).

27 Galland Adolf: *Die Ersten und die Letzten*, München 1984, pp. 96-97.

28 Prien Jochen…, op. cit., p. 311.

29 Prien Jochen, Stemmer Gerhard: *Messerschmitt Bf 109 im Einsatz bei Stab und I./Jagdgeschwader 3 1938-1945*, Eutin, p. 147.

30 Ibidem, op. cit. p. 146.

31 Paterson Michael: *Podniebne bitwy*, Warszawa 2006, p. 61.

32 Weal John: *Bf 109F/G/K Aces of the Western Front*, Oxford 1999, p. 16.

33 Caldwell Donald L.: *JG 26, Top Guns of the Luftwaffe*, New York 1993, p. 92.

34 Priller Josef: JG 26, *Geschichte eines Jagdgeschwaders*, Stuttgart 1980, pp. 113-114. According to Fw. Jäckel's report, he used 96 rounds from his MG 151 cannon and 679 rounds from the twin MG 17 machine guns to down the Stirling.

35 Lt. Peter Göring was Reichsmarschal Hermann Göring's nephew (author's note).

36 Heavy bombers in the Luftwaffe's vernacular (author's note).

37 Galland, p. 121.

38 Toliver Raymond F., Constable Trevor J.: *Das waren die deutschen Jagdflieger-Asse 1939-1945*, Stuttgart 1975, p. 52.

39 Weal…, op. cit. str. 28

40 Ibidem, str. 28-29

41 Scutts Jerry: *Bf 109 Aces of North Africa and the Mediterranean*, Oxford 2003, p. 16.

42 An Australian ace Clive "Killer" Caldwell, when asked by an interviewer about the origins of his famous nickname, replied: *"Perhaps because I was convinced that it was the right thing to shoot them in their 'chutes and strafe them on the ground. This was war. Our job was to win and in order to do that we had to inflict as much damage upon our enemy as possible. Hence, I considered it necessary to kill them in their parachutes, not because I was bloodthirsty or anything like that. I just didn't want them to get back to their units and come up another day to fight us."*

43 Prien Jochen: *Pik-As, Geschichte des Jagdgeschwaders 53*, Teil 1, Illertissen, p. 500.

44 Murawski Marek J.: *JG 27 w akcji*, vol. III, Lublin 2002, pp. 55-56.

45 Ring Hans, Shores Christopher: *Luftkampf zwischen Sand und Sonne*, Stuttgart 1972, p. 429.

46 *Ibidem, op. cit.*, p. 432.

47 Fernandez J., Ledet M., Kulikov V.: *Operation Barbarossa* (1 partie), 22 juin 1941: l'URSS pour cible. Batailles Aeriennes n 12, Outreau 2000.

48 Šnajdr Miroslav: Operace „Barbarossa", Letecká válka 22. června 1941, Praha 2003, p. 104.

49 *Ibidem*, p. 100.

50 Ishoven Armand van: *Messerschmitt Bf 109 at War*, London 1977, p. 62.

51 Prien Jochen, Stemmer Gerhard, *Messerschmitt Bf 109 im Einsatz bei der Stab und I./Jagdgeschwader 3*, Eutin, pp. 153-155.

52 Oblt. Hans Kolbow, the commander of 5./JG 51, began his combat career in the Condor Legion. During the campaign in the West he tallied 13 victories. After scoring his 27th, he was shot down and killed by Soviet anti-aircraft artillery on 16th July 1941 (author's note).

53 German pilots' 'war cry', which was a signal to commence the attack (author's note).

54 Josef Fözö had an opportunity to tackle with I-16 Ratas during the Spanish Civil War, where he was credited with three 'kills' (author's note).

55 In fact pilots of II./JG 51 were credited with 15 SB-2 bombers during this action (author's note).

56 Diminutive of Josef (author's note).

57 Fözö Josef: *Freie Jagd von Madrid bis Moskau, Ein Fliegerleben mit Mölders*, Berlin 1943, pp. 252-257.

58 Mombeek Eric, Bergström Christer, Pegg Martin: *Jagdwaffe, Barbarossa, the Invasion of Russia, June-December 1941*, Luftwaffe Colours, Volume Three Section 2, Hersham 2003, p. 102.

59 Prien Jochen: *Chronik des Jagdgeschwaders 53…, op. cit.*, p. 339.

60 Oddly, German pilots used the name "Curtiss" to identify the I-15, I-152 and I-153 (author's note).

61 Prien Jochen: *Chronik des Jagdgeschwaders 53…, op. cit.*, p. 339.

62 Due to an engine malfunction Lt. Schiess did not participate in the first mission of Stab/JG 53 that day (author's note).

63 Prien Jochen: *Chronik des Jagdgeschwaders 53…, op. cit.*, p. 340.

64 *Ibidem, op. cit.*, p. 343.

65 *Ibidem*.

66 First Air Corps (author's note).

67 Presently Puszcza Romincka, a large woodland at the Polish-Russian border (translator's note).

68 Presently Šiauliai in Lithuania (translator's note).

69 Memoirs by *Kommodore* of JG 54 Hannes Trautloft, dated to 22nd June 1941, in the author's possession, courtesy of the Knight's Cross holder Hans-Ekkehard Bob.

70 Presently Nesterov in Kaliningrad Oblast, Russia (translator's note).

Bf 109 F-1 bis F-4, Flugzeughandbuch

The following appendix presents excerpts from the original Bf 109 F-1/F-4 manual, first published in May 1941 by Messerschmitt A.G. in Augsburg. The included photographs and drawings offer a comprehensive and detailed overview of the Messerschmitt's design.

No.   Yes,

Luftfahrt-Archiv Hafner • German Aviation Technology 1930 to 1945

Reproductions of aircraft, powerplant and armament manuals, propeller documentations, assembly, maintenance and service instructions, equipment lists, spare parts' catalogues - offered as books and on CDs.

Luftfahrt-Archiv Hafner

Udo Hafner, Salonallee 5, D-71638 Ludwigsburg; tel. +49 (0) 7141-90 16 03, fax +49 (0) 7141-92 66 58

info@luftfahrt-archiv-hafner.de • www.luftfahrt-archiv-hafner.de

Luftfahrt-Archiv Hafner • Deutsche Luftfahrttechnik 1930–1945.

Reproduktionen von Flugzeug-, Motoren- u. Waffen-Handbüchern, Betriebs- Anleitungen, Ersatzteillisten, Bedienungsvorschriften, Luftschrauben-Anlagen, Montage- und Reparaturanleitungen, Ausrüstungsgerätelisten, Fl-Nummern-Listen in Buchform und als CD-ROM.

Luftfahrt-Archiv Hafner

Udo Hafner, Salonallee 5, D-71638 Ludwigsburg;Tel. +49 (0) 7141-90 16 03, Fax +49 (0) 7141-92 66 58

info@luftfahrt-archiv-hafner.de • www.luftfahrt-archiv-hafner.de

5. Schutzanstrich

Der Schutzanstrich erfolgt gemäß L. Dv. 521/1.

6. Beförderungsmöglichkeit

Das Flugzeug kann bei Beförderung mittels Eisenbahn auf einem Glt-Dresden-Wagen oder auf einem R-Stuttgart-Wagen verladen werden.

B. Flugwerk

1. Rumpf

a) Statischer Aufbau

Der aus plattiertem Dural bestehende Rumpf ist in Schalenbauweise ausgeführt. Die Rumpfschale besteht aus zwei Halbschalen, die aus Halbschüssen (1 a) zusammengesetzt sind. Zur Versteifung dienen die mit der Rumpfschale vernieteten Längsprofile (1 b, 2 a).

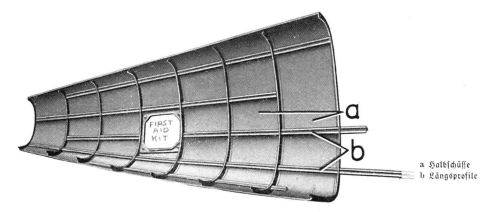

a Halbschüsse
b Längsprofile

Abb. 1: Rumpfhalbschale
Fuselage: port rear

Durch Stoßprofile (2 b) und Spantlaschen (2 c) sind die Halbschalen miteinander verbunden.

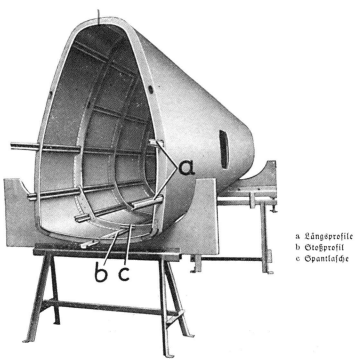

a Längsprofile
b Stoßprofil
c Spantlasche

Abb. 2: Blick in den hinteren Teil der Rumpfschale
hind part of rear fuselage

In Betriebsstellung ist der Radsporn durch einen Sperrbolzen verriegelt, der in eine oben im Rumpfende angeordnete Rastplatte greift. Beim Ausschwenken des Radsporns wird der mit der Kolbenstange des Arbeitszylinders verbundene Sperrbolzen durch die Kolbenstange aus der Sperrplatte gezogen.

Eine Anzeige der Spornstellung sowie Notauslösung für den Sporn sind nicht vorhanden.

Bei Versagen der Drucköleinlage ist eine Landung auf dem auch in eingeschwenktem Zustand noch etwas aus der Rumpfunterseite herausragenden Spornrad möglich.

3. Leitwerk

a) Höhenleitwerk

Das freitragende Höhenleitwerk besteht aus der Höhenflosse (10 b) und dem geteilten Höhenruder (10 c). Um Lastigkeitsmomente um die Querachse ausgleichen zu können, kann die Höhenflosse vom Führerraum aus verstellt werden.

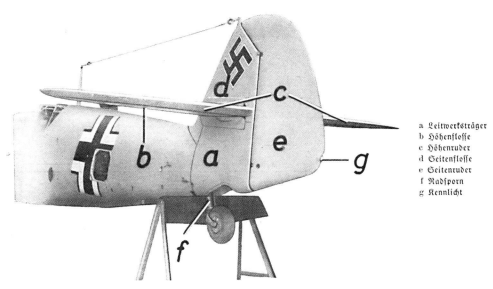

a Leitwerksträger
b Höhenflosse
c Höhenruder
d Seitenflosse
e Seitenruder
f Radsporn
g Kennlicht

Abb. 10: Leitwerksträger mit Leitwerk

Höhenflosse

Die Höhenflosse besteht aus plattiertem Duralblech und ist in Schalenbauweise ausgeführt. Jede Halbschale (Abb. 11) besteht aus der Beplankung und dem Z-förmigen Dural-Holm (11 a). Die Halbschalen sind durch Nasen- (11 b) und Endrippen (11 c) verstärkt, die mit dem Holm und der Beplankung vernietet sind. Die Nasenleiste (11 d) jeder Halbschale besteht aus einem angenieteten Gelenkband. Die Verbindung der Halbschalen ist an der Nase mittels Gelenkstiften und an der Hinterkante durch Vernietung der Endrippen an einem Punkt ausgeführt.

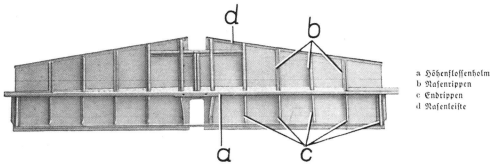

a Höhenflossenholm
b Nasenrippen
c Endrippen
d Nasenleiste

Abb. 11: Obere Halbschale der Höhenflosse ohne Randkappen

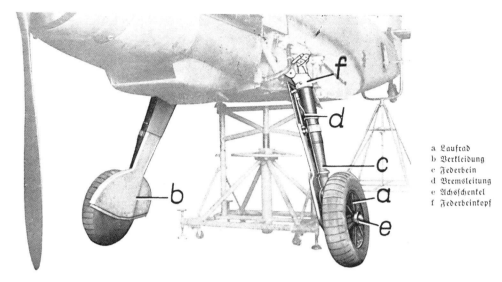

a Laufrad
b Verkleidung
c Federbein
d Bremsleitung
e Achsschenkel
f Federbeinkopf

Abb. 7: Fahrgestell mit Bremsleitungen und Verkleidungen
III: Main Landing Gear

d) Verkleidung

An den Federbeinen sind Verkleidungen (7 b) befestigt, die bei eingezogenem Fahrwerk den Streben-kanal und die Hälfte des Radausschnittes auf der Tragflächen-Unterseite abdecken.

e) Einziehvorrichtung (Drucköllanlage)

Das Ein- und Ausschwenken des Fahrwerks erfolgt durch Drucköl. Schema und Übersicht der Druck-ölanlage siehe Teil 8, Anlage 7.

Die Erzeugung des Öldrucks erfolgt durch eine am Presserabtrieb des Motors angeflanschte Schrau-benpumpe. Die Steuerung des Drucköls zur Betätigung der in den Tragflächen angeordneten Ar-beitszylinder (9 a) erfolgt durch einen automatischen Druckknopfschalter (25 m), der links an der Vorderseite der Rumpfstirnwand angeordnet ist. Die Knöpfe (30 q) für Betätigung des Druckknopf-schalters sind links in dem Gerätebrett gelagert. Nach Beendigung des Arbeitsganges springt der Druckknopfschalter selbsttätig in die Nullstellung zurück.

In Nullstellung des Druckknopfschalters fördert die Schraubenpumpe das Öl in geschlossenem Kreis-lauf über den Druckknopfschalter und den am linken Motorträger befestigten Ausgleichsbehälter (25 h) zurück zur Schraubenpumpe.

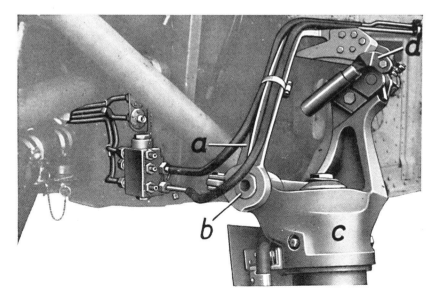

a Fahrwerksanschlußbock
b Schwenkachse
c Federbeinkopf
d Sperrklinke

Abb. 8: Federbeinanschluß am Rumpf links

Seitenfloffe

Die mit ihrem Vorder- (16 a) und Hinterholm (16 b) an dem Leitwerksträger befestigte Seitenfloffe ist ähnlich wie die Höhenfloffe aus zwei Duralblech-Halbschalen, der oberen Endkappe (16 d) und der Spaltabdeckung zusammengesetzt. Die Floffennase wird durch Gelenkbänder (16 e) gebildet. Die Verbindung der Halbschalen ist an der Nase mittels Gelenkstift und am Vorderholm mittels der Gleitbahn (12 c) und Schrauben ausgeführt. Die Verbindung am Hinterholm erfolgt durch Schrauben. Die Endkappe (16 d) ist oben an der Floffe und die Spaltabdeckung an dem Floffen-Vorderholm mit Schrauben befestigt. An der Endkappe befindet sich eine Öse (16 c) für die Antennenbefestigung.

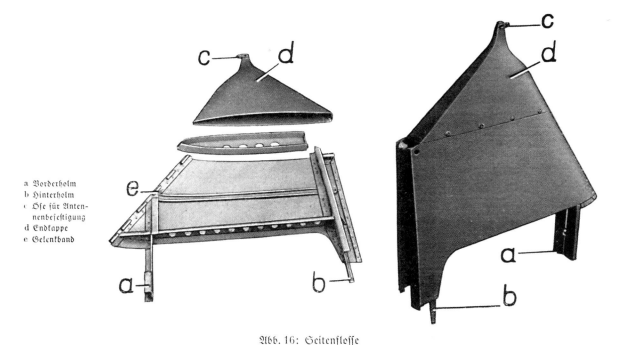

a Vorderholm
b Hinterholm
c Öse für Anten-
nenbefestigung
d Endkappe
e Gelenkband

Abb. 16: Seitenfloffe

Seitenruder

Das stoffbespannte Seitenruder ist an der Hinterkante der Höhenfloffe und dem Leitwerksträger gelagert. Durch ein Gewicht (Gußgewicht im Horn [17 d]) ist das Ruder maffenausgeglichen. In die Hinterkante des Seitenruders ist die Fassung (17 g) für das Kennlicht (10 g) eingebaut.

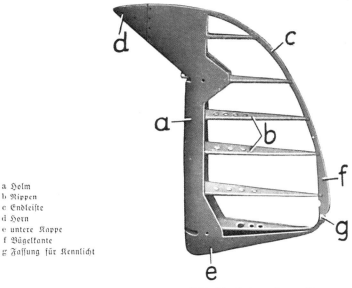

a Holm
b Rippen
c Endleiste
d Horn
e untere Kappe
f Bügelkante
g Fassung für Kennlicht

Abb. 17: Seitenrudergerüst
Rudder

und leicht abnehmbar. Die oberen Befestigungsbolzen sind als Heißösen zum Anheben des Flugzeuges mittels Heißvorrichtung ausgebildet.

Im äußeren hinteren Teil der Tragfläche sind die Querruder gelagert. Zwischen Rumpf und Querruder sind an der Unterseite der Tragfläche Wölbungsklappen angeordnet. Zwischen Rumpf und Wölbungsklappe befindet sich an der Ober- und Unterseite je eine Kühlerklappe. In jedem äußeren Teil der Tragflächenteile sind in der Flächennase Vorflügel angeordnet.

Alle Einbauteile im Tragwerk sind von der Flächen-Unterseite durch abgedeckte Rüstöffnungen zugänglich.

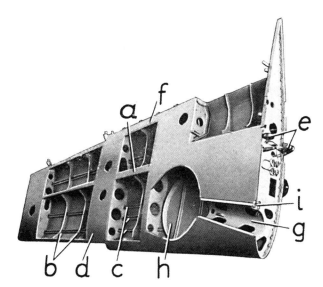

a Holm
b Rippen
c Längsprofile
d Beplankung
e Holmanschlußbeschläge
f Hilfsholm
g Strebenkanal
h Radausschnitt
i vorderer Tragflächen-Anschlußbeschlag

Abb. 21: Tragfläche ohne Rüstdeckel
V: Wing

b) Tragflächen

Die geteilte Tragfläche ist einholmig in Ganzmetallbauweise ausgeführt. Holm (21 a) und Beplankung (21 d) übernehmen gemeinsam die Biegekräfte. Die Verdrehkräfte werden von der Beplankung aufgenommen. Zur Aussteifung und Weiterleitung der Kräfte dienen Rippen (21 b) und Längsprofile (21 c).

Der I-Hauptholm (21 a) ist vollwandig aus Duralblech ausgeführt. Die Ober- und Untergurte sind durch beiderseits aufgenietete Duralwinkel gebildet. Die Holmanschlußbeschläge (21 e) aus Stahl sind mit Holmober- und -untergurt vernietet.

Im hinteren Teil jeder Tragfläche ist ein U-förmiger Hilfsholm (21 f) angeordnet.

Die Rippen sind mit dem Haupt- und Hilfsholm vernietet.

Die Beplankung besteht aus plattiertem Duralblech und ist durch Versenknietung mit dem Haupt- und Hilfsholm sowie den Rippen verbunden. Die Flächennase ist durch eine innen aufgeniete Formleiste verstärkt und die Beplankung durch längsverlaufende Formleisten versteift.

Die Randkappen sind mit Paßstiften an den Tragflächenenden befestigt.

Zur Aufnahme des Fahrwerks in eingezogenem Zustand ist in jeder Unterseite der Tragflächenteile ein Strebenkanal (21 g) und ein Radausschnitt (21 h) angeordnet.

An der Vernietung zwischen Strebenkanalbeplankung und Untergurt der Rippe 1 ist der vordere Tragflächen-Anschlußbeschlag (21 i) angebracht, der mit einem Sechskantbolzen an einem Schäkel des Fahrwerksbockes befestigt ist.

c) Wölbungsklappen

An Stelle der sonst üblichen Landeklappen ist dieses Flugzeug mit Wölbungsklappen (Abb. 23) ausgerüstet.

Je eine Wölbungsklappe ist links und rechts an dem inneren Teil der Tragflächen-Unterseite zwischen angeordnet. Außerdem ist vor jedem Kühler eine verstellbare vordere Kühlerklappe angebracht. Die Verstellung der Klappen, die miteinander gekuppelt sind, erfolgt durch einen Arbeitszylinder, der mit der Drucköltanlage verbunden ist. Der in die Kühlstoffvorlaufleitung eingebaute Thermostat steuert den Ölein- und -austritt des Arbeitszylinders und bewirkt somit die Verstellung der Kühlerklappen. Die Kühlerklappen sind mit den Wölbungsklappen (29 d) gekuppelt und werden beim Anstellen der Wölbungsklappen mit angestellt.

a Kühlstoffkühler
b obere Kühlstoffkühlerklappe
c untere Kühlstoffkühlerklappe
d Wölbungsklappe

Abb. 29: Anordnung der Kühlstoffkühler
VI: Radiator

11. Auspuffanlage

Die Ableitung der Auspuffgase aus dem Motorraum ins Freie erfolgt durch kurze als Rückstoßer ausgebildete Auspuffstutzen (25 i) (Strahldüsen) mit Flammendämpfung bei Nachtflug. Die Auspuffstutzen sind gemeinsam mit dem linken und rechten Haubenträger am Motor befestigt.

12. Luftschraubenverstellanlage

(Siehe auch Teil 8, Anlage 9.)

Der Motor ist mit einer dreiflügeligen VDM-Verstell-Luftschraube ausgerüstet. Die Verstellung der Luftschraubenblätter erfolgt durch eine elektrische Luftschraubenverstellautomatik.

Die Luftschraubenverstellautomatik besteht aus dem auf der Motoroberseite angeordneten Fliehkraftregler und dem an der Motorunterseite befestigten Einheitsverstellgerät sowie einem Relaiskasten. Der Fliehkraftregler betätigt die Verstellung der Luftschraube im Sinne einer vom Flugzustand unabhängigen, gleichbleibenden Motordrehzahl.

Der auf eine beliebige Drehzahl einstellbare Fliehkraftregler wird durch das Zwischengetriebe vom Flugmotor angetrieben. Bei einer Abweichung der Drehzahl von der eingestellten Reglerdrehzahl werden im Regler Kontakte betätigt. Dadurch wird über das Relais das Einheitsverstellgerät der Luftschraube links- oder rechtsdrehend je nach Drehzahlabweichung geschaltet und damit die Schraube im Sinne einer gleichbleibenden Drehzahl verstellt.

Die Einstellung der Drehzahl am Regler erfolgt über ein Gestänge mit Kurvenscheibe vom Gashebelgestänge aus. Schaltung auf Segelstellung erfolgt von Hand durch Betätigung des Daumenschalters am Gashebel. Die Verstellautomatik läßt sich durch den unter dem Gashebelkasten sitzenden Wechselschalter E 26 ausschalten. Bei Versagen der Verstellautomatik ist die Blattsteigung durch den Daumenschalter (30 t) einzuschalten.

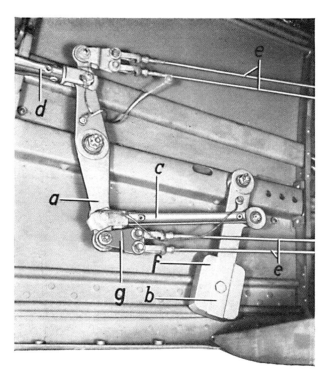

a Zwischenhebel
b Schwinghebel
c Stoßstange
d Stoßstange
e Steuerzüge
f Massenausgleich
g Gabel

Abb. 44: Zwischenhebel mit Massenausgleich für Höhensteuerung

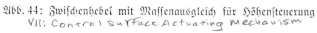
VII: Control Surface Actuating Mechanism

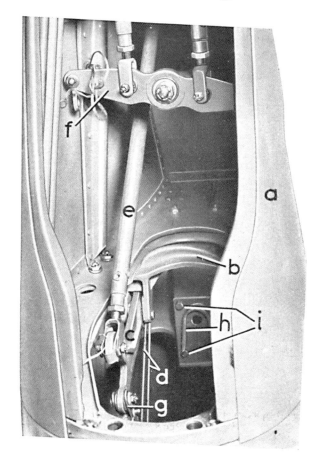

a Leitwerksträger
b Hebelbrücke
c Zwischenhebel
d Steuerzüge
e Stoßstange
f Zwischenhebel
g Gabel
h Spornlagerplatte

Abb. 45: Steuerung im Rumpfende

Den **hinteren Zwischenhebel** (45 c, 46 f) an der Hebelbrücke (45 b) - im Leitwerksträger (45 a) -
lagern und mit Zwischenhebel (44 a, 46 d) wie folgt durch doppelte Steuerzüge (44 e, 46 g) ver-

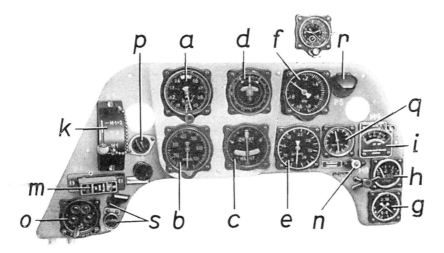

a Fein- und Grobhöhenmesser
b Fahrtmesser
c Elt-Wendezeiger
d Führertochterkompaß
e Nachdrehzahlmesser
f Ladedruckmesser
g Kraft- und Schmierstoff-Druckmesser
h Kraftstoffvorratsmesser
i Elt. Anzeigegerät für Kühlstoffaus-
   und Schmierstoffeintrittstemperatur
k Zündschalter
m Anlaßschalter
n Reststandswarnlampe
o Fahrwerksanzeigegerät
p Netzausschalter
q Stellungsanzeiger
r Steckdose
s Führungen

Abb. 88: Anordnung der Geräte in der Gerätetafel
VIII: Instrument Panel

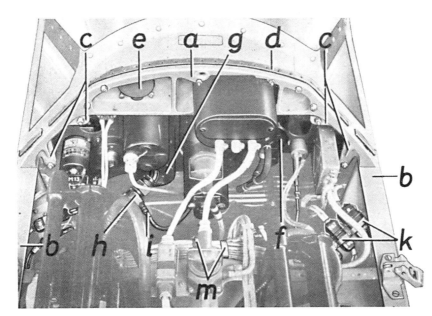

a Gerätetafelträger
b Rumpfobergurte
c Knaggen
d Metallgummiband
e Borduhr
f Fahrtmesser
g Nachdrehzahlmesser
h Entöler
i Stutzen
k Bügel
m Schellen

Abb. 89: Einbau der Gerätetafel

Auf Oberseite Gerätetafel-Träger sowie seitlich an diesem Metallgummibänder (89 d) anbringen und in Träger Borduhr (89 e, 103 a) einsetzen.

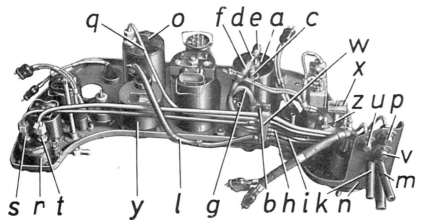

a Fein- und Grobhöhenmesser
b Fahrtmesser
c Gummischlauch
d T-Stück
e Gummischlauch
f Gummischlauch
g Gummischlauch
h Rohrleitung
i Rohrleitung
k Schlauch
l Entölerleitung
m Schlauch
n Flanschträger
o Ladedruckmesser
p Flanschstutzen
q Ladedruckleitung
r Kraft- und Schmierstoffdruckmesser
s Stutzen
t Stutzen
u Flanschstutzen
v Flanschstutzen
w Schelle
x Mitnehmer des Anlaßschalters
y Nachdrehzahlmesser
z Welle des Anlaßschalters

Abb. 90: Leitungsanschlüsse auf Gerätetafelrückseite

ſchraube (94 h) ſtreifen und Schraube in Annietmutter (94 i) einſchrauben. Hierbei muß die Laſche auf der Formleiſte liegen (ſ. Abb. 94).

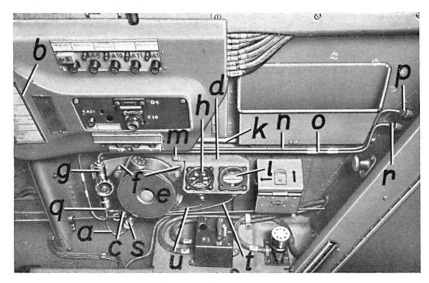

a Verbindungsleitung
b Rohrleitung
c Stutzen am Höhenatmer
d Halterung
e Höhenatmer
f Abſtandsrohre
g Bedienventil
h Druckmeſſer
i O₂-Wächter
k Formleiſte
m Laſche
n Auffülleitung
o Entnahmeleitung
p Anſchlußſtutzen
q Anſchlußſtutzen
r Stutzen
s Stutzen
t Rohrleitung

Abb. 95: Einbau der Höhenatmungsanlage im Führerraum

Die beiden Sauerſtoff-Flaſchen (96 a, b) unter der Gepäckraumdecke aufhängen und zwar Flaſche (96 a) mit Doppelanſchluß am Ventil (96 c) rechts und Flaſche (96 b) links. Flaſche von hinten durch die Spannbänder (96 d) in die Töpfe (96 f) einſetzen und Spannbänder mit Sechskantſchraube, Feder-ring, ſowie Sechskantmutter verſchließen. Beide Flaſchen durch das Rohr (96 g) verbinden.

Verſchlußmutter von Außenbordanſchluß (96 e) abſchrauben und Außenbordanſchluß vom Rumpf-innern durch die rechte Rumpfwand führen, Leitungs-Anſchlußſtutzen zeigt nach unten. Befeſtigungs-ſchrauben des Außenbordanſchluſſes von innen nach außen einſetzen. Unter eine Sechskantmutter Sicherungskette der Verſchlußmutter legen.

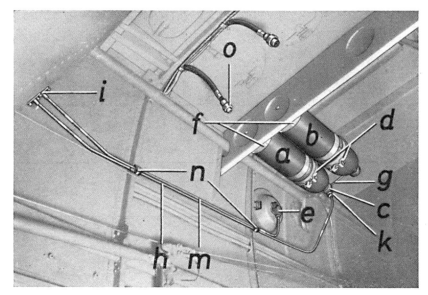

a rechte Sauerſtofflaſche
b linke Sauerſtofflaſche
c Flaſchenventil
d Spannbänder
e Außenbordanſchluß
f Flaſchentöpfe
g Verbindungsrohr
h Entnahmeleitung
i Schraubflanſch
k Leitungsanſchluß
m Auffülleitung
n Inſtallationsband
o Elt-Leitung für Kraftſtoffpumpe

Abb. 96: Einbau der Sauerſtoff-Flaſchen
IX: Starboard side of Cockpit
with oxygen bottles

Rechts an den Spanten je einen Winkel mit Linſenſchraube befeſtigen.

b) Leitungen

Die Leitungsrohre ſind wie folgt zu verlegen und nach Anlage 8 anzuſchließen. **Achtung!** Nicht ver-geſſen die Alu-Dichtringe einzuſetzen.

X

a Vorduhr
b Abdeckung für Anzeigegerät
c Anzeigegerät für Kühlstoff- und *Combined coolant exit & oil intake temps. indicator* Schmierstofftemperatur
d Sicherungsfeder
e Netzausschalter (A 5)
f Zündschalter (B 5) *ignition switch*
g Anlaßschalter (B 4)
h Anzeigegerät für Fahrwerk
i Daumenschalter
k Führertochterkompaß *repeater compass*
m Wendezeiger *Artificial horizon/bank indicator*
n Gashebel
o Reststandswarnlampe
p Einsatztafel
q Druckmesser für Kraftstoff und *oil & fuel content guage* Schmierstoff
r Zuggriff für Fahrwerksnotauslösung
s Handhebel für Brandhahnschaltung
t Steuerknüppel *Control column w/ KG12A grip.*

Abb. 103: Eingebaute Gerätetafel

X: Cockpit Interior

Verdunkler C 10 (104 d) mit Linsenschrauben an der Frontplatte (104 f) befestigen.

Die Befestigung der Steckdose C 11 (38 m) erfolgt im Leitwerksträger an der rechten Seite mittels Schelle (38 i); Preßstoffunterlage (38 k) beilegen. Befestigung der Schelle und Unterlage erfolgt mit Sechskantschrauben.

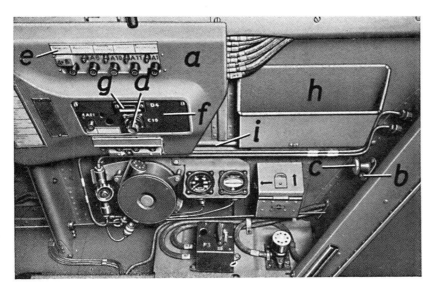

a Deckel der Hauptverteilertafel
b Durchführung für Seilzug
c Handknopf
d Verdunkler
e Leisten
f Frontplatte
g Schauzeichen
h Kartenkasten
i Formleiste

Abb. 104: Eingebaute Verteilertafel

D-Anlage (Elektrische Heizung)

Schauzeichen D 4 (104 g) mit Linsenschrauben an Frontplatte (104 f) befestigen.

E-Anlage (Elektrische Antriebe einschl. Überwachung)

Auf Geräteträger (97 a) unter dem Signalhorn (97 k) den Relaiskasten E 3 (97 m) aufschrauben.

Brandschottdose E 5 (174 k) an Halterung (183 a) anbringen und mit Linsenschrauben befestigen.

Winkelsteckdose E 11 (157 h) an der linken Rumpfaußenwand und die beiden Signalschalter E 12 (105 h) und E 13 am linken (105 a) bzw. rechten Federbeinlager wie folgt anbauen:

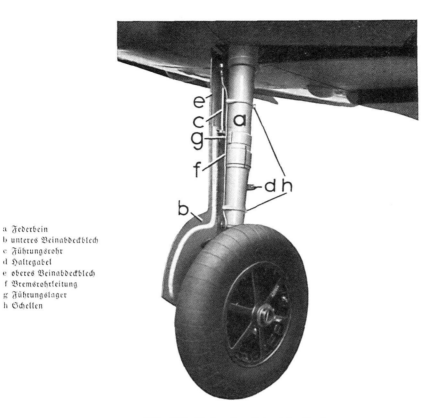

a Federbein
b unteres Beinabdeckblech
c Führungsrohr
d Haltegabel
e oberes Beinabdeckblech
f Bremsrohrleitung
g Führungslager
h Schellen

Abb. 126: Anbau der Federbeinabdeckung

X: Main Landing Gear Strut & wheel cover

Zugseil (127 n) streifen und Zugseil (127 n) mittels Kausche an Lasche (127 c) befestigen. Unter Fußboden an der rechten Rumpfwand eine Halterung mit zwei Umlenkrollen (127 f) anbringen. An der losen Rolle (127 e) ein Zugseil (127 o) und an dessen Ende eine lose Rolle (127 g) befestigen. Um die Rollen (127 f, g) ein Zugseil (127 p) legen. Das eine Ende des Seiles (127 p) ist durch die rechte Rumpfwand zu ziehen und wird später mit dem Seil (159 g) in der Fläche verbunden. An das andere Ende ist ein zweites Seil (127 k) mittels Spannschloß (127 i) anzuschließen und dann durch die linke Rumpfwand zu führen. Auch dieses Ende wird mit dem Seil in der linken Fläche verbunden.

a Zuggriff
b Umlenkrolle
c Lasche
d Spannschloß
e lose Rolle
f Umlenkrollen
g lose Rolle
h Zwischenlaschen
i Spannschloß
k Zugseil
m Zugseile in den
   Tragflächen
n Zugseil
o Zugseil
p Zugseil

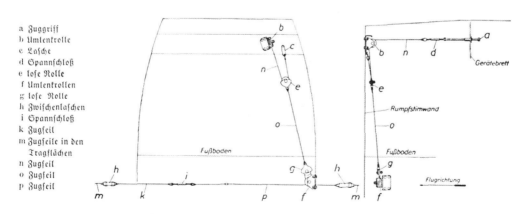

Abb. 127: Anordnung des Seilzuges für Fahrwerksnotauslösung

3. Radsporn

Der Einbau des Radsporns (114 k) wird nach Anbau des Leitwerksträgers wie folgt ausgeführt. Im Rumpfende an der oberen Spornhalterung (128 a) die Spornlagerplatte (45 h, 128 b) mit Sechskantschrauben (45 i) und niedrigen Kronenmuttern befestigen. Schrauben von unten einsetzen.

Unten am Rumpfendspant die beiden Augenbolzen (128 c) einsetzen, vom Rumpfinnern je eine Scheibe überstreifen und je eine niedrige Kronenmutter aufschrauben.

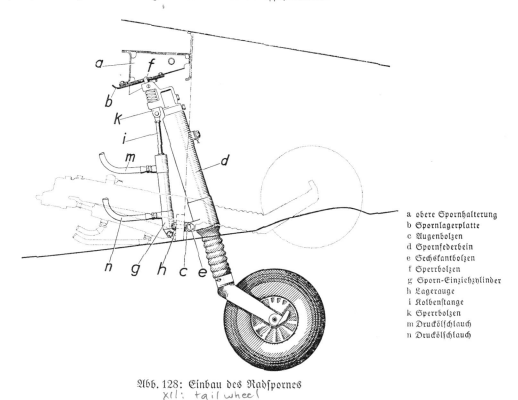

a obere Spornhalterung
b Spornlagerplatte
c Augenbolzen
d Spornfederbein
e Sechskantbolzen
f Sperrbolzen
g Sporn-Einziehzylinder
h Lagerauge
i Kolbenstange
k Sperrbolzen
m Drucköljchlauch
n Drucköljchlauch

Abb. 128: Einbau des Radspornes

XII: tail wheel

Hierauf das Federbein (128 d) des zusammengebauten Radspornes (Zusammenbau s. Vorschrift der Elektron-Co. m. b. H. Cannstatt) in den Rumpf einführen und zwischen den beiden Augenbolzen (128 c) mit einem Sechskantbolzen (128 e) lagern. Den Bolzen von links einsetzen, eine Scheibe überstreifen und eine niedrige Kronenmutter aufschrauben.

Den Radsporn nach unten drücken, damit der Sperrbolzen (128 f) oben am Federbein in die Lagerplatte (128 b) einrastet.

Hierauf den Sporn-Einziehzylinder (128 g) vom Innern des Rumpfes an das Lagerauge (128 h) und die Kolbenstange (128 i) an den Sperrbolzen (128 k) mit Sechskantbolzen Scheiben und Kronenmuttern befestigen.

Den Drucköljchlauch (128 m) an den oberen Stutzen, den Drucköljchlauch (128 n) an den unteren Stutzen des Einziehzylinders (128 g) anschließen.

E. Anbau der Tragflächen an den Rumpf

1. Einbauten in den Tragflächen

Bevor die Tragflächen an den Rumpf angebaut werden, sind sämtliche Tragflächeneinbauten in die Flächen einzubringen und zu befestigen.

a) Steuerung (s. Anlage 12)

In die Tragflächen sind die Umlenkhebel und Gestänge für Quersteuerung und Wölbungsklappenverstellung einzubringen.

Den Zwischenhebel (129 a) für die Quersteuerung wie folgt zusammenbauen: In die Nabe des Hebels (130 a) das Abstandsstück (130 b) und die Seeger-Innensicherungen (130 c) einsetzen. Die beiden Kugellager (130 d) in die Nabe einbringen. Hierauf den Hebel (130 a) zwischen die Lagerbleche (130 e) setzen und mit Sechskantbolzen befestigen. Sechskantbolzen von unten einführen; auf beiden Seiten der Nabe eine Abdeckscheibe (130 f) anbringen.

Anſchlußbeſchläge

Nun in den Kühlerausſchnitt Abb. 138 der Tragfläche die Anſchlußbeſchläge (138 a, b) einbauen. Die Beſchläge ſind mit je drei Sechskantbolzen an die Rippe 1 bzw. 4 anzuſchrauben.

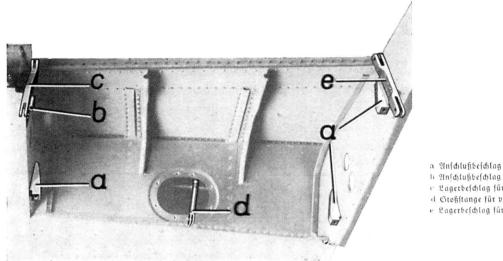

a Anſchlußbeſchlag
b Anſchlußbeſchlag
c Lagerbeſchlag für Kühlerklappe
d Stoßſtange für vordere Kühlerklappe
e Lagerbeſchlag für Kühlerklappe

Abb. 138: Anordnung der Beſchläge für Kühlſtoffkühler- und Kühlerklappenlagerung

Der Beſchlag (138 b) wird zuſammen mit dem Lagerbeſchlag (138 e, c) für die Kühlerklappen an die Rippe 4 angeſchraubt (Muttern im Kühlerausſchnitt).

Der einbaufertige Kühler iſt anzuheben und in den Flächenausſchnitt einzubringen. Von unten ſind darauf die vier Befeſtigungsbolzen (143 c) durch die Ausſchnitte (139 g) in die Verkleidung (139 d) einzuführen und mittels Steckſchlüſſel feſtzuſchrauben. Sicherung des Bolzens durch Draht.

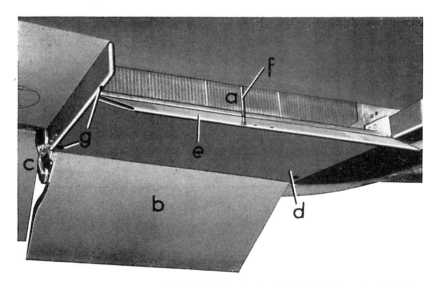

a Kühlſtoffkühler
b hintere Kühlerklappe
c Wölbungsklappe
d Kühlerverkleidung
e vordere Kühlerklappe
f Stoßſtange
g Ausſchnitt für Kühlerbefeſtigungs-
  bolzen

Abb. 139: Eingebauter Kühlſtoffkühler mit Kühlerklappen
VI: Radiator

Nach Einbau des Kühlers (139 a) iſt die Stoßſtange (138 d, 139 f) an die vordere Kühlerklappe (139 e) anzuſchließen.

Anmerkung: Abſtand zwiſchen vorderer Kühlerklappe und Unterkante der Kühlerverkleidung muß im geſchloſſenen Zuſtand 55 mm betragen.

Rohrleitung (180 r, 184 f, 192 q) anschließen, die zweimal am Motor mit Schellen (180 m, 192 r) gehaltert werden. Die Schellen werden an den Zylinderdeckeln des Motors (Gewindelöcher vorhanden) mit Sechskantschrauben und Federringen befestigt. Auf die Enden dieser Rohre je einen Schlauch (174 r, 192 s) schieben, die mit ihren Verschraubungen (174 s) an die Rohrkrümmer (80 a, b) angeschlossen werden.

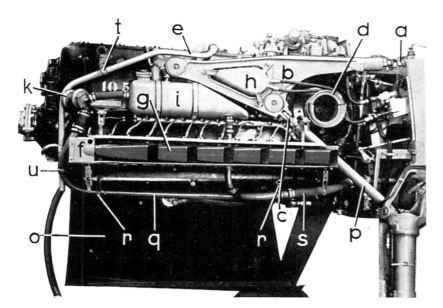

a	Anschlußbeschlag für Biegungsträger am Rumpf
b	Biegungsträger
c	Ofenkopf der Abfangstrebe
d	Ansaugstutzen am Lader
e	Rohrleitung
f	linker Haubenträger
g	Auspuffstutzen
h	Ölbehälter
i	Kühlstoff-Ausgleichsbehälter
k	Dampfabscheider
o	unteres Haubenteil
p	Abfangstrebe
q	Rohrleitung
r	Schellen
s	Schlauchleitung
t	Rundschelle
u	Rundschelle

Abb. 192: Kühlstoff- und Entlüftungsleitung auf linker Motorseite

Ferner werden die Dampfabscheider (191 h, 192 k) mit den vorne liegenden Stutzen (191 n) der Ausgleichsbehälter durch einen Schlauch (191 o) verbunden. Eine Ausgleichs-Rohrleitung (191 p) wird an die oben liegenden Stutzen (191 q) der Ausgleichsbehälter angebracht. Auf der rechten Motorseite ist das Ausgleichsrohr (191 p) mit dem Druckausgleichsventil (191 e) durch eine Rohrleitung (191 r) über eine Schlauchmuffe zu verbinden.

An dem Druckausgleichsventil eine Rohrleitung (191 s) anschrauben. Nach dem Anbau des rechten Haubenträgers (191 t) wird das Rohr (191 s) in das Rohr (191 u) der Halterung (191 v) eingesetzt. Für die Motorblockentlüftung auf der linken und rechten Motorseite je eine Rohrleitung (191 w, 188 a) an die Dampfabscheider (191 h) anschließen.

Sämtliche Schläuche und Gummimuffen werden mit Installationsbändern befestigt.

h) Verschiedene Anbauteile

Auf der rechten Motorseite die Andrehwelle für den Schwungkraftanlasser mit ihrem Gelenk (188 n) in den Anlasser einsetzen und mit Splintbolzen befestigen.

Über die Welle das Lagerblech (188 o) streifen und Lagerblech am rechten Biegungsträger (188 e) mit Sechskantschrauben befestigen. Die vordere Befestigungsschraube ist gleichzeitig die Befestigungsschraube für die Halterung des Winkelgetriebes (175 f). Das mit Gummimuffe (161 q) und Gummimanschette (188 p) versehene **Belüftungsrohr (188 q, 161 p) des Stromerzeugers** durch das Lagerblech (188 o) führen, auf den Stutzen des Stromerzeugers (161 b) setzen und an diesem mit einem Splint befestigen. Das Belüftungsrohr muß mit blauem Kennzeichnungslack versehen sein.

Für die **Motorgehäuse-Entlüftung** die mit blauem Kennzeichnungslack versehene Rohrleitung (170 i, 192 e) mittels Gummimuffe (170 m) an dem Entlüfter (170 n) oben auf dem Motor befestigen. Die Gummimuffe an dem Stutzen und der Rohrleitung mit Verbindern haltern, Rohrleitung mit zwei Rundschellen (192 t) haltern, die an der linken vorderen Transportöse bzw. an der Rundschelle (192 w) befestigt werden.

An das **linke obere Haubenteil** (195 a) die Ansaughuße (194 b, 195 b) mit Senkschrauben befestigen. Hierauf das Haubenteil an den oberen Haubenträger (196 f) setzen und den Gelenkdraht in die Gelenkbänder einschieben.

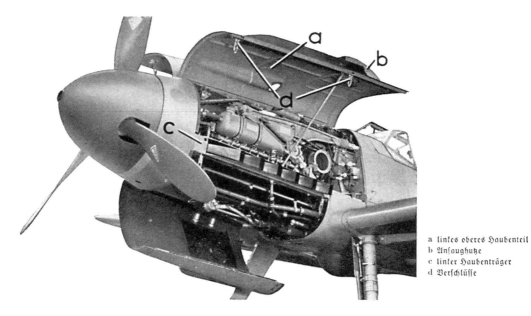

a linkes oberes Haubenteil
b Ansaughuße
c linker Haubenträger
d Verschlüsse

Abb. 195: Geöffnete Haubenteile von links gesehen

Das **rechte obere Haubenteil** (196 a) ebenfalls an den oberen Haubenträger (196 f) setzen und mit Gelenkdraht befestigen.

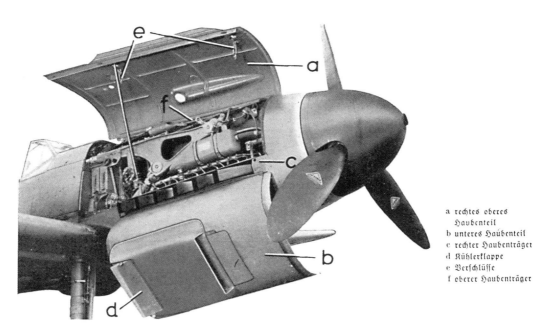

a rechtes oberes
   Haubenteil
b unteres Haubenteil
c rechter Haubenträger
d Kühlerklappe
e Verschlüsse
f oberer Haubenträger

Abb. 196: Geöffnete Haubenteile von rechts gesehen

Nachdem in das **untere Haubenteil** (194 c, 196 b) der Schmierstoffkühler und die Klappenbetätigung eingebaut ist (s. f. Schmierstoffanlage, Seite 119), wird das Haubenteil an den rechten Haubenträger (196 c) mit einem Gelenkdraht befestigt. Die Kühlerklappe (194 d, 196 d) an der Kühlerverkleidung (194 e) ebenfalls mit Gelenkstift lagern.

a Ladedruck-Leitung
b Kraftstoffdruck-Leitung
c Schmierstoffdruck-Leitung
d Entöler-Leitung
e Staurohr-Leitungen
f Einspritz-Leitung
g Biegsame Welle für Drehzahlmesser
h Biegsame Welle für Luftschrauben-Automatik
i Ladedruckmesser
k Fahrtmesser
l Fein- und Grobhöhenmesser

m Drehzahlmesser
n Kraft- und Schmierstoffdruckmesser
o Anzeigegerät für Luftschraube
p Einspritzpumpe
q Staurohr

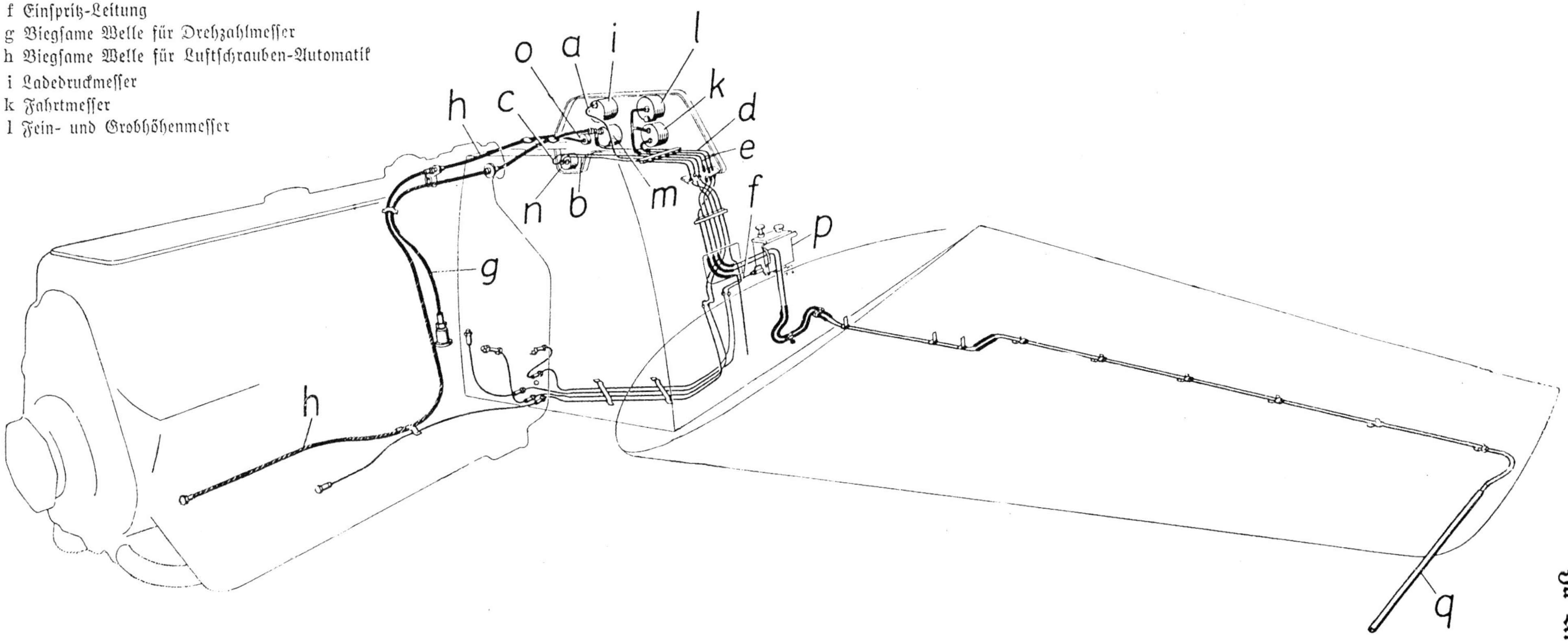

Leitungen der Betriebsgeräte BF 109 F

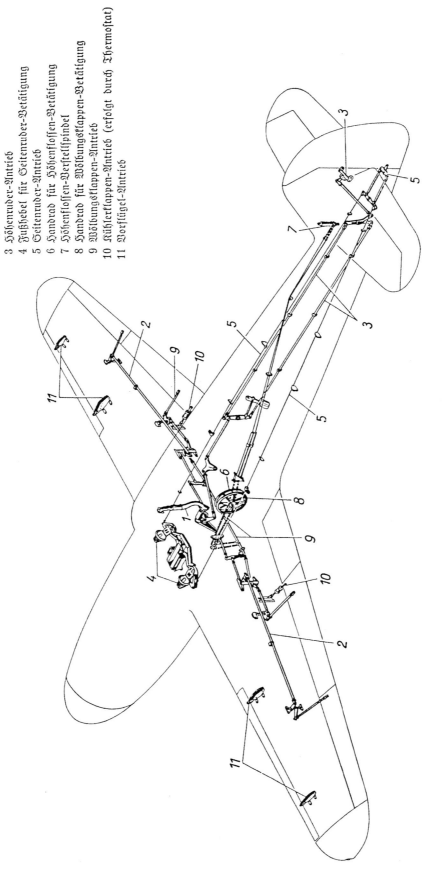

1 Steuerknüppel mit Lagerung (für Quer- und
  Höhenruder-Betätigung)
2 Querruder-Antrieb
3 Höhenruder-Antrieb
4 Fußhebel für Seitenruder-Betätigung
5 Seitenruder-Antrieb
6 Handrad für Höhenflossen-Betätigung
7 Höhenflossen-Verstellspindel
8 Handrad für Wölbungsklappen-Betätigung
9 Wölbungsklappen-Antrieb
10 Kühlerklappen-Antrieb (erfolgt durch Thermostat)
11 Vorflügel-Antrieb

Übersicht der Steuerung BF 109 F

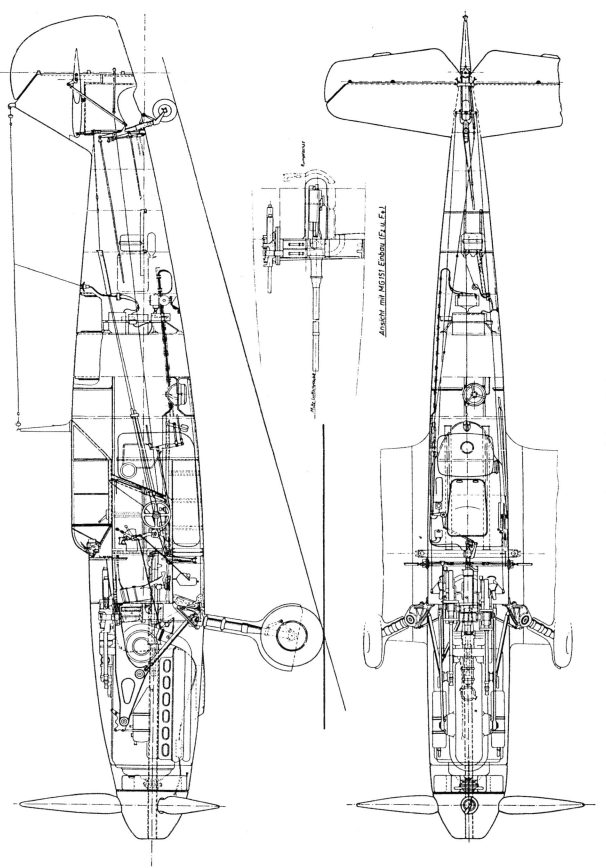

Ansicht mit MG151 Einbau (F₂ u. F₃)

Flugzeug-Zusammenstellung
Längsschnitt und Draufsicht

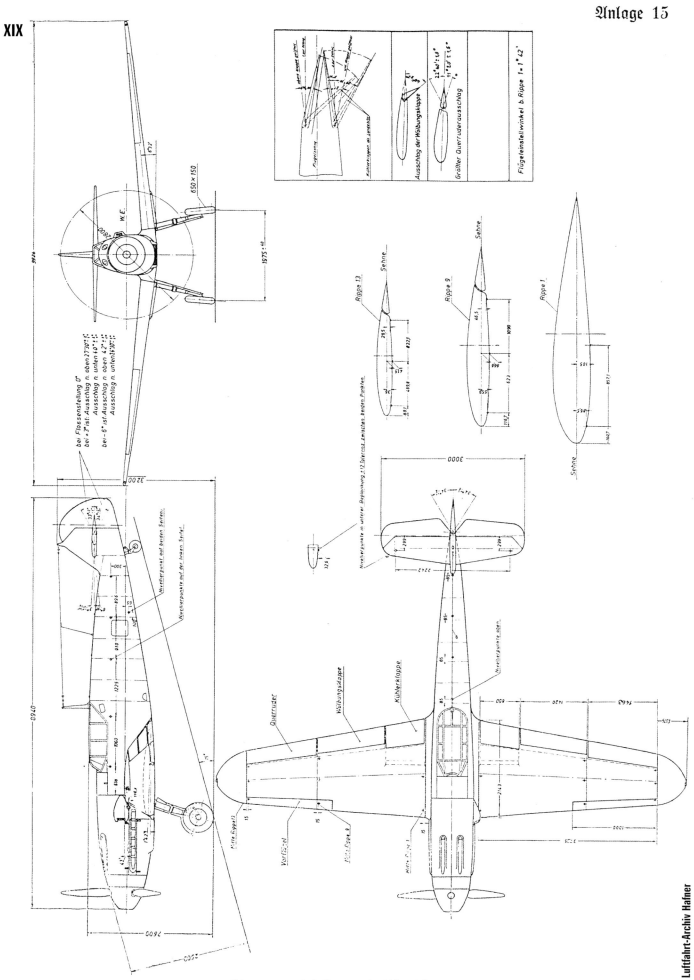

Steuerausschläge und Nivellierpunkte

Sheet 01

Drawings: Mariusz Łukasik

The drawings have been prepared using previously published literature, documentary evidence and contemporary photographs.

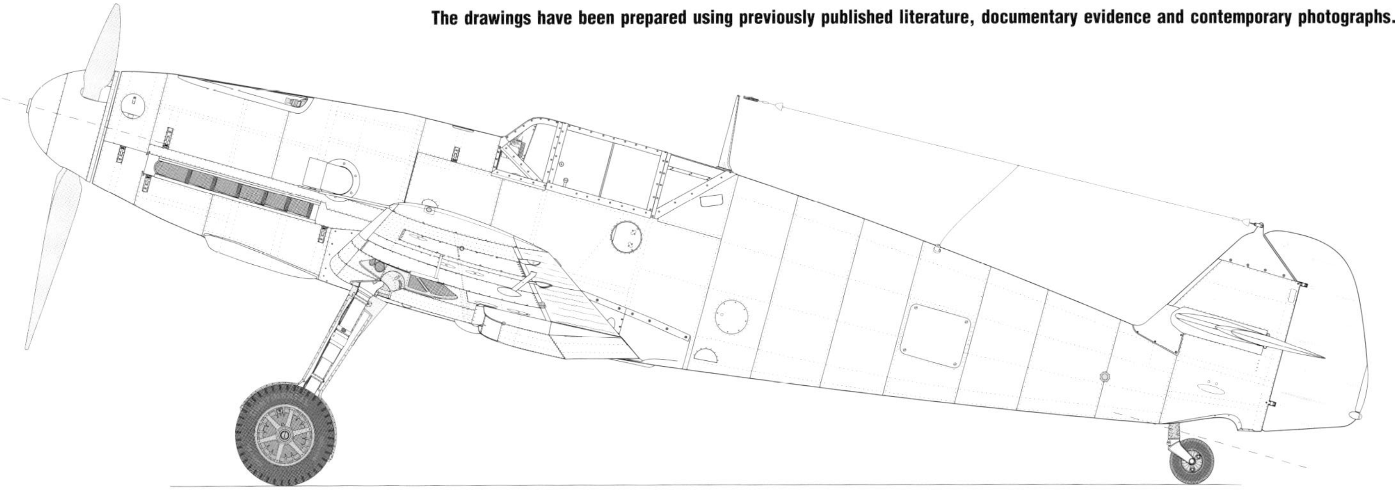

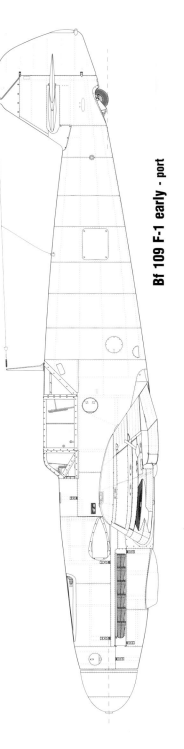

Bf 109 W.Nr. 1801 CE+BP - port

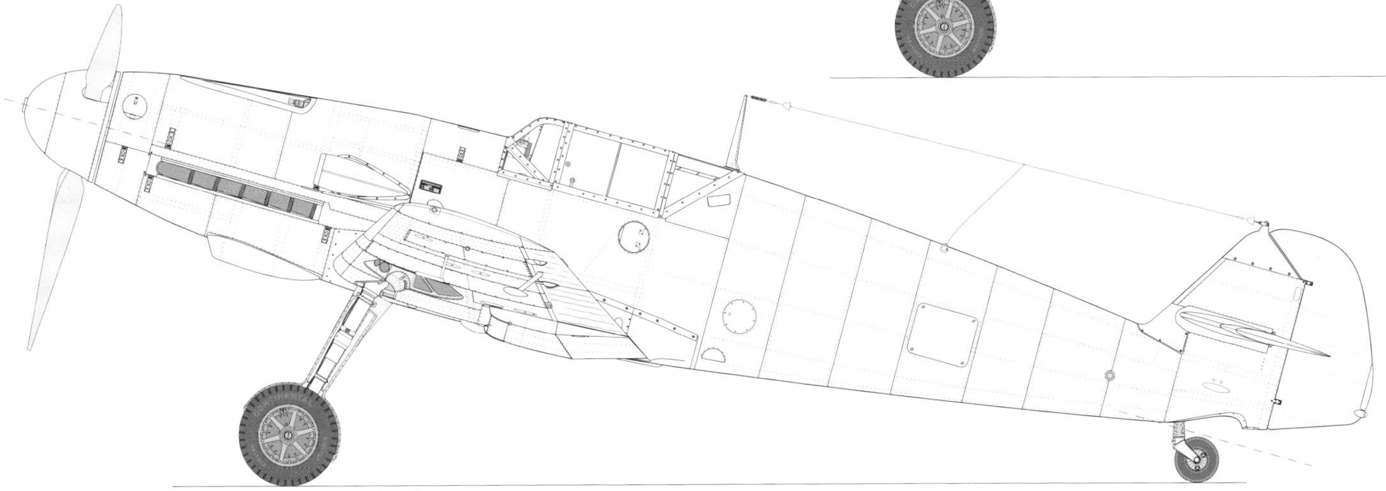

Bf 109 W.Nr. 5604 VK+AB - port

Bf 109 F-1 early - port

Bibliography

J.R. Beaman Jr., *Messerschmitt Bf 109 part 2*, Carrolton, 1983
M. Griehl, *Messerschmitt Bf 109 F*, Illertissen, 1999
R Grinsell, *Messerschmitt Bf 109*, New York, 1980
T.H. Hitchcock, *Bf 109 F*, Sturbridge, 1990
A. van Ishoven, *Messerschmitt aircraft designer*, London, 1973
J. Ledwoch, *Messerschmitt Bf 109 F*, Warszawa, 1997
R. Michulec, *Messerschmitt Bf 109 part 1-5*, Gdańsk, 1999
M.J. Murawski, *Messerschmitt Bf 109 F vol.1*, Lublin, 2007
H. Nowarra, *German Guided Misilles*, Atglen, 1993
H. Nowarra, *The Messerschmitt Bf 109*, Letchworth, 1963
W. Radinger & W. Otto, *Bf 109 F-K*, Atglen, 1999
Bf 109 F-1 bis F-4 Flugzeughandbuch, Augsburg, 1941

Attention! In some views the course of riveted joints have been simplified for the drawings clearness

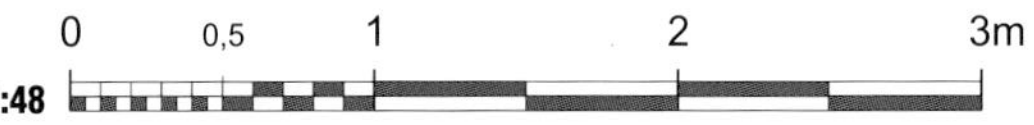

3m 2 1 0,5 0

Scale 1:48

MONOGRAFIE LONOGRAFIS

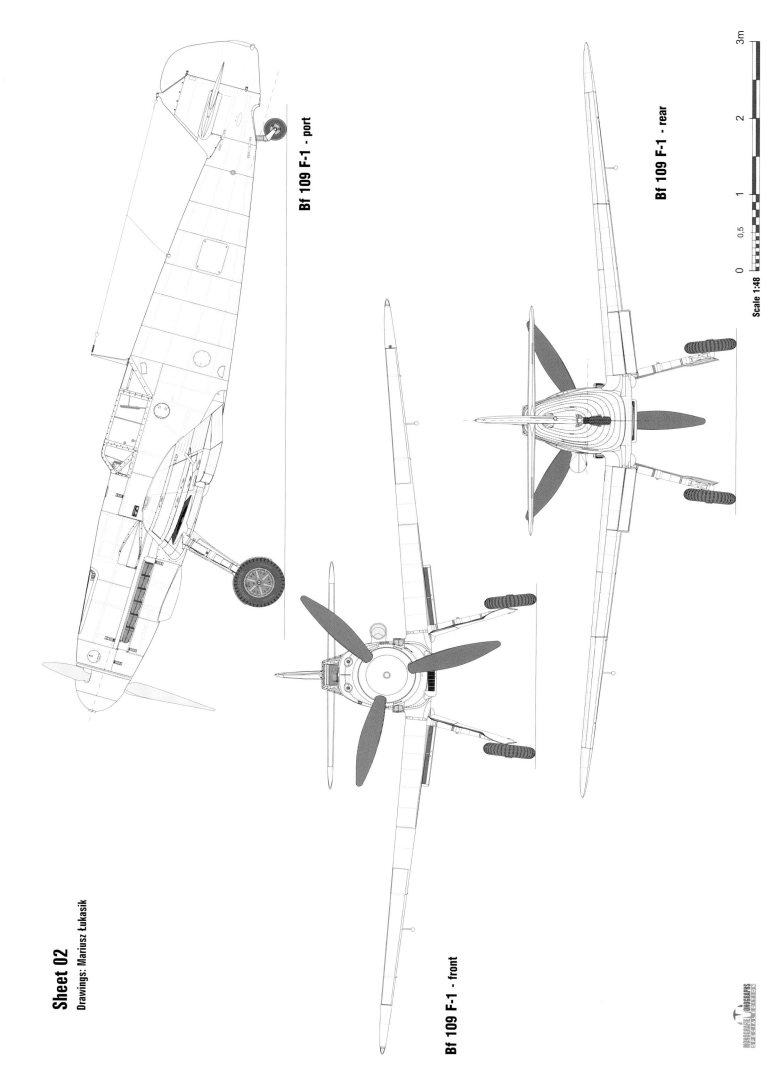

Sheet 02

Drawings: Mariusz Łukasik

Bf 109 F-1 - port

Bf 109 F-1 - front

Bf 109 F-1 - rear

Scale 1:48

0   0,5   1   2   3m

MONOGRAFIE LOTNICZE
SPECIAL EDITION

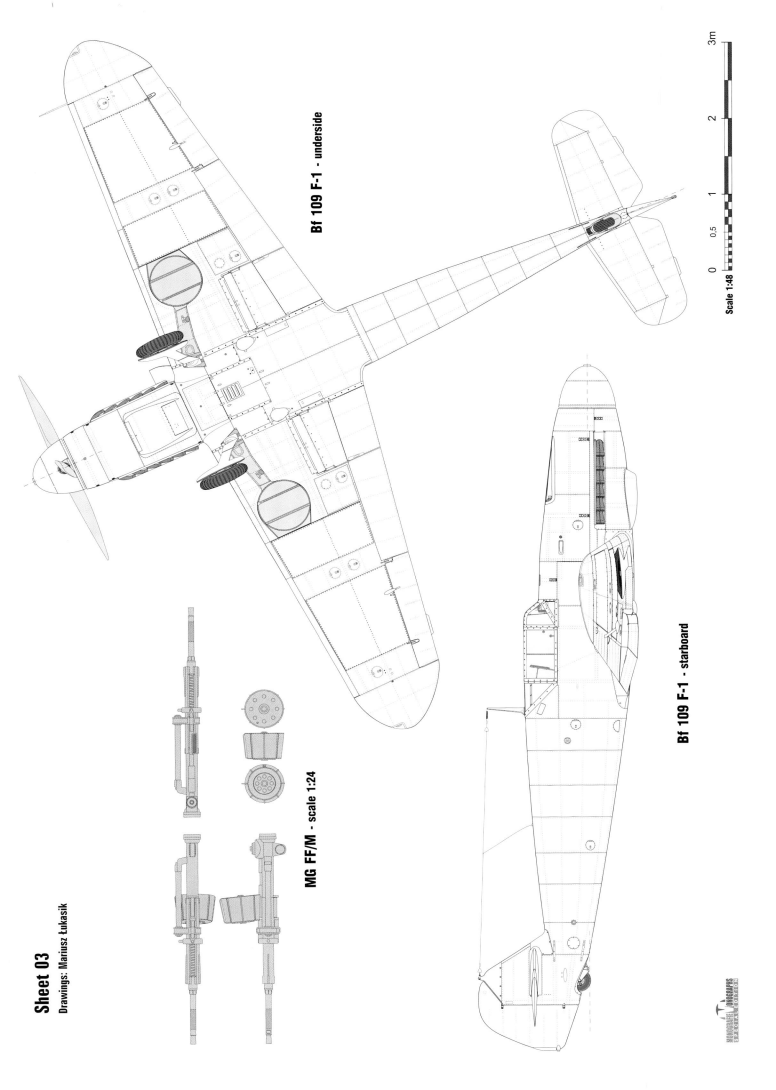

Bf 109 F-1 - underside

Bf 109 F-1 - starboard

MG FF/M - scale 1:24

Scale 1:48

0   0,5   1   2   3m

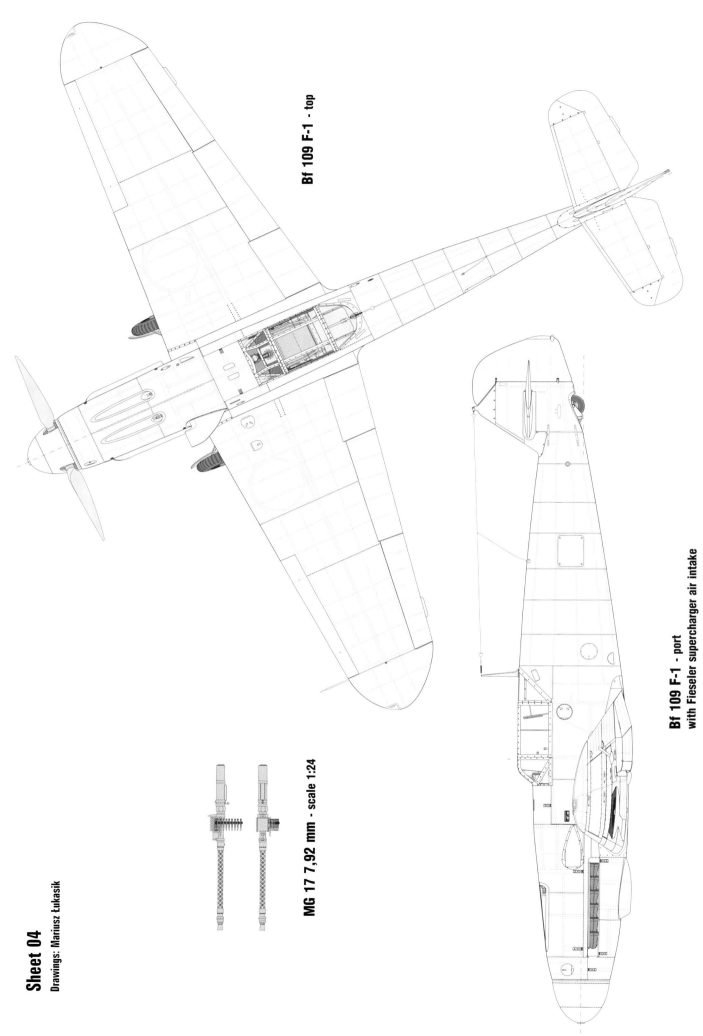

Sheet 04
Drawings: Mariusz Łukasik

Bf 109 F-1 - top

MG 17 7,92 mm - scale 1:24

Bf 109 F-1 - port
with Fieseler supercharger air intake

Scale 1:48

0   0,5   1   2   3m

Sheet 05

Drawings: Mariusz Łukasik

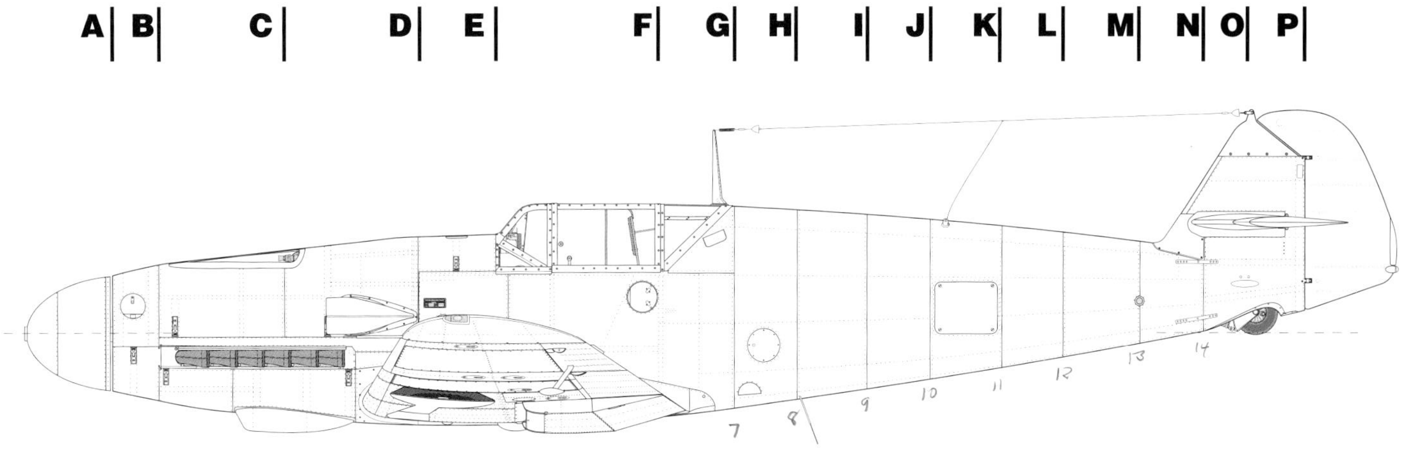
A B C D E F G H I J K L M N O P
7 8 9 10 11 12 13 14

Bf 109 F-2 - port

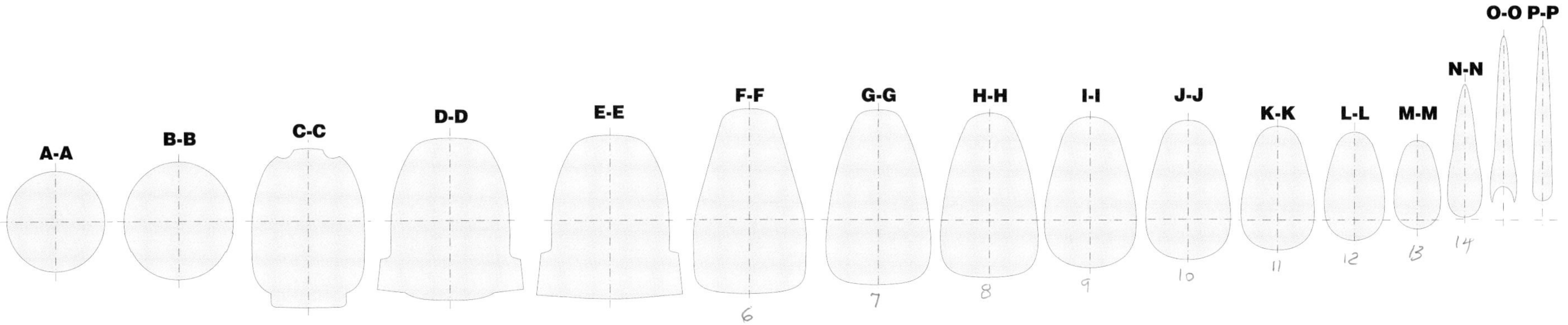
A-A
B-B
C-C
D-D
E-E
F-F
G-G
H-H
I-I
J-J
K-K
L-L
M-M
N-N
O-O
P-P
6 7 8 9 10 11 12 13 14

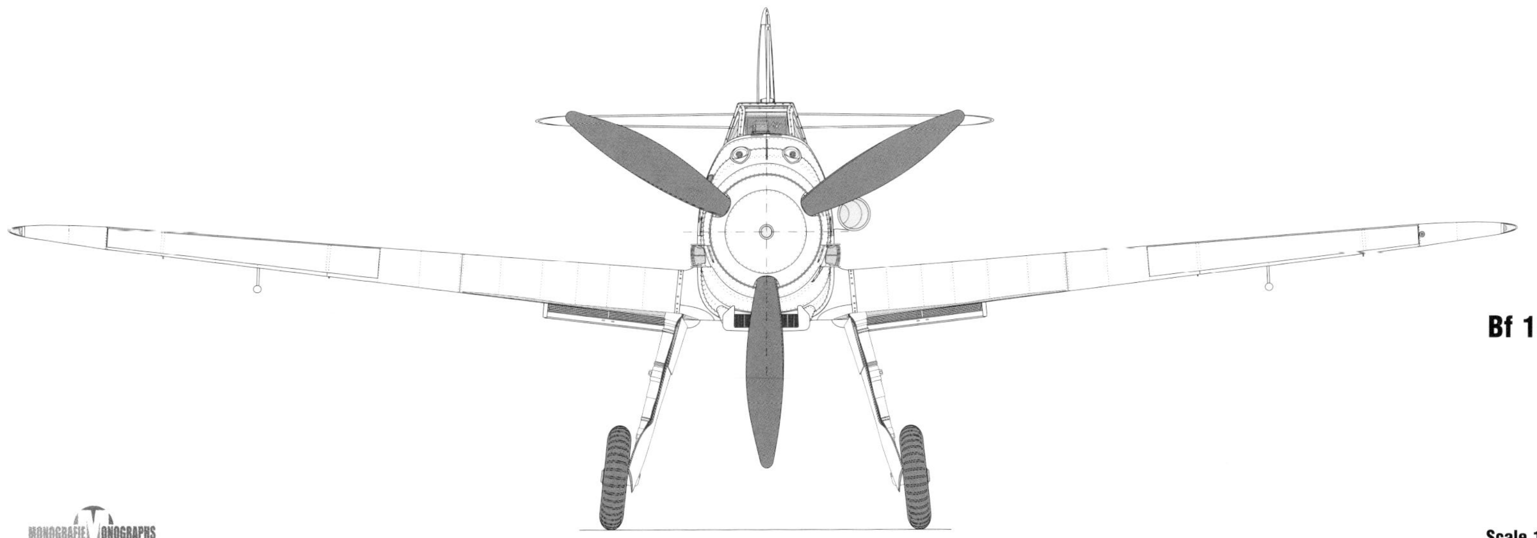

Bf 109 F-2 - front

Scale 1:48

0 0,5 1 2 3m

MONOGRAFIE MONOGRAPHS SPECIAL EDITION

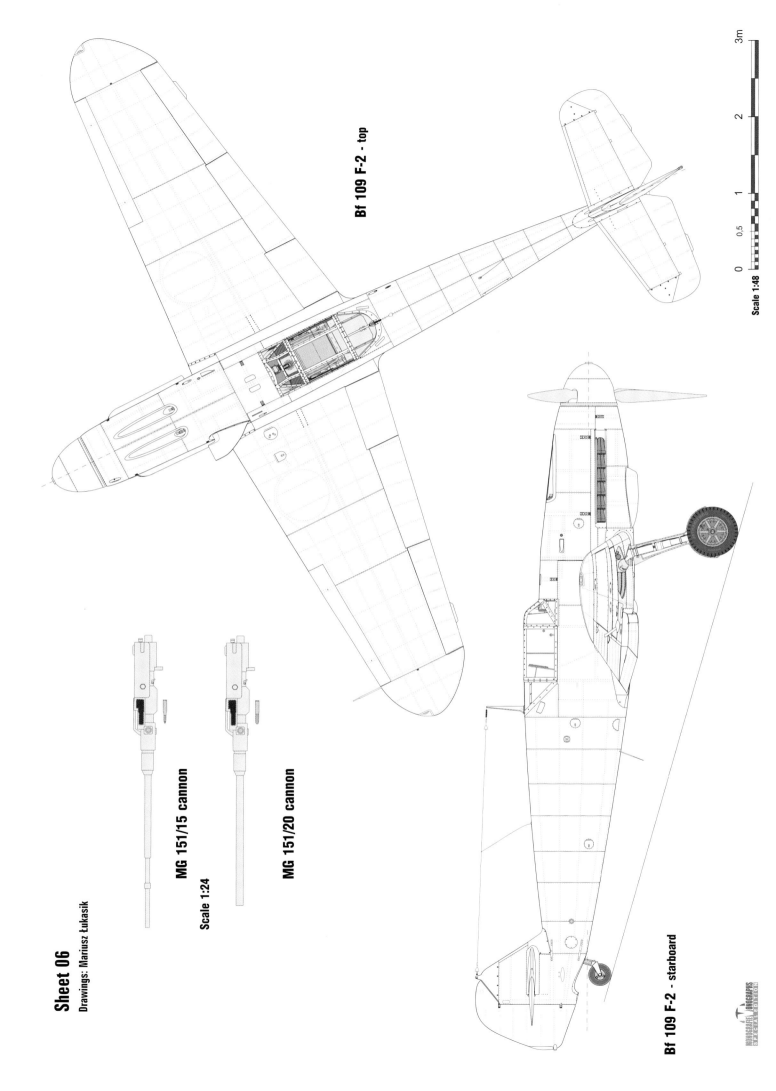

Sheet 06

Drawings: Mariusz Łukasik

Bf 109 F-2 - top

MG 151/15 cannon

Scale 1:24

MG 151/20 cannon

Bf 109 F-2 - starboard

Scale 1:48

3m
2
1
0,5
0

MONOGRAFIE LONOGRAPHS

Sheet 07

Drawings: Mariusz Łukasik

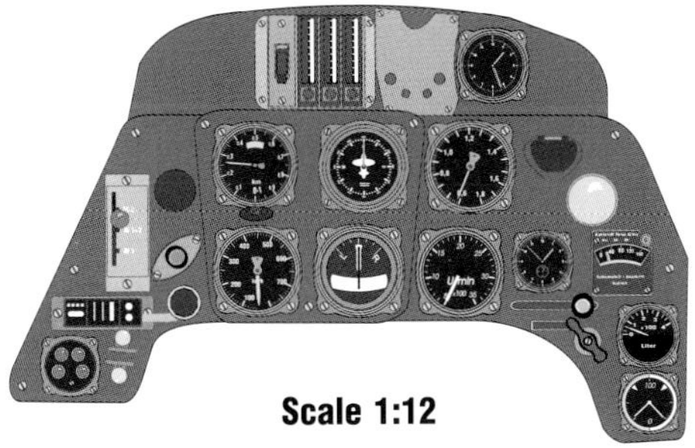

Bf 109 F-2 - underside

S3

S2

S1

S1

S2

S3

Bf 109 F-2 - instrument panel

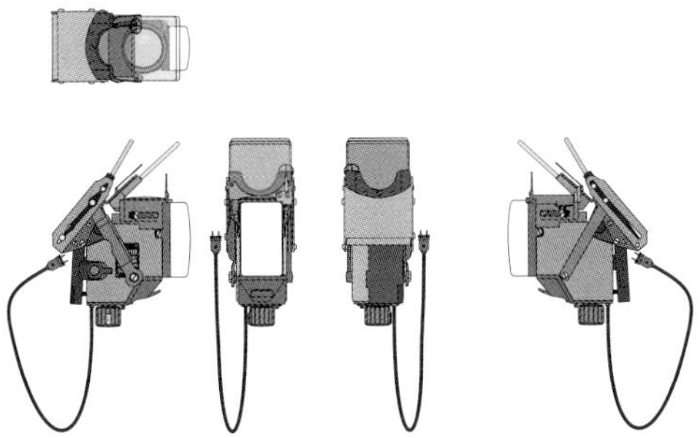

Scale 1:12

Revi C12/D

Scale 1:12

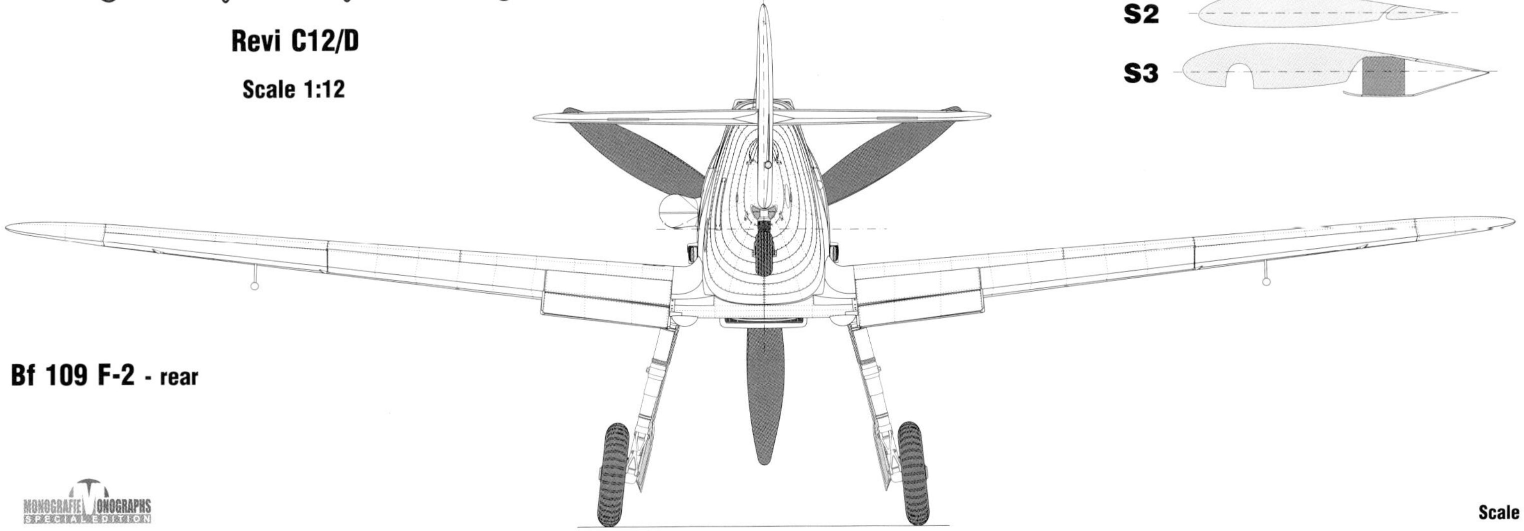

Bf 109 F-2 - rear

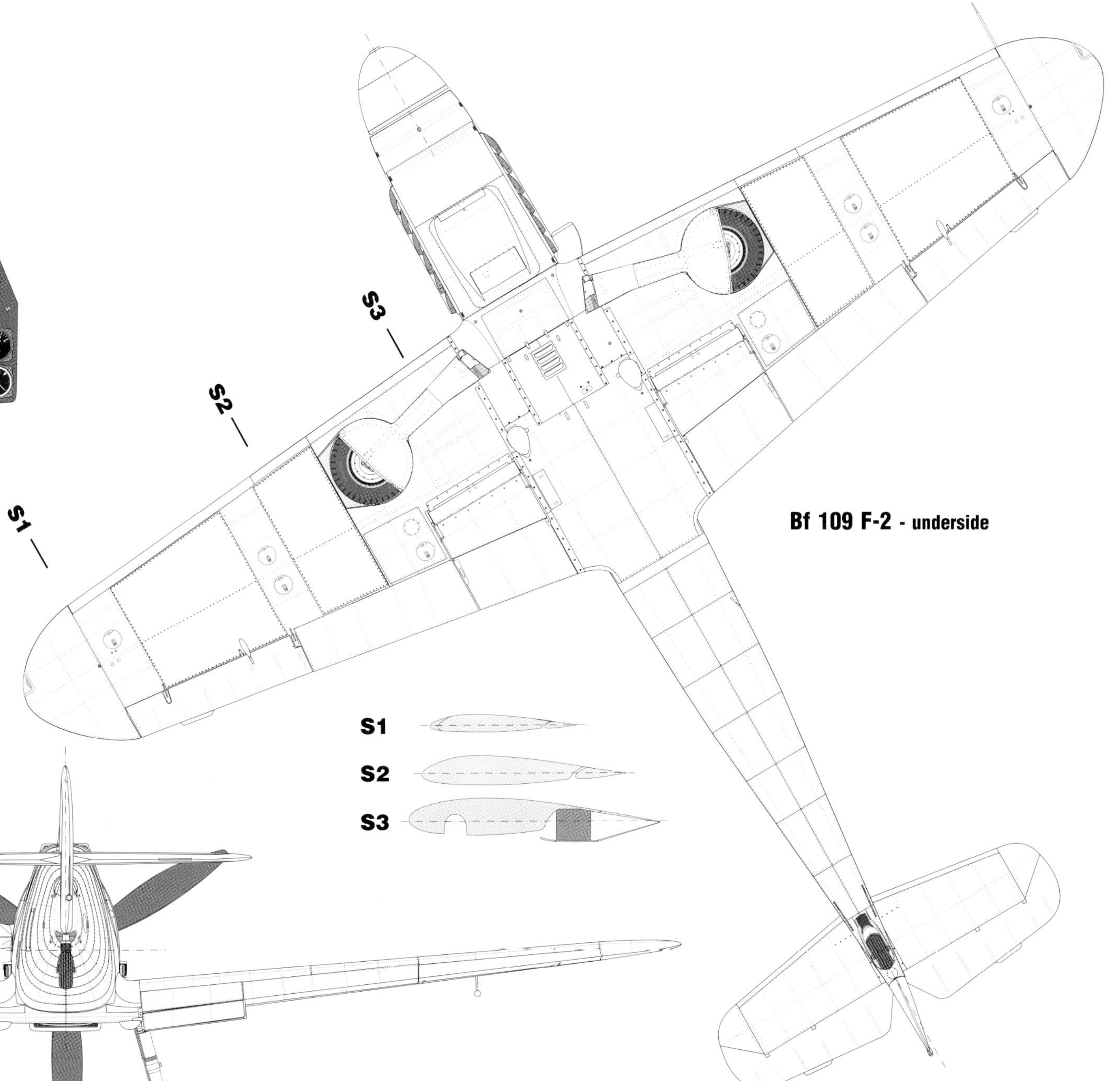

3m

2

1

0,5

0

Scale 1:48

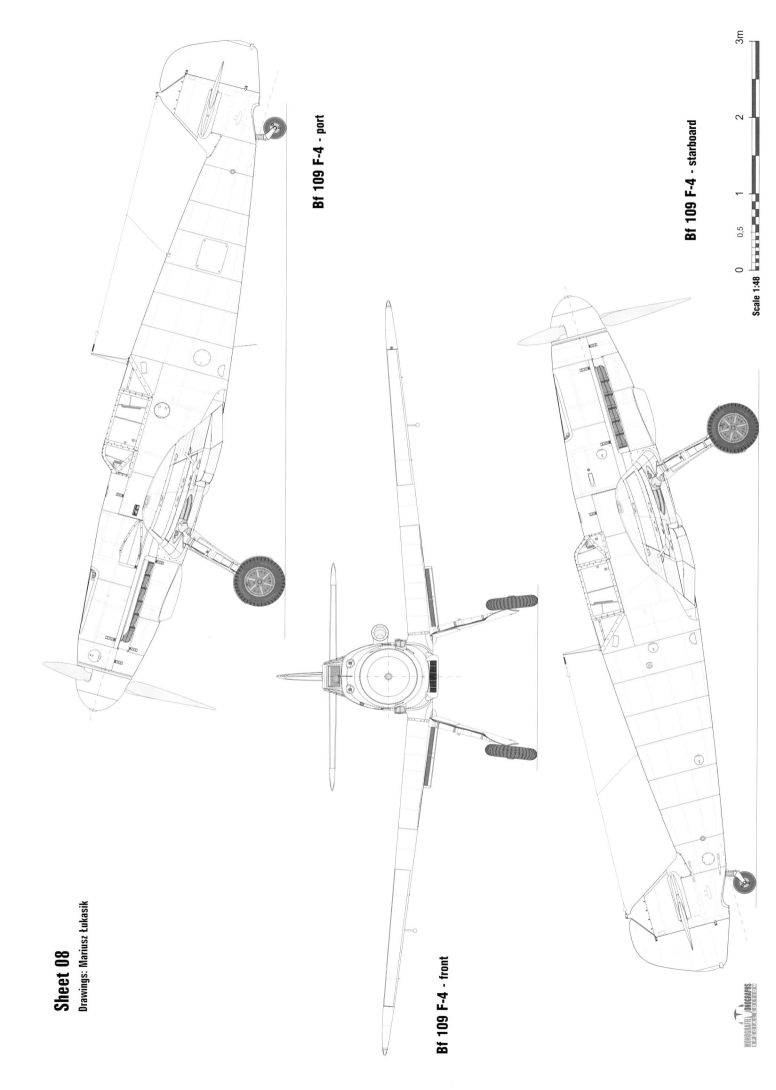

Sheet 08

Drawings: Mariusz Łukasik

Bf 109 F-4 - port

Bf 109 F-4 - front

Bf 109 F-4 - starboard

Scale 1:48

0   0,5   1   2   3m

Sheet 09

Drawings: Mariusz Łukasik

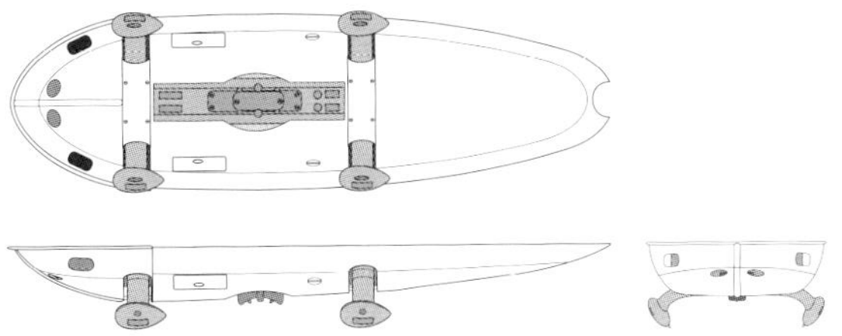

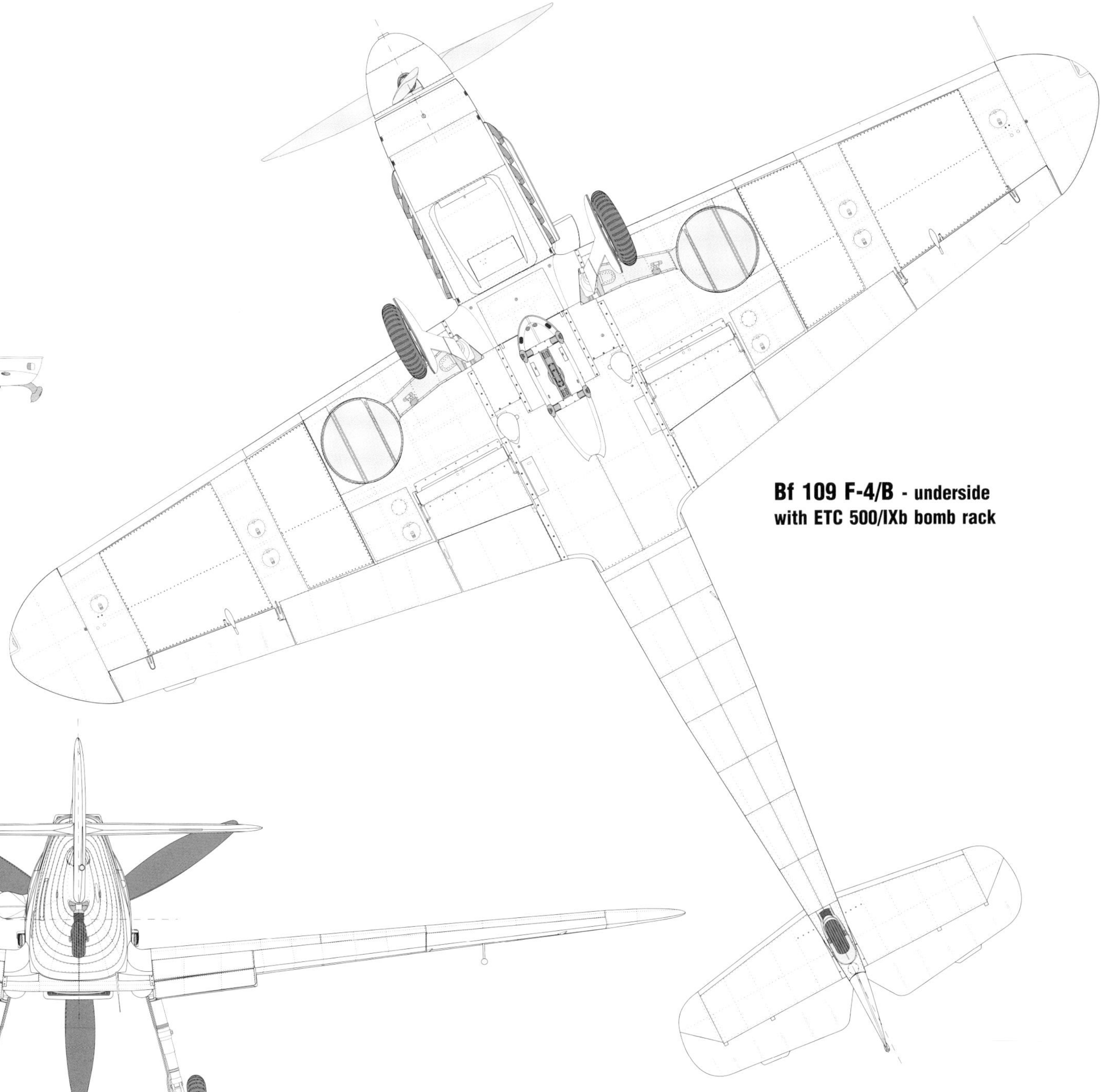

Bf 109 F-4/B - underside
with ETC 500/IXb bomb rack

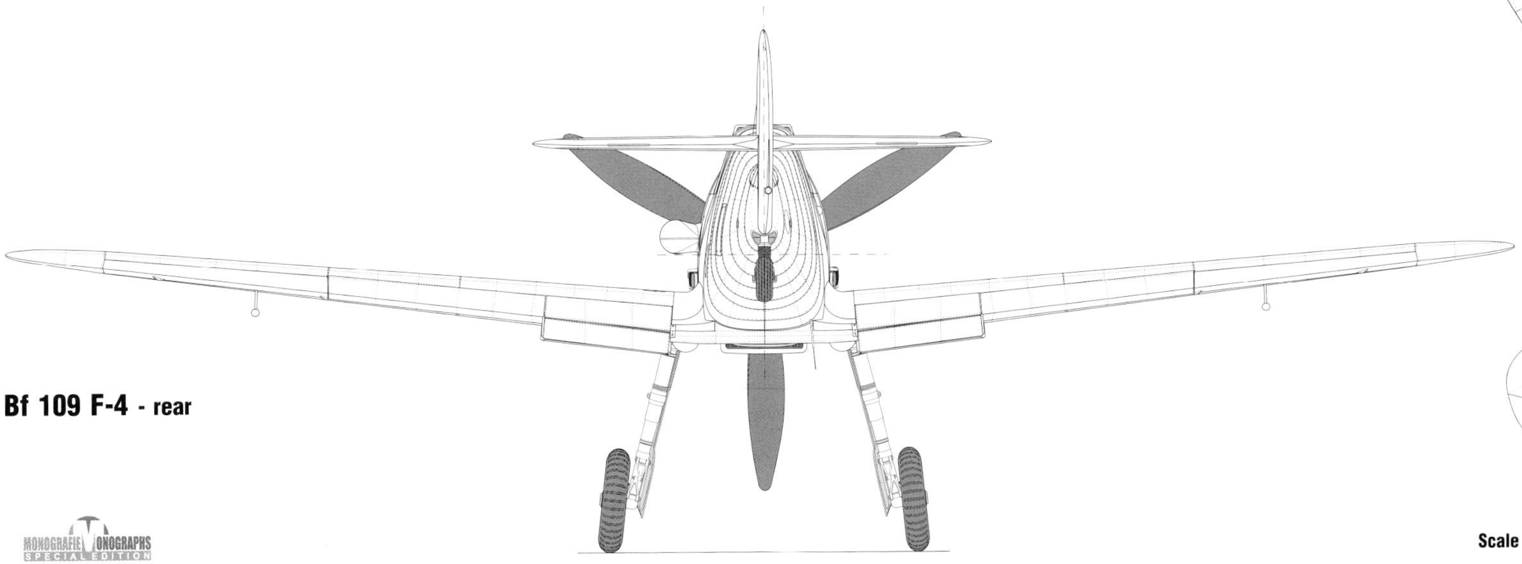

Scale 1:24

ETC 500/IXb bomb rack

Bf 109 F-4 - rear

Scale 1:48

0   0,5   1   2   3m

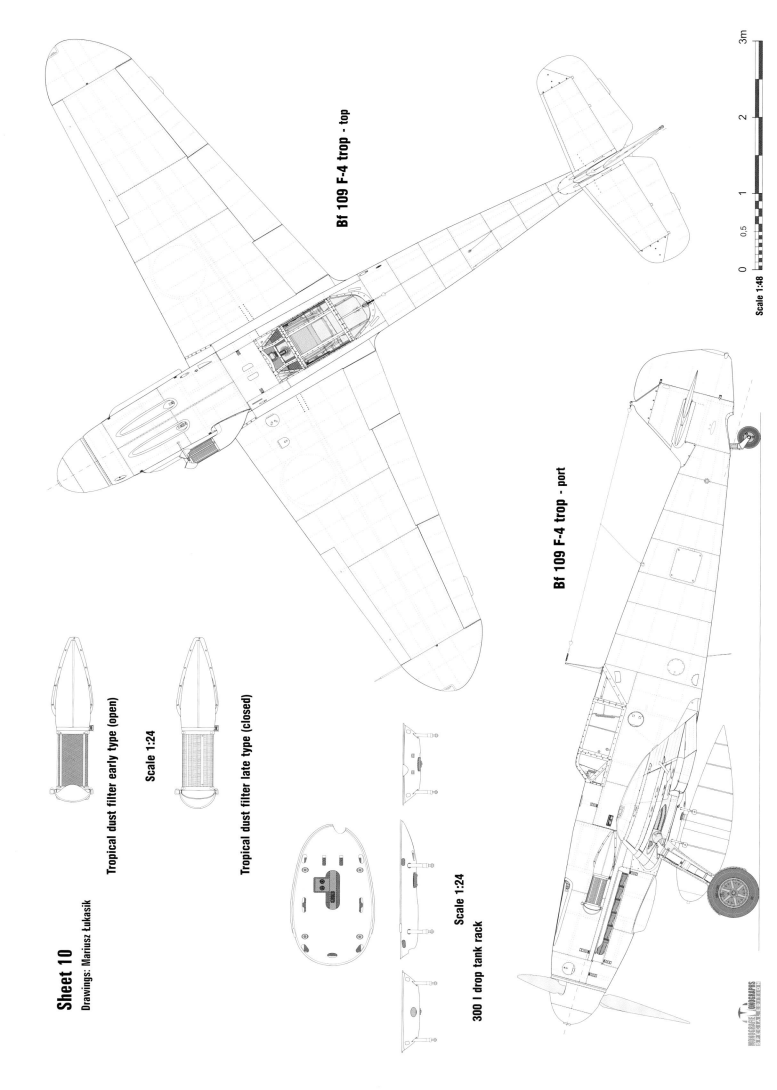

Sheet 10

Drawings: Mariusz Łukasik

Tropical dust filter early type (open)

Scale 1:24

Tropical dust filter late type (closed)

Scale 1:24

300 l drop tank rack

Bf 109 F-4 trop - top

Bf 109 F-4 trop - port

Scale 1:48

3m 2 1 0,5 0

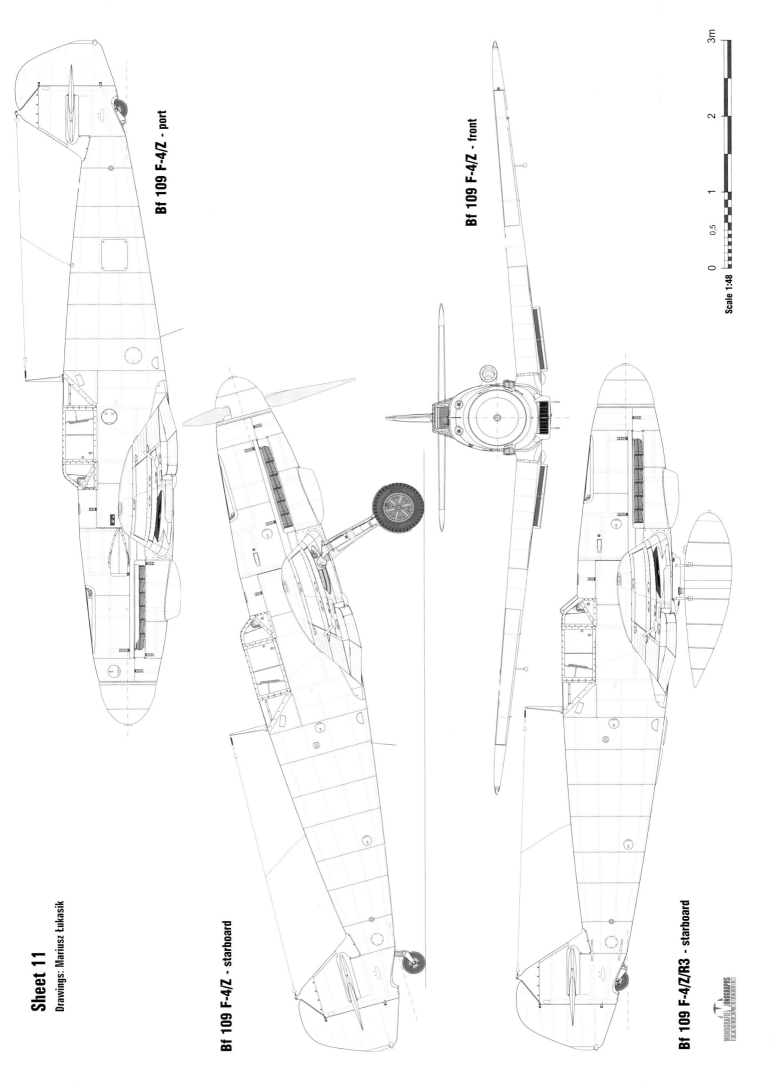

Sheet 11

Drawings: Mariusz Łukasik

Bf 109 F-4/Z - port

Bf 109 F-4/Z - starboard

Bf 109 F-4/Z - front

Bf 109 F-4/Z/R3 - starboard

Scale 1:48

0   0,5   1   2   3m

Sheet 12

Drawings: Mariusz Łukasik

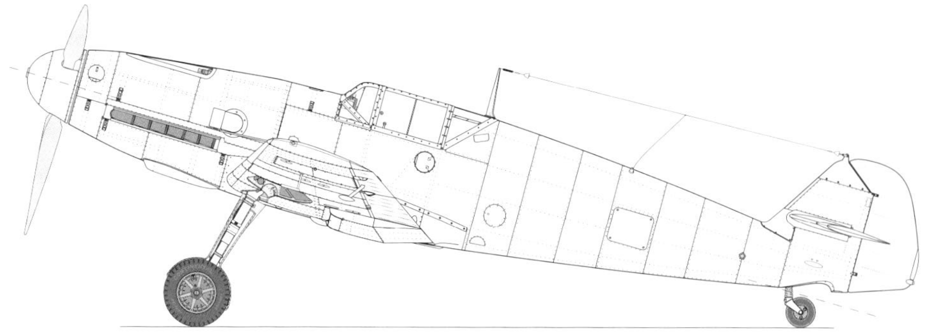

Bf 109 W.Nr. 1801 CE+BP - port

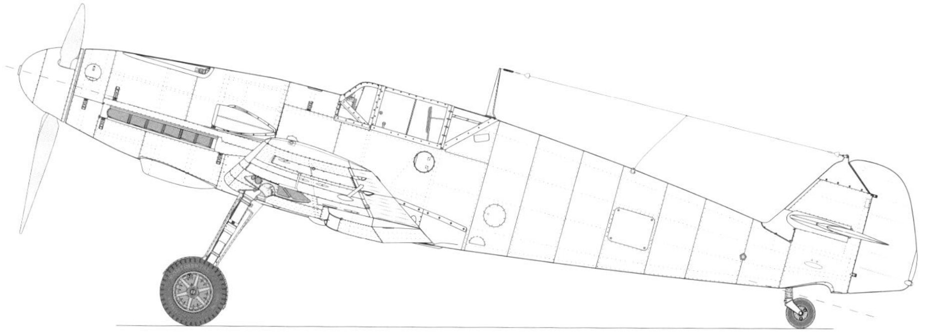

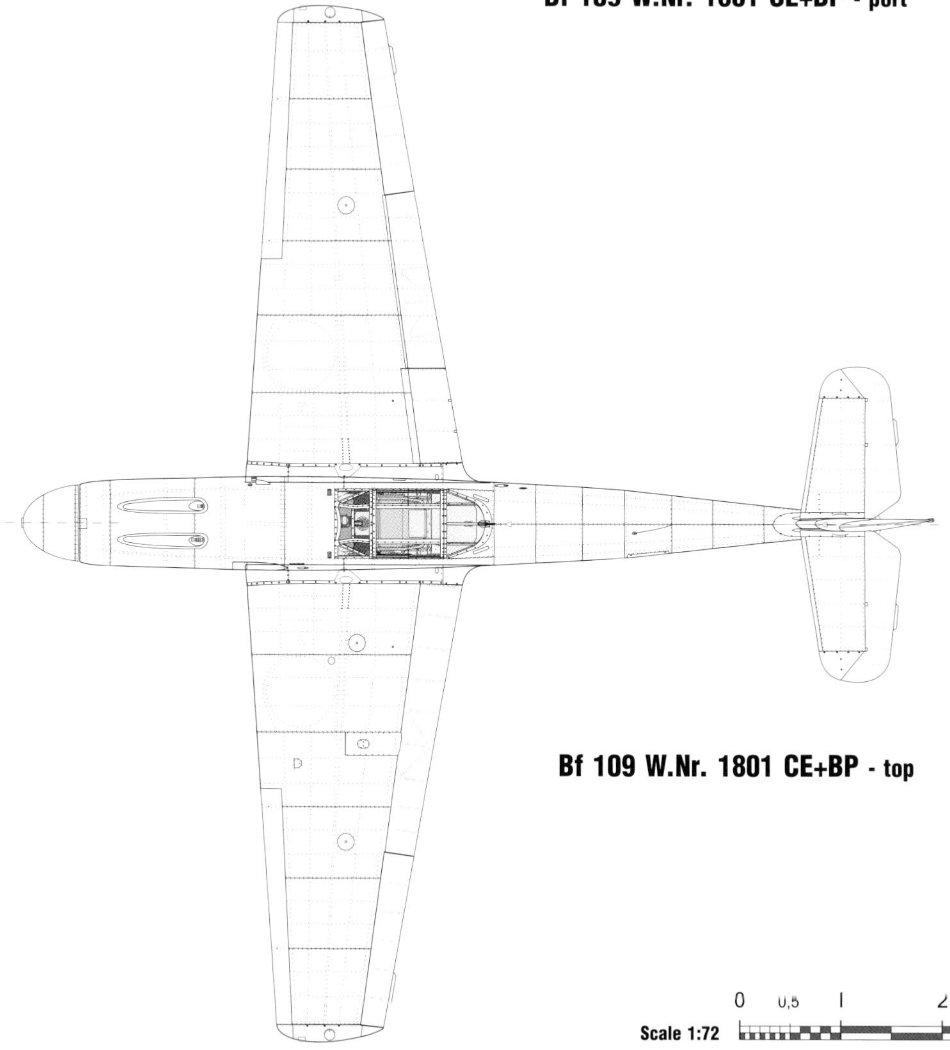

Bf 109 W.Nr. 1801 CE+BP - top

Bf 109 W.Nr. 5604 VK+AB - port

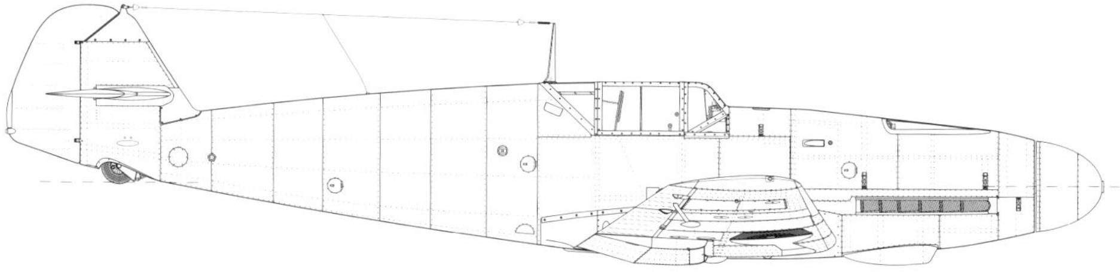

Bf 109 W.Nr. 5604 VK+AB - starboard

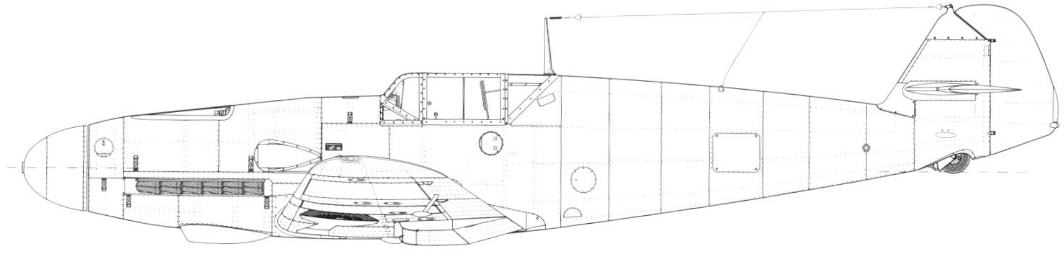

Bf 109 F-1 early - port

Scale 1:72

0   0,5   1   2   3m

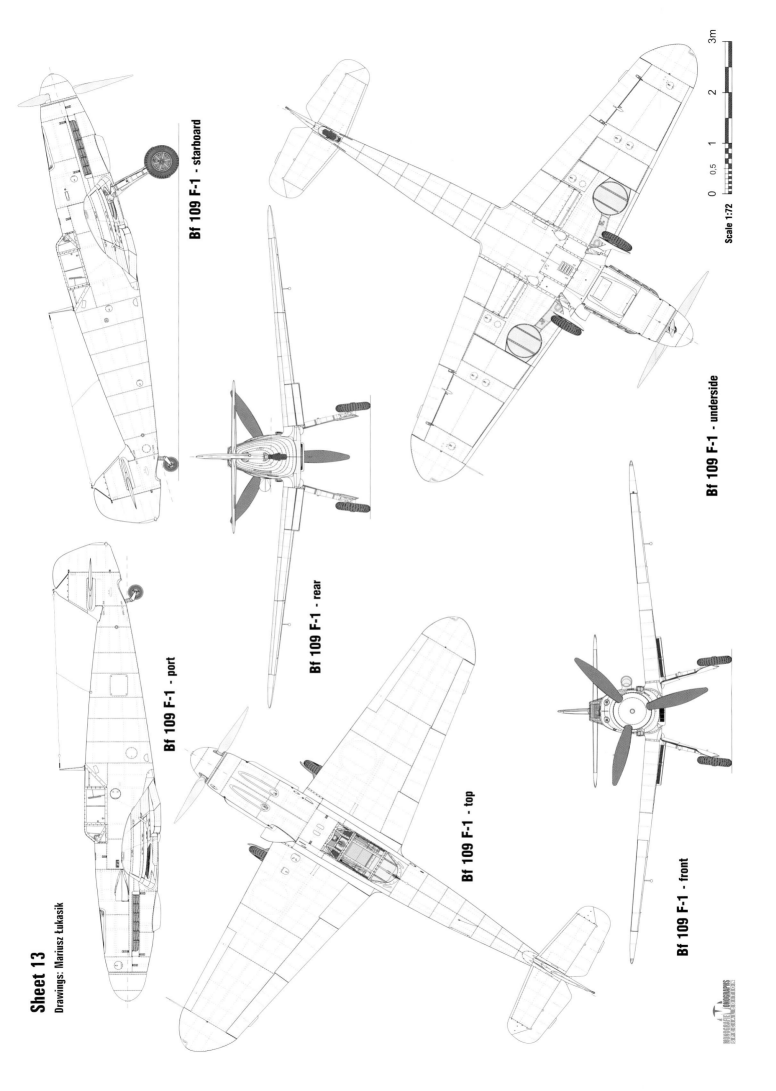

Sheet 13

Drawings: Mariusz Łukasik

Bf 109 F-1 - starboard

Bf 109 F-1 - port

Bf 109 F-1 - underside

Bf 109 F-1 - rear

Bf 109 F-1 - top

Bf 109 F-1 - front

Scale 1:72

0   0,5   1   2   3m

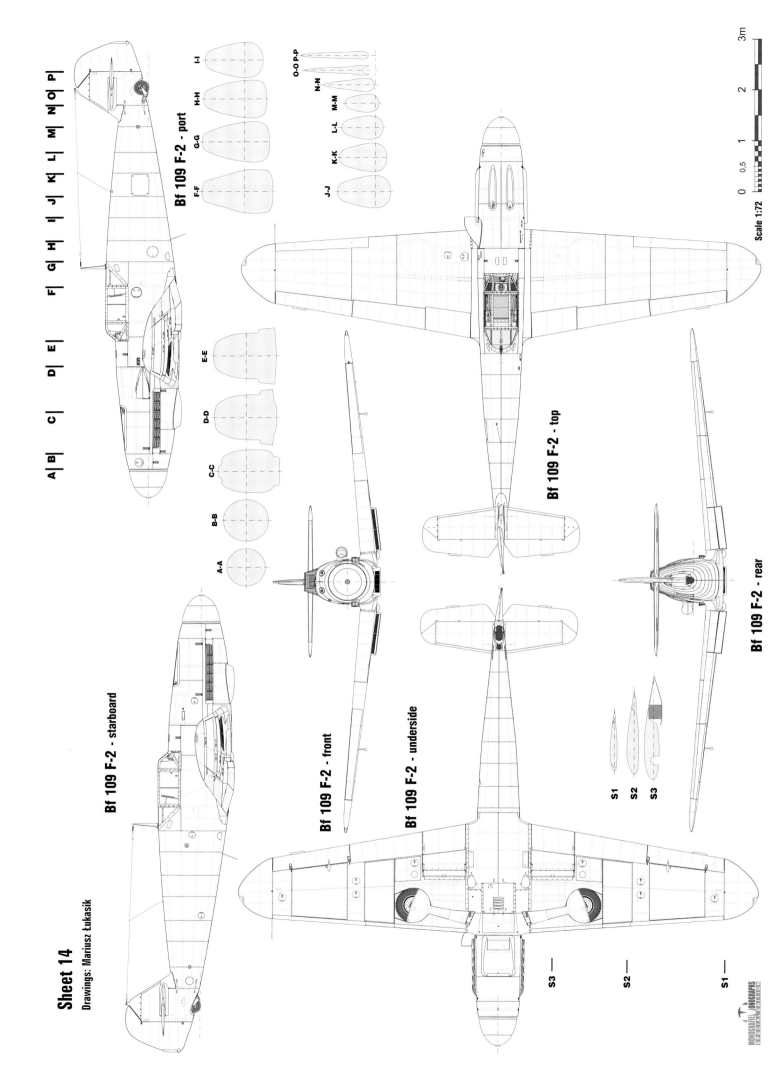

Sheet 14

Drawings: Mariusz Łukasik

A | B | C | D | E | F | G | H | I | J | K | L | M | N | O | P |

Bf 109 F-2 - port

F-F G-G H-H I-I

J-J K-K L-L M-M N-N O-O P-P

A-A B-B C-C D-D E-E

Bf 109 F-2 - starboard

Bf 109 F-2 - front

Bf 109 F-2 - underside

Bf 109 F-2 - top

Bf 109 F-2 - rear

S1
S2
S3

S3 —
S2 —
S1 —

Scale 1:72

0   0,5   1   2   3m

Sheet 15

Drawings: Mariusz Łukasik

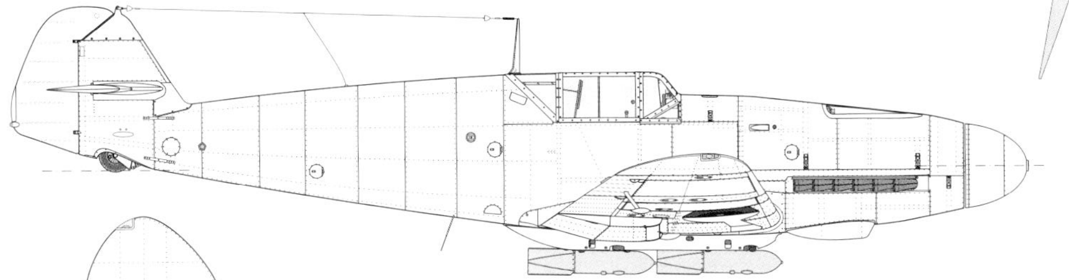

Bf 109 F-2/B - starboard
with ETC 50/VIIId bomb rack and four 50 kg bombs

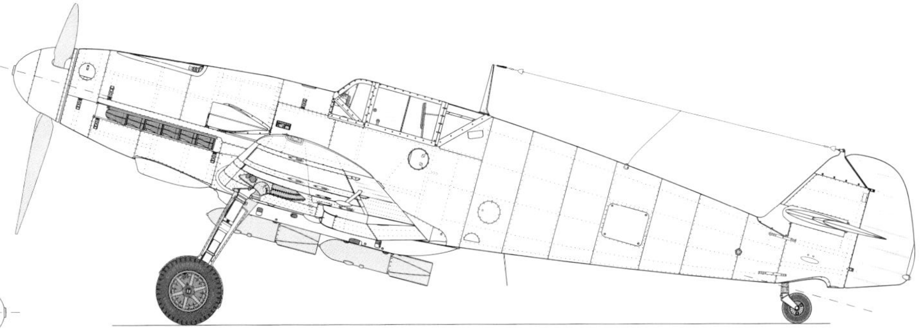

Bf 109 F-2/B - port
with ETC 50/VIIId bomb rack and four 50 kg bombs

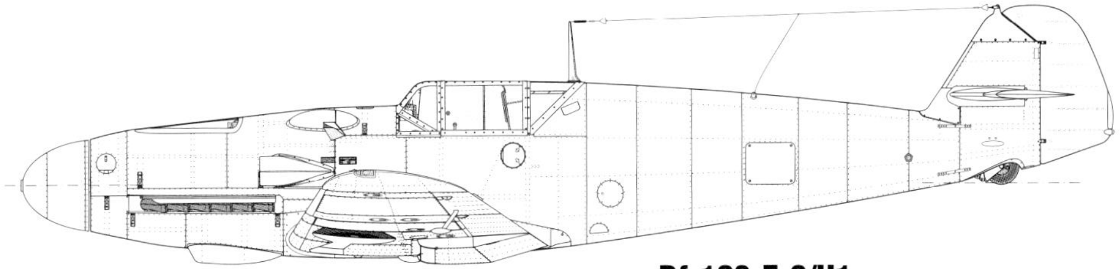

Bf 109 F-2/U1 - port

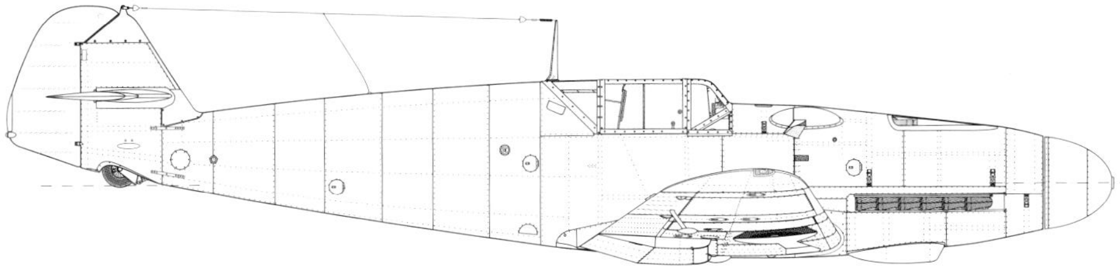

Bf 109 F-2/U1 - starboard

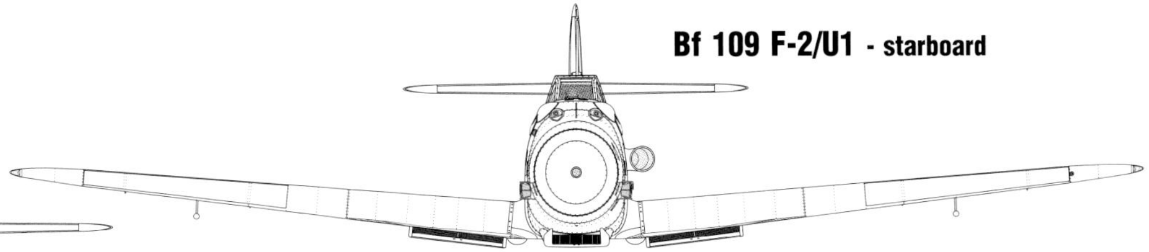

Bf 109 F-2/U1 - front

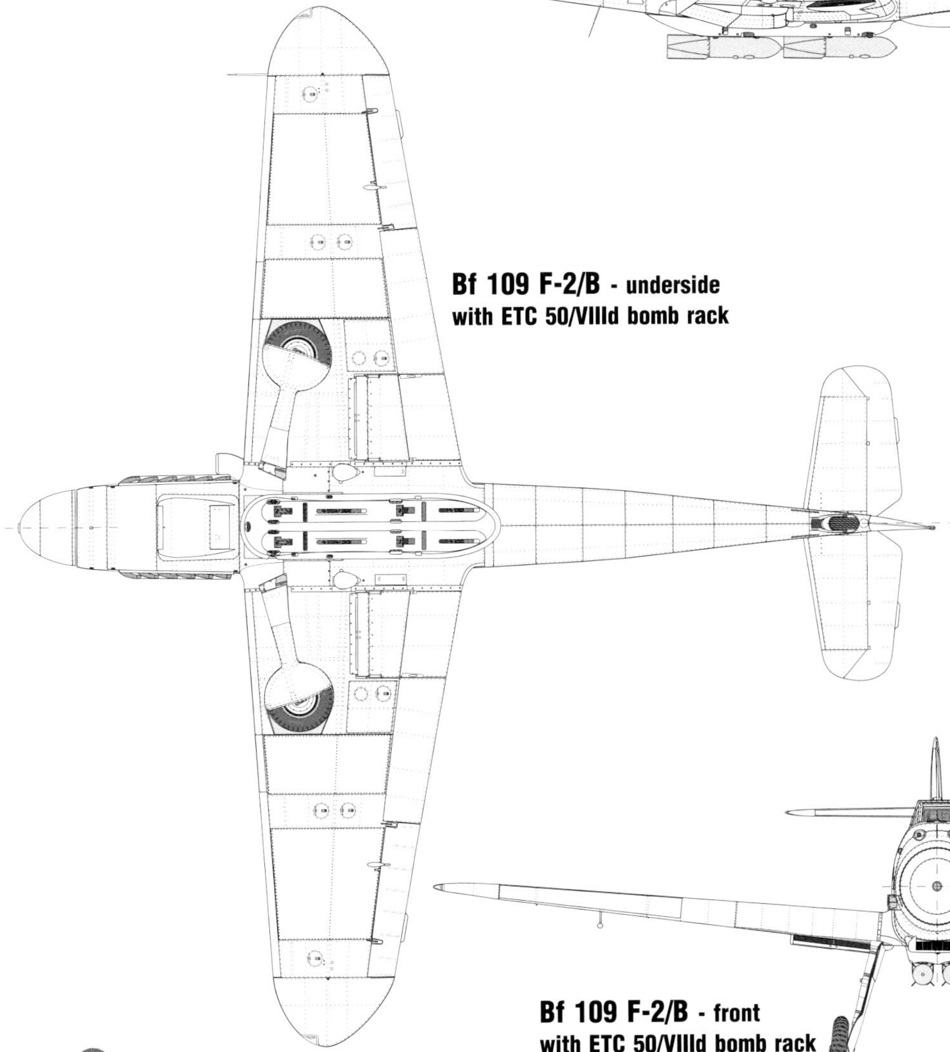

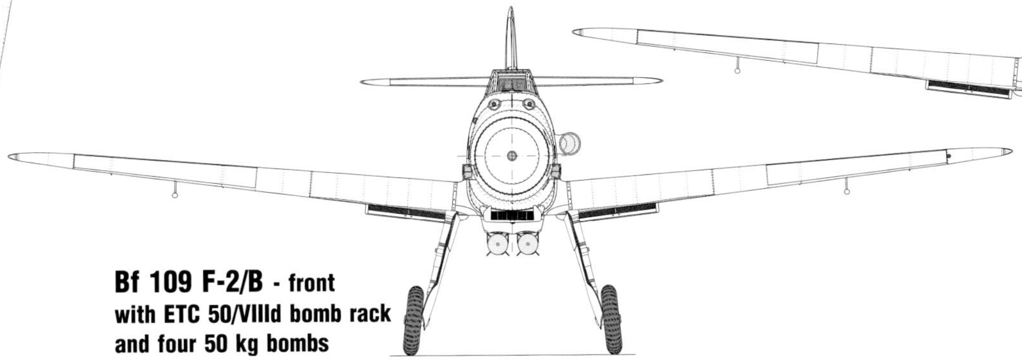

Bf 109 F-2/B - underside
with ETC 50/VIIId bomb rack

Bf 109 F-2/B - front
with ETC 50/VIIId bomb rack
and four 50 kg bombs

Scale 1:72

0   0,5   1   2   3m

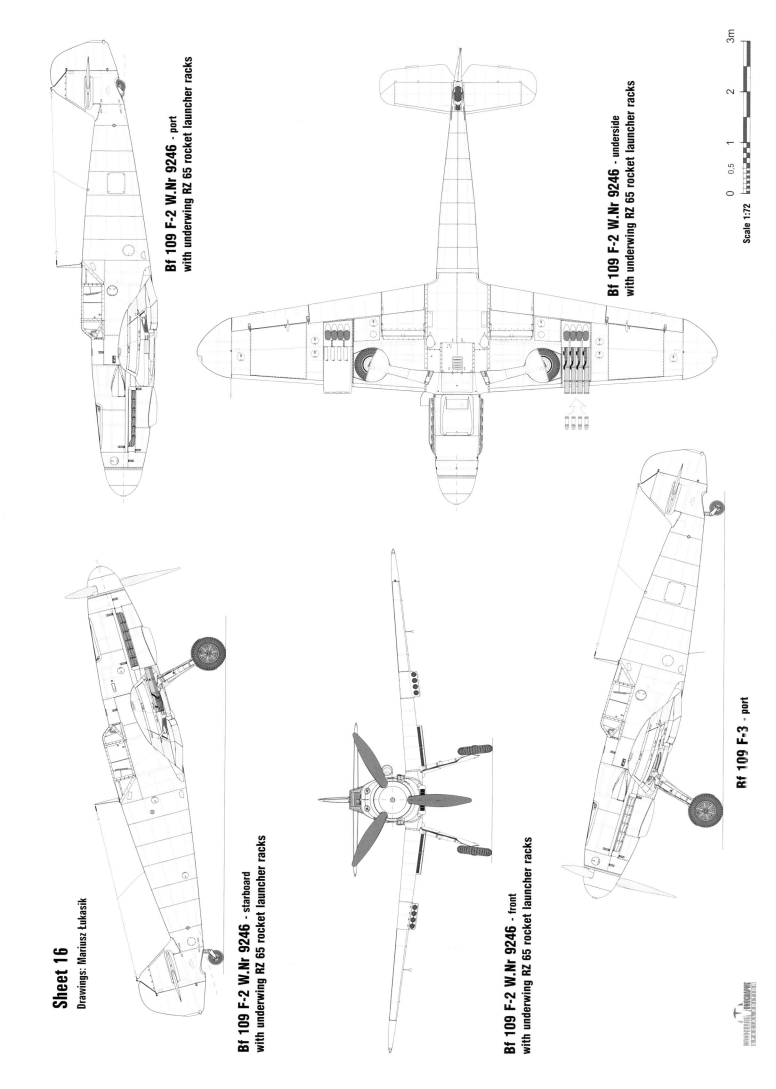

Sheet 16

Drawings: Mariusz Łukasik

Bf 109 F-2 W.Nr 9246 - port
with underwing RZ 65 rocket launcher racks

Bf 109 F-2 W.Nr 9246 - underside
with underwing RZ 65 rocket launcher racks

Bf 109 F-2 W.Nr 9246 - starboard
with underwing RZ 65 rocket launcher racks

Bf 109 F-2 W.Nr 9246 - front
with underwing RZ 65 rocket launcher racks

Rf 109 F-3 - port

Scale 1:72

0   0,5   1   2   3m

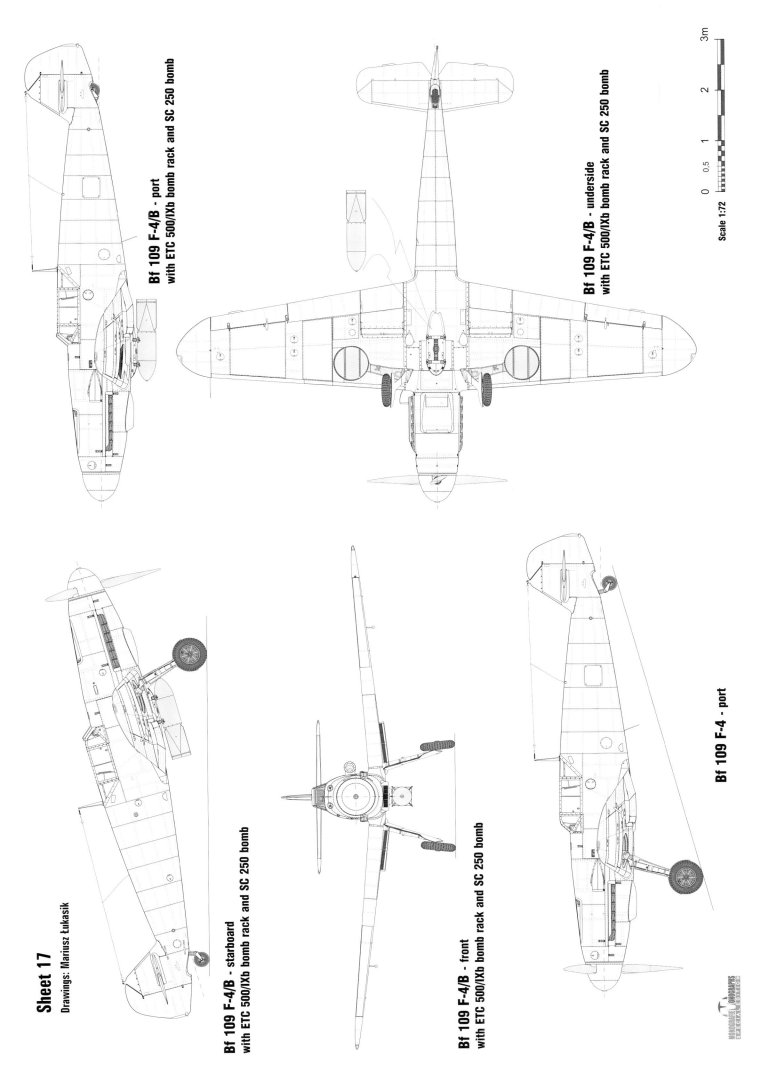

Sheet 17

Drawings: Mariusz Łukasik

Bf 109 F-4/B - port
with ETC 500/IXb bomb rack and SC 250 bomb

Bf 109 F-4/B - underside
with ETC 500/IXb bomb rack and SC 250 bomb

Scale 1:72

0   0,5   1   2   3m

Bf 109 F-4/B - starboard
with ETC 500/IXb bomb rack and SC 250 bomb

Bf 109 F-4/B - front
with ETC 500/IXb bomb rack and SC 250 bomb

Bf 109 F-4 - port

MONOGRAFIE LOTNICZE SPECIAL EDITION

Drawings: Mariusz Łukasik

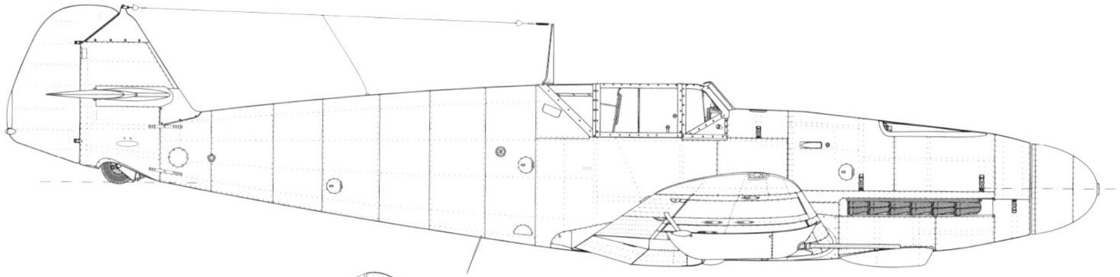

Bf 109 F-4/R1 - starboard
with MG 151/20 underwing cannons

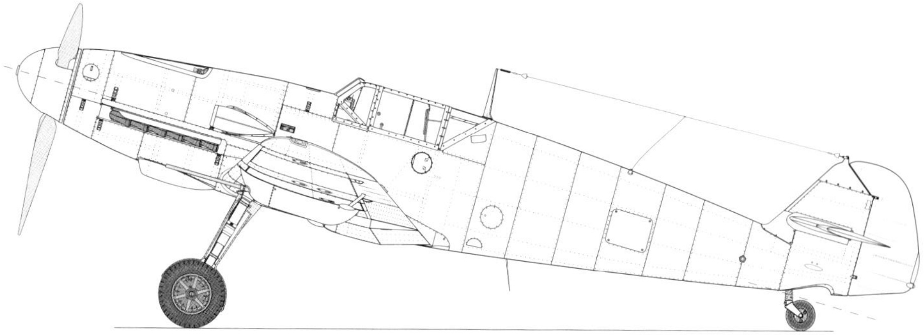

Bf 109 F-4/R1 - port
with MG 151/20 underwing cannons

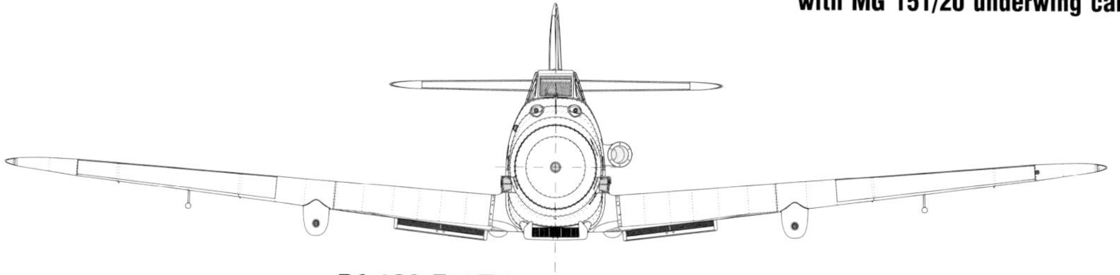

Bf 109 F-4/R1 - front
with MG 151/20 underwing cannons

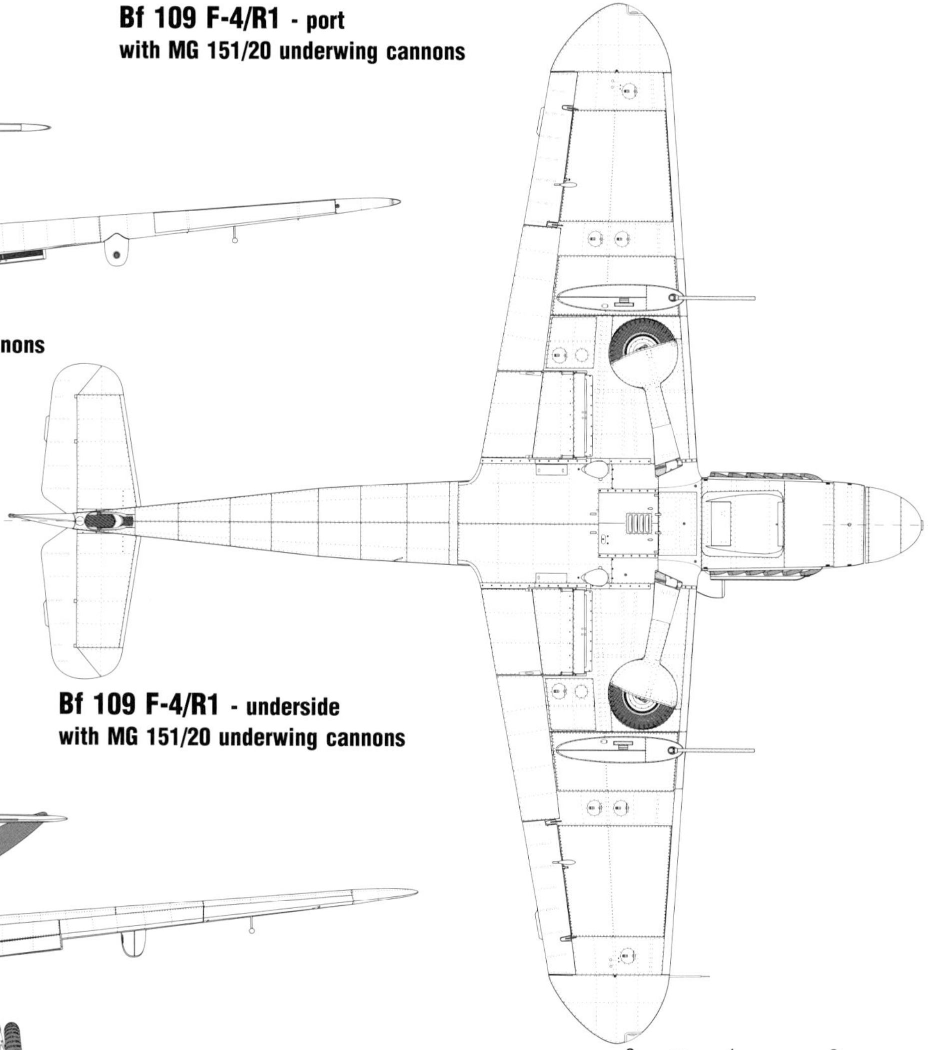

Bf 109 F-4/R1 - underside
with MG 151/20 underwing cannons

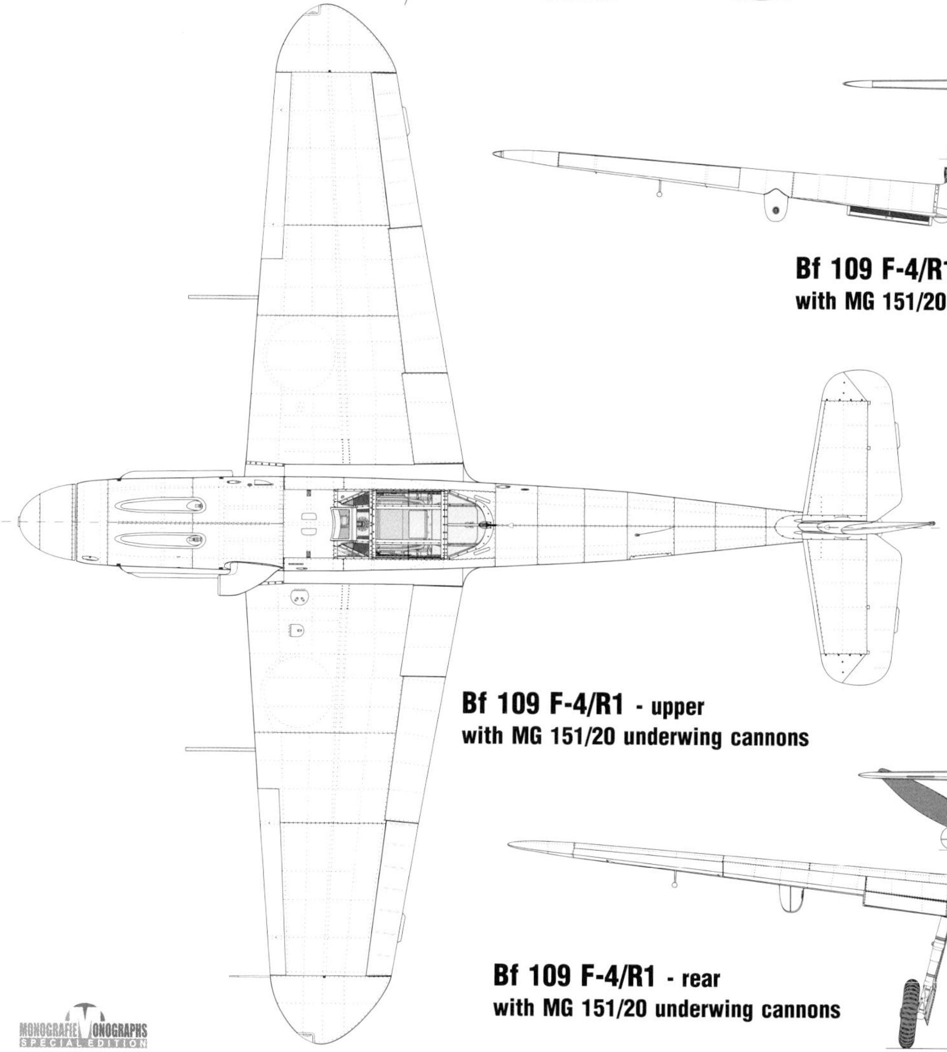

Bf 109 F-4/R1 - upper
with MG 151/20 underwing cannons

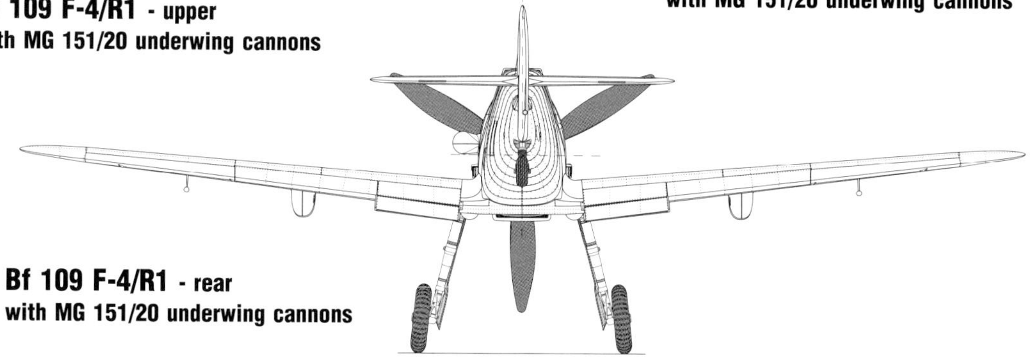

Bf 109 F-4/R1 - rear
with MG 151/20 underwing cannons

Scale 1:72

0   0,5   1   2   3m

Sheet 19

Drawings: Mariusz Łukasik

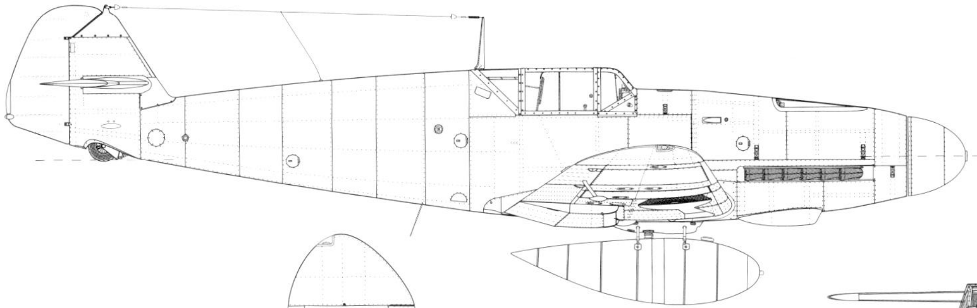

Bf 109 F-4 trop - starboard
with 300 l drop tank

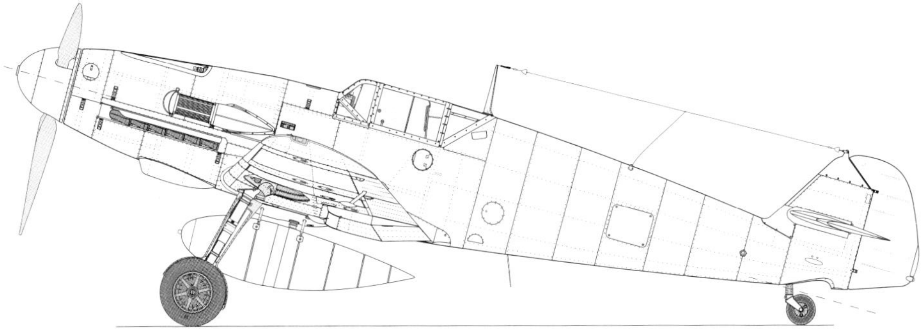

Bf 109 F-4 trop - port
with 300 l drop tank

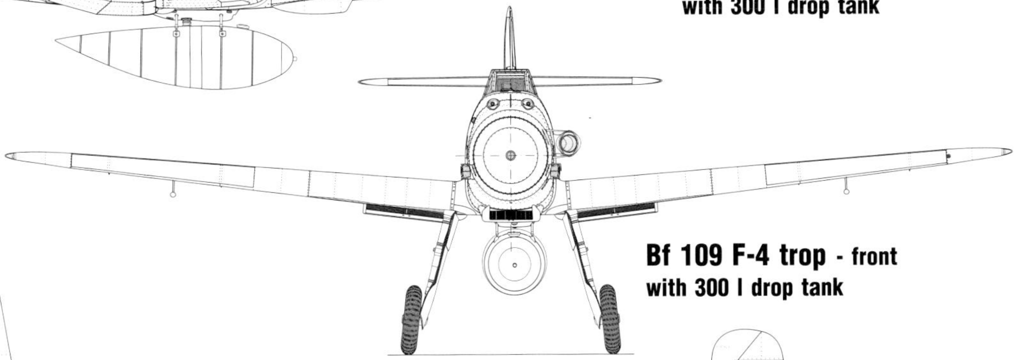

Bf 109 F-4 trop - front
with 300 l drop tank

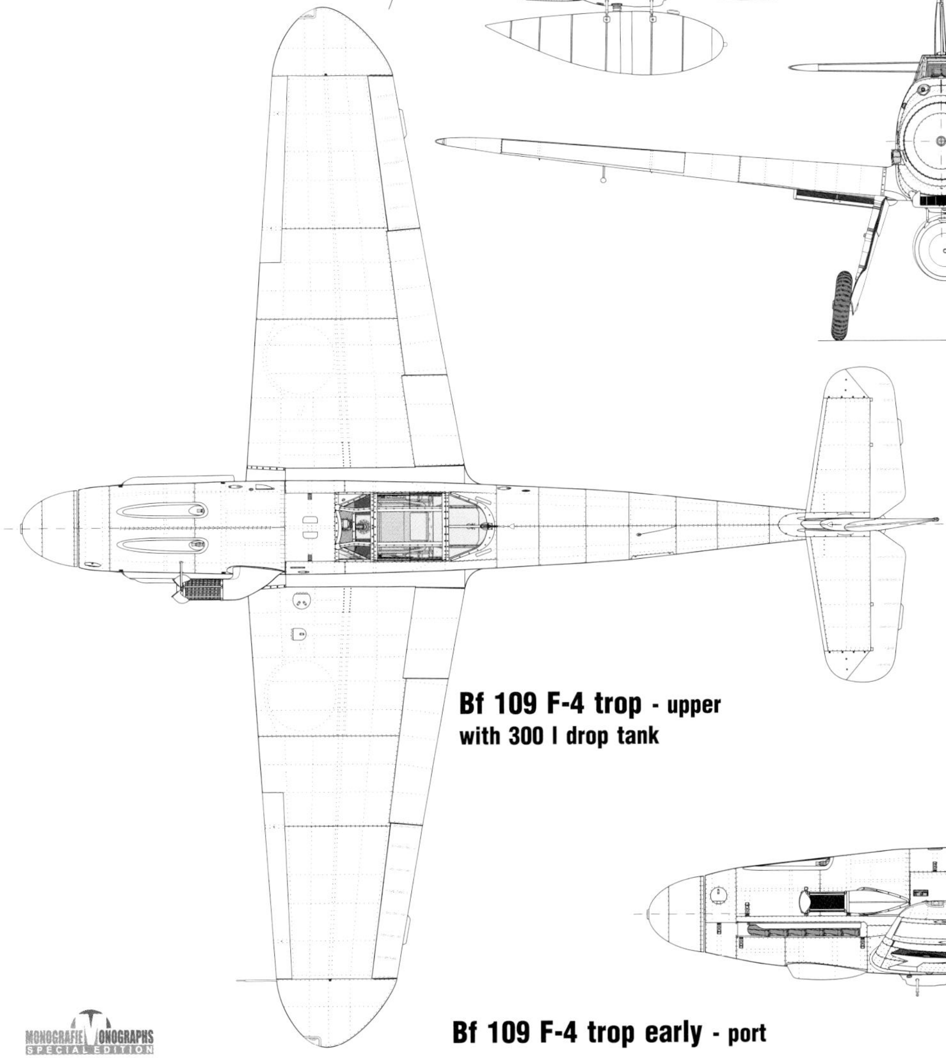

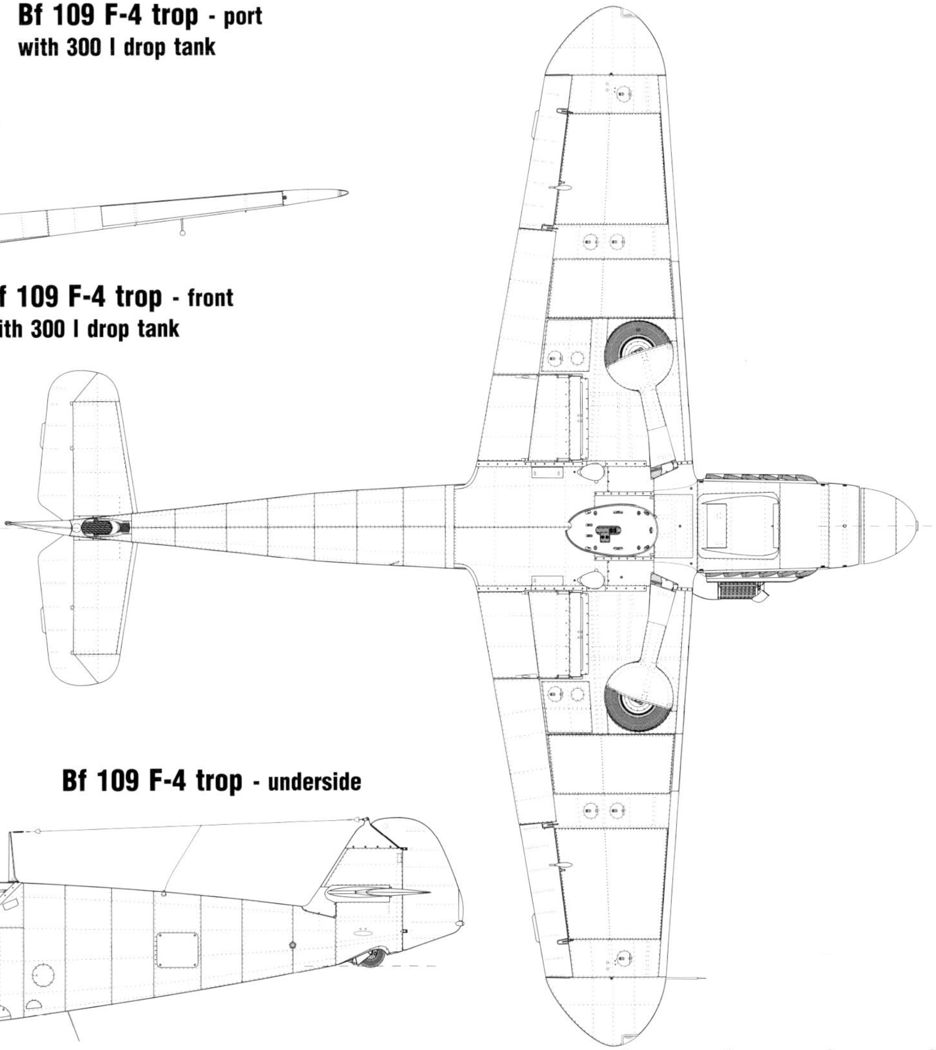

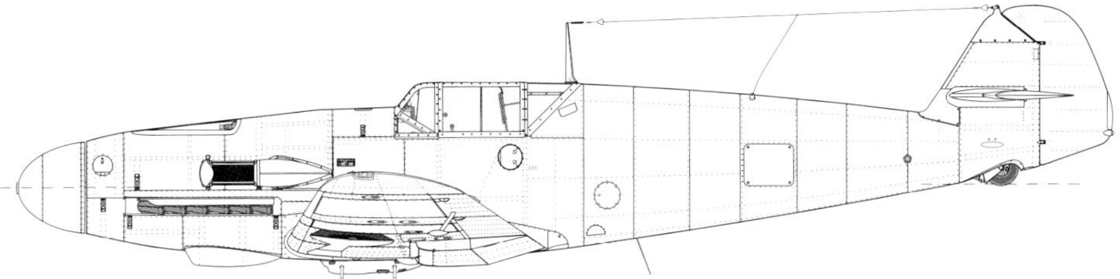

Bf 109 F-4 trop - upper
with 300 l drop tank

Bf 109 F-4 trop - underside

Bf 109 F-4 trop early - port

MONOGRAFIE MONOGRAPHS SPECIAL EDITION

Scale 1:72

0 0,5 1 2 3m

Specification of external changes

Bf 109 F-1

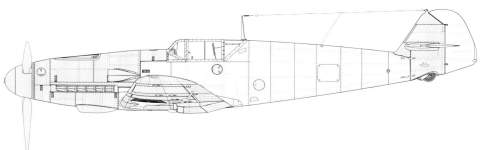

New VDM 9-11207A propeller
New spinner
DB 601 N engine
MG-FF/M engine-mounted cannon
Modified engine cowling panels
Enlarged oil cooler
New supercharger air intake
Fuel tank filler point under the cockpit sill on the port fuselage
Master compass hatch in the fuselage between Frame 2 & 3
Modified tail assembly
External stiffeners on the rear fuselage
Semi-retractable tailwheel
Wing with elliptical wingtips
Pitot tube on the port wingtip
Modified slats and flaps
New wing-mounted coolant radiators

Bf 109 F-2

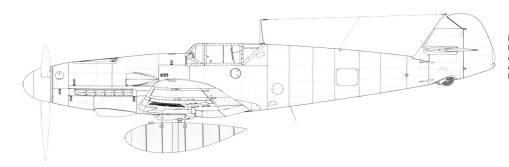

MG-151/15 engine-mounted cannon
FuG 25 IFF set antenna
Adaptation to install 300 l drop tank
Adaptation to install under-fuselage bomb racks
in fighter-bomber variants

Bf 109 F-3

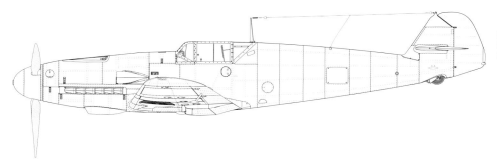

DB 601 E engine
VDM 9-12010A propeller
MG-FF/M engine-mounted cannon

Bf 109 F-4

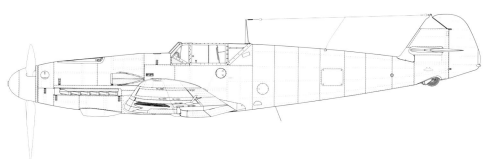

MG 151/20 engine-mounted cannon
Modified supercharger air intake (not applicable to early-built aircraft)
External stiffeners on the rear fuselage deleted in the course
of series production
External armour-glass panel on the front of the windscreen
retrofitted more frequently than to the Bf 109 F-2
Circular wheel wells in majority of produced aircraft

Bf 109 F-4/Z

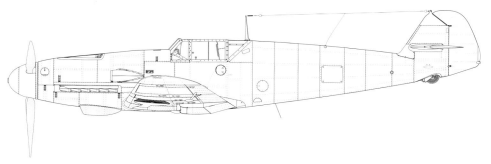

Deeper Fö 870 oil cooler
VDM 9-12087A propeller with wider blades in several aircraft

Sheet 20

Drawings: Mariusz Łukasik

0   0,5   1   2   3m

Scale 1:72

Changes

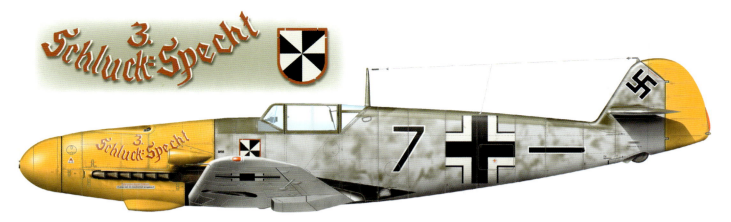

Messerschmitt Bf 109 F-2; 'Black 7', flown by Lt. Horst Buddenhagen of 5./JG 3, Darmstadt-Griesheim, April 1941.

Messerschmitt Bf 109 F-2; 'White 1', flown by Oblt. Kurt Sochatzy, *Staffelkapitän* of 7./JG 3, France, May-June 1941.

Messerschmitt Bf 109 F-2, W.Nr. 8165, flown by Oblt. Karl-Heinz Leesmann, *Gruppenkommandeur* of I./JG 52, Leeuwarden, June 1941.

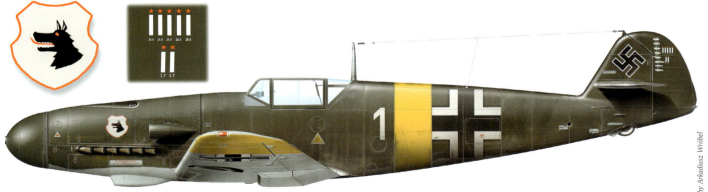

Messerschmitt Bf 109 F-4; W.Nr. 8334, 'White 1', flown by Oblt. Wolfdieter Huy, *Staffelkapitän* of 7./JG 77, Jassy, 5th July 1941.

Painted by Arkadiusz Wróbel

Messerschmitt Bf 109 F-2; W.Nr. 5749, flown by Hptm. Hans 'Assi' Hahn, *Gruppenkommandeur* of III./JG 2, St. Pol, mid-July 1941.

Messerschmitt Bf 109 F-4; W.Nr. 7087, flown by Maj. Hanns Trübenbach, *Geschwaderkommodore* of JG 52, Bucharest-Pipera, 15th July 1941.

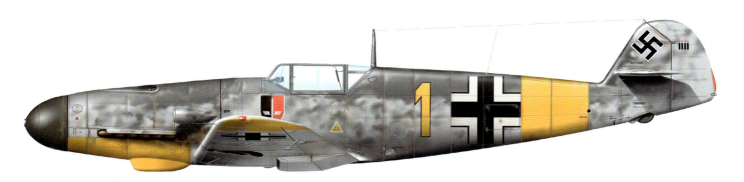

Messerschmitt Bf 109 F-2; W.Nr. 12848, 'Yellow 1', flown by Oblt. Rudolf Resch, *Staffelkapitän* of 6./JG 52, Andreyeva, 30th July 1941.

Messerschmitt Bf 109 F-2; 'White 9', flown by Oblt. Hans Philipp, *Staffelkapitän* of 4./JG 54, Mal. Owsischtschi, 10th August 1941.

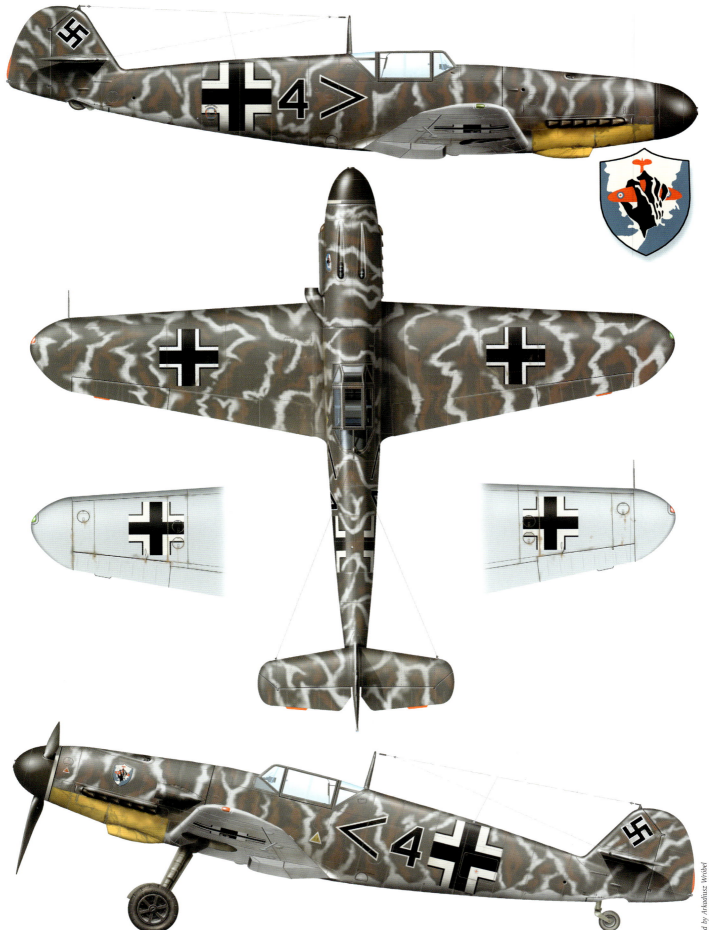

Messerschmitt Bf 109 F-2; W.Nr. 8165, flown by Uffz. Fritz Geissler of Stab I./JG 52, Katwijk, September 1941.

Painted by Arkadiusz Wróbel

Messerschmitt Bf 109 F-4/Z; W.Nr. 7308, 'Black 1', flown by Oblt. Günther Rall, *Staffelkapitän* of 8./JG 52, Stschastliwaja, 30th August 1941.

Messerschmitt Bf 109 F-4; 'Black 13', flown by Oblt. Kurt Ubben, *Staffelkapitän* of 8./JG 77, Berislav, early September 1941.

Messerschmitt Bf 109 F-4; W.Nr. 7017, 'White 8', flown by Fw. Josef Zwernemann of 7./JG 52, Berislav, 14th September 1941.

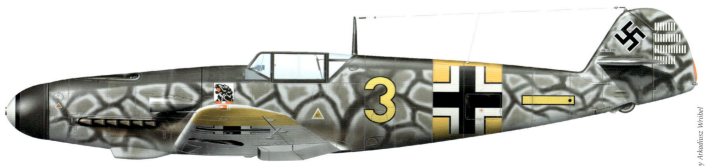

Messerschmitt Bf 109 F-2; W.Nr. 9588, 'Yellow 3', flown by Hptm. Franz Eckerle, *Staffelkapitän* of 6./JG 54, Staraja Russa, October 1941.

Painted by Arkadiusz Wróbel

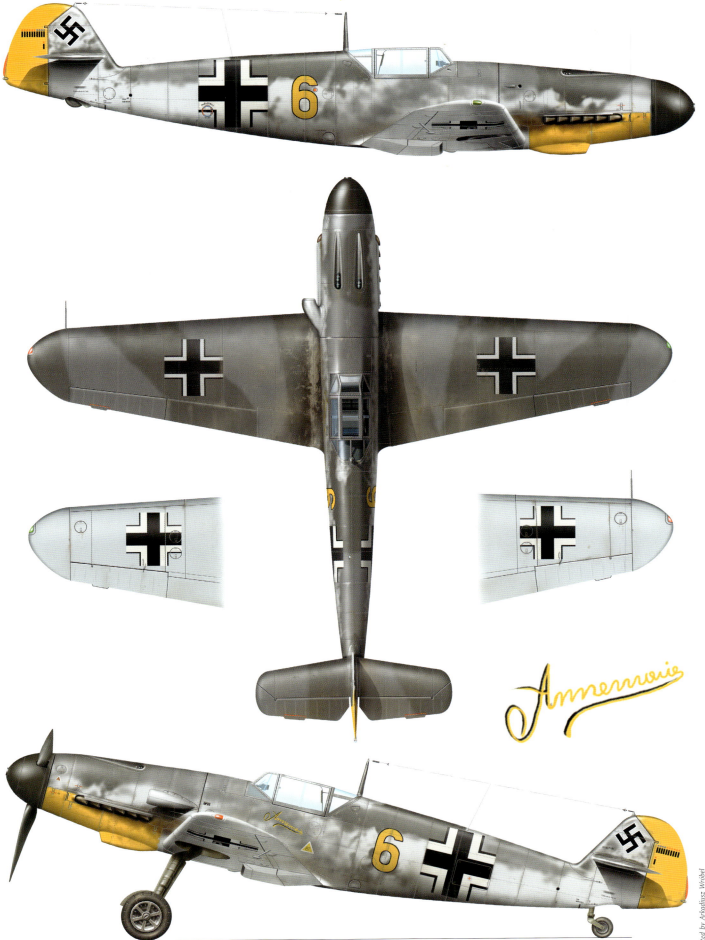

Messerschmitt Bf 109 F-4; W.Nr. 7194, 'Yellow 6', flown by Uffz. Karl Willius of 3./JG 26, St. Omer, autumn 1941.

Painted by Arkadiusz Wróbel

Messerschmitt Bf 109 F-4; W.Nr. 7187, 'White 4', flown by Fw. Fritz Dinger of 4./JG 53, Sologubovka, October 1941.

Messerschmitt Bf 109 F-2; 'Black 12', flown by Uffz. Peter Bremer of 2./JG 54, Russia, late autumn 1941.

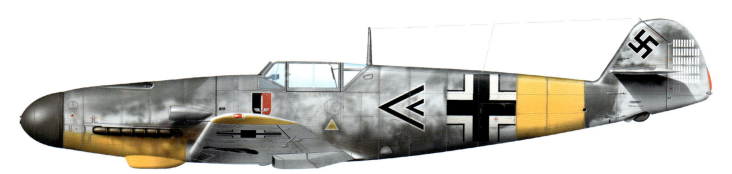

Messerschmitt Bf 109 F-4; W.Nr. 13744, flown by Oblt. Johannes Steinhoff, *Gruppenkommandeur* of II./JG 52; Klin, 3rd December 1941.

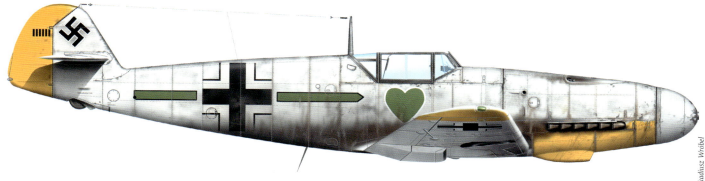

Messerschmitt Bf 109 F-4; probable W.Nr. 7243, flown by Oblt. Otto Kath, *Geschwader Adjutant* of JG 54, Siverskaya, Winter of 1941/1942.

Painted by Arkadiusz Wróbel

Messerschmitt Bf 109 F-2; 'Black 8', flown by Fw. Herbert Brönnle of 2./JG 54, Krasnogvardeisk, 16th March 1942.

Painted by Arkadiusz Wróbel

Messerschmitt Bf 109 F-2; flown by Hptm. Hans Philipp, *Gruppenkommandeur* of I./JG 54, Krasnogvardeisk, 22nd March 1942.

Messerschmitt Bf 109 F-4/Z; W.Nr. 7391, 'Black 5', flown by Fw. Gerhard Köppen of 8./JG 52, Kharkov, spring 1942.

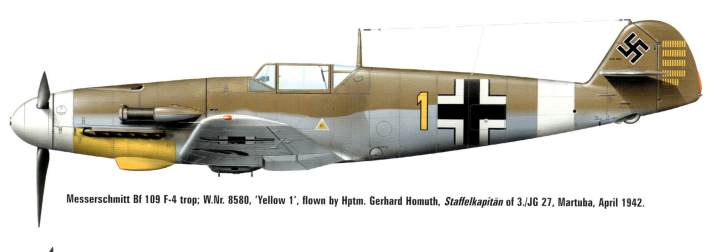

Messerschmitt Bf 109 F-4 trop; W.Nr. 8580, 'Yellow 1', flown by Hptm. Gerhard Homuth, *Staffelkapitän* of 3./JG 27, Martuba, April 1942.

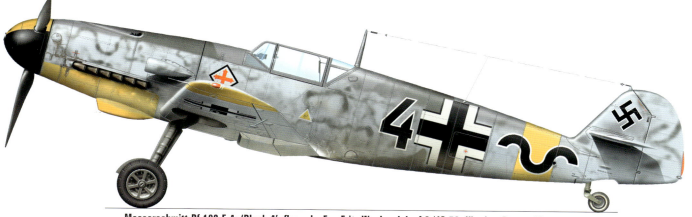

Messerschmitt Bf 109 F-4; 'Black 4', flown by Fw. Fritz Wachowiak of 8./JG 52, Kharkov-Rogan, May 1942.

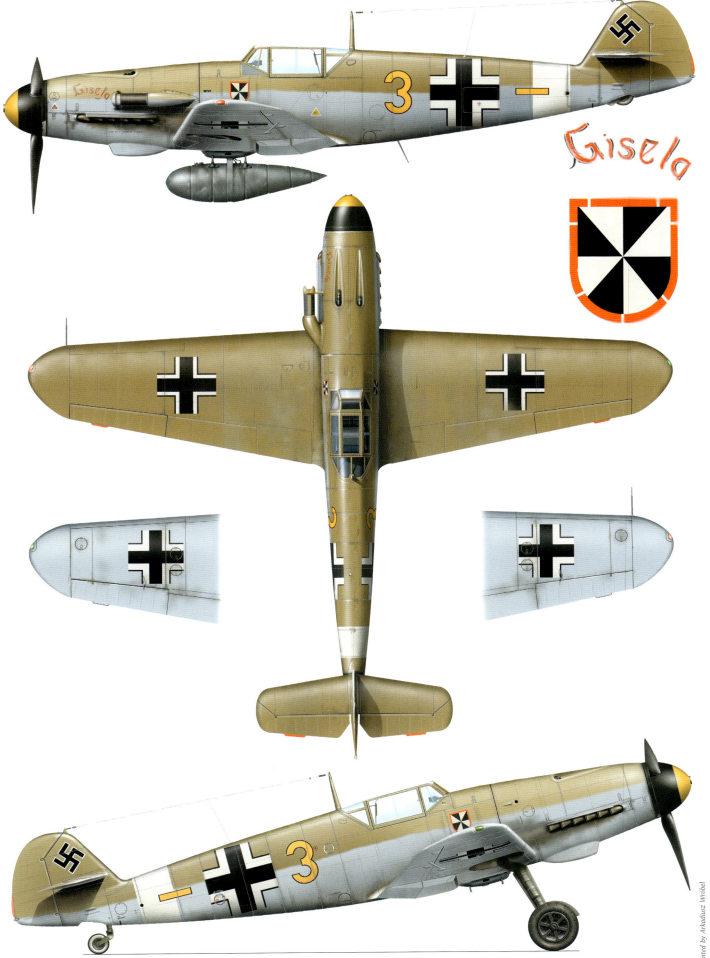

Gisela

Messerschmitt Bf 109 F-4 trop; 'Yellow 3', flown by Uffz. Franz Schwaiger of 6./JG 3, Martuba, April 1942.

Painted by Arkadiusz Wróbel

Messerschmitt Bf 109 F-4; 'Yellow 5', flown by Fw. Alfred Grislawski of 9./JG 52, Kharkov-Rogan, May 1942.

Messerschmitt Bf 109 F-4/R1; W.Nr. 13206, 'Black 1', flown by Oblt. Siegfried Simsch, *Staffelkapitän* of 5./JG 52, Grammatikovo, May 1942.

Messerschmitt Bf 109 F-4/Z trop; 'White 5', flown by Lt. Jürgen Harder of 7./JG 53, Martuba, 17th June 1942.

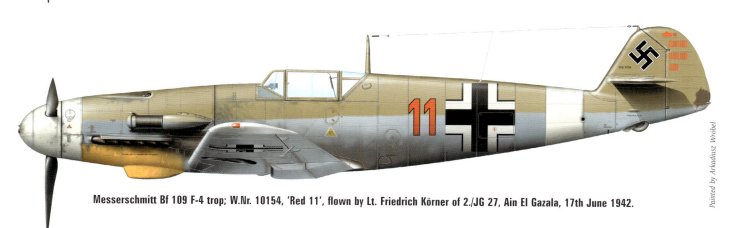

Messerschmitt Bf 109 F-4 trop; W.Nr. 10154, 'Red 11', flown by Lt. Friedrich Körner of 2./JG 27, Ain El Gazala, 17th June 1942.

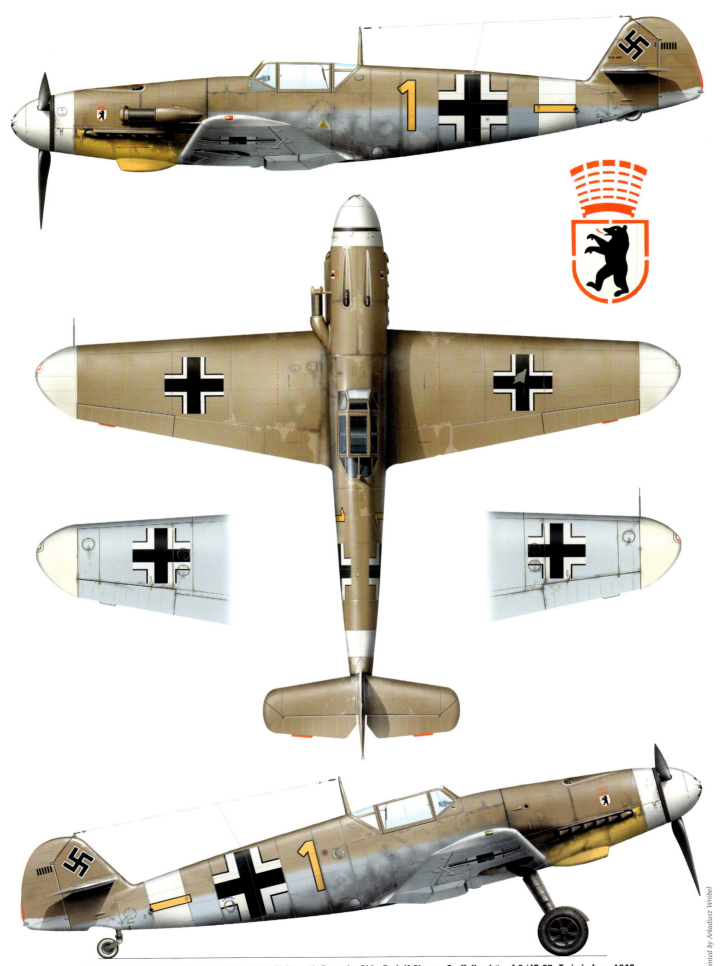

Messerschmitt Bf 109 F-4 trop; W.Nr. 8687, 'Yellow 1', flown by Oblt. Rudolf Sinner, *Staffelkapitän* of 6./JG 27, Tmimi, June 1942.

Painted by Arkadiusz Wróbel

Messerschmitt Bf 109 F-4; 'White 1', flown by Oblt. Werner Pichon-Kalau vom Hofe, *Staffelkapitän* of 7./JG 54, Utti, 23rd or 24th June 1942.

Messerschmitt Bf 109 F-4; 'Yellow 10', flown by Fw. Hans Döbrich of 6./JG 5, Petsamo, 30th June 1942.

Messerschmitt Bf 109 F-4; flown by Lt. Heinrich Graf von Einsiedel, *Gruppen Adjutant* of III./JG 3, Gortschetnoje, July 1942.

Messerschmitt Bf 109 F-4; 'Black 5', flown by Oblt. Anton Hackl, *Staffelkapitän* of 5./JG 77, Kastornoje, 26th July 1942.

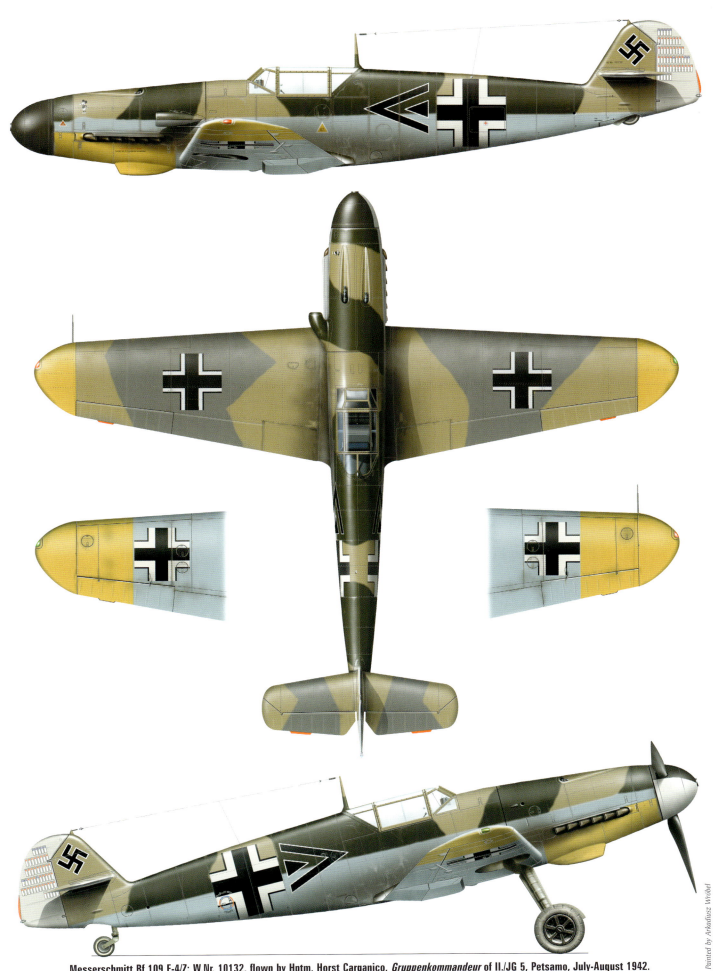

Messerschmitt Bf 109 F-4/Z; W.Nr. 10132, flown by Hptm. Horst Carganico, *Gruppenkommandeur* of II./JG 5, Petsamo, July-August 1942.

Painted by Arkadiusz Wrobel

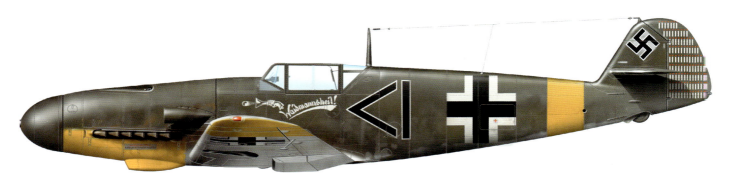

Messerschmitt Bf 109 F-2; flown by Obfw. Franz-Josef Beerenbrock of Stab IV./JG 51, Dugino, 1st August 1942.

Messerschmitt Bf 109 F-2; W.Nr. 6661, 'Black 12', flown by Obfw. Heinz Klöpper of 11./JG 51, Dugino, August 1942.

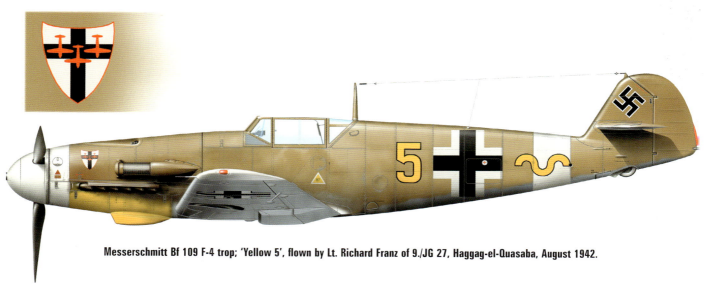

Messerschmitt Bf 109 F-4 trop; 'Yellow 5', flown by Lt. Richard Franz of 9./JG 27, Haggag-el-Quasaba, August 1942.

Messerschmitt Bf 109 F-4 trop; 'White 12', flown by Ofw. Franz Stiegler of 4./JG 27, Quotaifiya, August 1942.

Painted by Arkadiusz Wróbel

Messerschmitt Bf 109 F-4 trop; W.Nr. 8673, 'Yellow 14', flown by Oblt. Hans-Joachim Marseille, *Staffelkapitän* of 3./JG 27, Quotaifiya, 5th September 1942.

Painted by Arkadiusz Wróbel

Messerschmitt Bf 109 F-4/Z trop; W.Nr. 8567, 'Black 1', flown by Lt. Werner Schroer, *Staffelkapitän* of 8./JG 27, Haggag-el-Quasaba, early September 1942.

Messerschmitt Bf 109 F-4 trop; W.Nr. 8635, 'White 3', flown by Fw. Alfred Krumlauf of 4./JG 27, El Hammam, 20th September 1942.

Messerschmitt Bf 109 F-2; flown by Hptm. Hartmann Grasser, *Gruppenkommandeur* of II./JG 51, Jesau, autumn 1942.

Messerschmitt Bf 109 F-4; flown by Hptm. Franz Hahn, *Gruppenkommandeur* of I./JG 4, Mizil, autumn 1942.

Painted by Arkadiusz Wróbel